SAUL BELLOW AND THE DECLINE OF HUMANISM

New Directions in American Studies
General Editor: Eric Homberger, Lecturer in American Studies, University of East Anglia

'American Studies' however diversely defined has been dominated by the preoccupations of scholars in the United States, for whom the discovery of a 'usable past' and the definition and redefinition of literary tradition went hand in hand with the changing agendas of nationalism. Foreign writers and scholars have occasionally made significant contributions to the debate in the United States, but they have seldom possessed a collective sense of the uniqueness of their perspective upon American civilisation. This series is designed to foster a distinctively 'European' perspective upon American culture. It will contain books which range widely across disciplines. There is much talk of the end of the Cold War and an increased concern at the ecological crisis of industrial societies. The rapidity of social and political change around the world, and the extent to which the American people are themselves in the midst of a muddled and sometimes contradictory reappraisal of the very foundations of the post-war political settlement, have begun to raise questions about literature and culture and their relations to the social order. The contributors to the series will not necessarily all be Europeans, nor will they speak with a single voice about America and its culture. But they are asking the kind of questions about the American experience which urgently need to be asked.

Denis Lacorne, Jacques Rupnik and Marie-France Toinet (*editors*)
THE RISE AND FALL OF ANTI-AMERICANISM: A Century of French Perception

Mark Shechner
THE CONVERSION OF THE JEWS AND OTHER ESSAYS

Michael K. Glenday
SAUL BELLOW AND THE DECLINE OF HUMANISM

Series Standing Order

If you would like to receive future titles in this series as they are published, you can make use of our standing order facility. To place a standing order please contact your bookseller or, in case of difficulty, write to us at the address below with your name and address and the name of the series. Please state with which title you wish to begin your standing order. (If you live outside the United Kingdom we may not have the rights for your area, in which case we will forward your order to the publisher concerned.)

Customer Services Department, Macmillan Distribution Ltd
Houndmills, Basingstoke, Hampshire, RG21 2XS, England.

Saul Bellow and the Decline of Humanism

Michael K. Glenday

Senior Lecturer in American Studies
Liverpool Institute of Higher Education

M

MACMILLAN

First published 1990

Published by
THE MACMILLAN PRESS LTD
Houndmills, Basingstoke, Hampshire RG21 2XS
and London
Companies and representatives
throughout the world

Filmset by Wearside Tradespools,
Fulwell, Sunderland

Printed and bound in Great Britain by
WBC Ltd, Bristol and Maesteg

British Library Cataloguing in Publication Data
Glenday, Michael K., *1952–*
Saul Bellow and the decline of humanism. – (New
directions in American studies).
1. Fiction in English. American writers. Bellow, Saul
– Critical studies
I. Title   II. Series
813'. 52

ISBN 0–333–49023–1

For my mother and father

Contents

Acknowledgements

I would like to express my thanks to the staff of the University of Kent Library, of the John Rylands University Library of Manchester, and of the Liverpool Institute of Higher Education Library for their friendliness and efficiency in obtaining relevant material for my research.

I would also like to thank Dr Hilda Spear of the University of Dundee, who first nourished my interest in American literature and who has continued to offer her kind support and encouragement in the preparation of this book. Thanks are also due to Mr A. Robert Lee of the University of Kent for providing me with opportunities to discuss and refine my arguments. I am particularly indebted to Mr Henry Claridge of the University of Kent. For his tactful and sound criticism, and for his friendship and professional generosity throughout my period of research, I am most grateful.

The author and publishers wish to thank the following for permission to use the extracts from Saul Bellow's works quoted in this study:

The extracts from *Humboldt's Gift* (© 1973, 1974, 1975 by Saul Bellow) and from *Him With His Foot in His Mouth and Other Stories* (Copyright © 1974, 1978, 1982, 1984 by Saul Bellow Limited) are reprinted by permission of Martin Secker & Warburg Limited.

Extracts from the following works are reprinted by permission of the author and the author's agents, Harriet Wasserman Literary Agency Inc, 137 East 36th Street, New York, NY 10016: *Dangling Man*, *The Victim*, *The Adventures of Augie March*, *Seize the Day*, *Henderson the Rain King*, *Herzog*, *Mr Sammler's Planet*, *Humboldt's Gift*, *The Dean's December*, *More Die of Heartbreak*, *A Theft*, *Mosby's Memoirs and Other Stories*, *Him With His Foot in His Mouth and Other Stories*, and *To Jerusalem and Back*.

Parts of this study originally appeared in essay form and grateful acknowledgement is made to the following publishers for permission to reprint these extracts: Chapter 1, pp. 20–6 from my essay '"The Consummating Glimpse": *Dangling Man*'s Treacherous Reality', *Modern Fiction Studies*, 25 (Spring 1979). *Modern Fiction Studies*, copyright © by Purdue Research Foundation, West Lafayette, Indiana 47907. Reprinted with permission. Chapter 3, pp. 71–80 is a revised version of part of my essay 'Some Versions of Real: The

Novellas of Saul Bellow', which appeared in The Modern American *Novella*, edited by A. Robert Lee (London: Vision Press and New York: St. Martin's Press, 1989), © 1989 by Vision Press Ltd.

M.K.G.

They have science, but in science there is nothing but what is subject to the senses. The spiritual world, however, the higher half of man's being, is utterly rejected, dismissed with a sort of triumph, even with hatred. And that is why the idea of service to humanity, of brotherhood and of the solidarity of men is more and more dying out in the world.

(Fyodor Dostoyevsky, *The Brothers Karamazov*)

It was conceivable, even, that science had drawn all the capacity for deeper realizations out of the rest of mankind and monopolized it. This left everyone else in a condition of great weakness. In this weakness people did poetry, painting, humanism, fiddle-faddle – idiocy.

(Saul Bellow, *The Dean's December*)

1

Introduction: Saul Bellow and Humanism

'One of my themes is the American denial of real reality, our devices for evading it, our refusal to face what is all too obvious and palpable.'[1] Thus Saul Bellow, speaking about his novel *The Dean's December* (1982). The reality to which he refers, and the suggestion that there is in American culture a desire to escape into an inauthentic version of reality are concepts which bear upon the central aesthetic and ethical tenets of his writing. He has said that 'without art, it is impossible to interpret reality ... the degeneration of art and language leads to the decay of judgement'.[2] Bellow's novels have shown an increasing concern with the haemorrhage to 'real reality' in America, caused by that culture's indifference to anything but what Charles Olsen once called the 'poor crawling actuarial "real"'.[3] The novelist must, Bellow believes, 'find enduring intuitions of what things are real and what things are important. His business is with these enduring intuitions which have the power to recognise occasions of suffering or occasions of happiness, in spite of all distortions and blearing'.[4] There is in Bellow's thought none of that philosophical scepticism about the nature of reality which has so characterised the postmodern literary aesthetic over the past 25 years.[5] Reality is not philosophically problematic for Bellow; it is, rather, cognitively available, is 'all too obvious and palpable' to the mind which seeks an authentic relationship with it. Bellow's fiction takes as one of its explicit concerns the access to reality, the need to discover its essence.

Bellow's critique of what passes for reality in American culture is carried through by using the novel as his means of exposing the inauthenticity of the everyday, that system of reality which is dominant in American life. This system derives its imperatives from the worlds of business, technology, entrepreneurial guile, from the submission of the humanistic channels of thought and feeling to the ascendancy of scientific rationalism. Bellow does not

1

deny that this pragmatic and empirical value system has its place, but his fiction argues that the dominance of such values acts to repress that competing mode of being, contingent upon emotional and spiritual release, upon what E.M. Forster called 'the tender core of the heart that is so seldom used'.[6] 'To have a soul, to *be* one – that today is a revolutionary defiance of received opinion',[7] so Bellow believes. He foresees man's future as dependent upon the possibilities for intimate human interaction and the honest communication of emotional states. My study of his fiction concludes, however, that he does not place much faith in the regenerative promises of a communal ethic. For as long as the American people are exposed to an irresponsible, basely-babbling phalanx of media agencies, as long as communication and entertainment culture (too often these are indistinguishable) contribute to the wholesale 'degeneration of art and language', Bellow's heroes must face the lonely character of their enlightenment.

In a passage from *To Jerusalem and Back* Bellow indicts the media for trivialising the fundamental realities of existence:

> Our media make crisis chatter out of news and fill our minds with anxious phantoms of the real thing – a summit in Helsinki, a treaty in Egypt, a constitutional crisis in India, a vote in the U.N., the financial collapse of New York ... Worse yet, what is going on will not let us alone. Neither the facts nor the deformations, the insidious platitudes of the media (tormenting because the underlying realities are so huge and so terrible), can be screened out.[8]

The nerve-consuming journalism of our existence is omnipresent and is the backdrop against which Bellow's later heroes move towards their strategies of withdrawal from this debased reality. Bellow once said that 'the modern revolution can no longer be a revolution of machinery. It will have to do with the internal state'.[9] Since *Henderson the Rain King* his heroes have more and more appeared as revolutionaries of this sort. Their efforts to elevate the reality of their lives have led them towards bold reorientations. We think of Charlie Citrine's involvement with theosophy and Albert Corde's desperate attacks on Chicagoan vice in his *Harper's* essays. Of the former of these two dissenters, Bellow attempted to explain to a 'stumped' interviewer what it was that drew Citrine towards his interest in meditation and mysticism:

It was, in a word, the recognition that everything which Charlie had taken to be commonsensical, realistic, prudent, normal – his ambitions, marriage, love affairs, possessions, business relations – was a mass of idiocies. 'A serious human life? This! You've got to be kidding!' And from demonic absorption in the things of this world, he turns to an invisible world in which he thinks his Being may be founded . . . 'Science' with the aid of modern philosophy – what we call the positive outlook – has driven the 'invisible' into the dark night where enlightenment says it belongs . . . Charlie Citrine does not accept being intimidated by the representatives of 'scientific' respectability.[10]

Here again we find the castigation of that restrictive reality founded upon the scientific and excessively rationalistic ideologies. And Citrine's rejection of the normative world seriously called into question the critical consensus which had the author billed as a robust humanist. Along with Herzog, Corde, and most recently Benn Crader in *More Die of Heartbreak* (1987), Citrine's decision to withdraw from the 'mass of idiocies' comprising life in the contemporary USA implied Bellow's dismissal of humanism with its emphasis upon the necessary strength of the human community and its sceptical regard for the supernatural.

Bellow's work has, of course, attracted a huge body of critical attention. Most of his admirers unite in regarding him as a writer working the humanist seam, and have applauded him for producing an art which confirms and celebrates the ultimately noble and perfectible nature of man, one which places an axiomatic faith in community and the ameliorative prospects that lie within man's physical grasp. There is certainly a potent critical tradition that has seen his fiction as essentially affirmative and promissory.[11] Daniel Fuchs in one of the most recently published book-length studies of the fiction draws on this humanist consensus in his introduction, telling us that Bellow 'wishes to make art possible for life. Where the artist-hero sought isolation, the Bellow protagonist longs for community'.[12] And again later Fuchs places Bellow firmly within the humanist grain finding that 'Bellow's humanism is . . . a humanism of civilized possibility':

For Bellow there generally is a politics of civility, a possibility of more than fragmentary consensus, a middle grasped from the periphery in an often exasperating but finally decent society which represents a civilization worth preserving.[13]

And Fuchs' description of the fiction as one concerned to show 'the humanist's search for the dignity of the ordinary'[14] is echoed in Jeanne Braham's study, published also in 1984. The emphasis is again upon Bellow the humanist battler and Braham's introduction recites the consensual judgement of a writer dedicated to communitarian ethics – 'to Bellow, the individual's life is incapable of being defined in isolation; to realize meaning, man must try to relate himself to society, to its institutions and communal values'.[15] Like Fuchs, Braham presents the novelist as having 'implicit faith' in 'the community's "ordinary life"'.[16] However, Fuchs' more rigorous and probing study seems to realise the inadequacy of such judgements at least with regard to Bellow's later work, describing *The Dean's December* as a novel in which we see him 'playing a humanist's version of end-game'.[17] But such a view is rare. Introducing a special Saul Bellow issue of the periodical *Studies in the Literary Imagination*, its editor specifically includes the later novels in a total authorial vision described as 'a contest that necessitates one's accepting the community of man'.[18] And Malcolm Bradbury, while acknowledging that in the postwar universe 'the new humanism was hard to forge', nevertheless sees this as Bellow's commitment as he became 'a primary voice of a time when the Jewish-American writer . . . concerned to distil a morality and a possible humanism from a bland, material, encroaching reality . . . moved to the centre of American writing'.[19] I take the following to be an exact *summa* of the consensus reception of Bellow's work:

> What distinguishes Bellow from many other contemporary American novelists is the tension he manages to create between the actual world and the trust he puts in man. He does not exclude from his fiction the violent, chaotic, corrupt, and dangerous world he sees out there; he plants his characters firmly in it. But he does not describe the situation as totally hopeless and absurd; nor does he give us an interpretation of history as ineluctably leading to utter destruction. Sarcasm and nihilism are not his cup of tea. Reason, human reason, is still of paramount importance to Bellow, for it enables man to understand . . . In Bellow's novels, therefore, the individual is seen in conflict with society and with himself. But Bellow remains well within the humanist tradition. Indeed he is conscious of the chaos of the world and of the arbitrary quality of civilised society

... but he sees no choice for man but to go on living among those elements. He sees escape or refusal as impossible or impractical.[20]

Only the most recent work of Bellow criticism, Jonathon Wilson's *On Bellow's Planet: Readings From the Dark Side* (1985), sets out to revise this consensus. This study attempts to explain the reasons why the majority view of Bellow as 'a lone voice on the apocalyptic battlefields, still sounding the virtues of humanism, upholding the values of community' is one that represents 'an error of some magnitude'.[21] Although I certainly agree with this view and welcome Wilson's argument inasmuch as it does challenge the fundamental premises on which the consensus view rests, I am unable to accept his reading of the novels. Dangling between humanist dream and persecuted reality, Wilson proposes that Bellow's fiction resolves itself into a 'static dialectic' with masochistic heroes who 'persistently attack the objects of their own desire and behaviourally contradict their most cherished ideals'.[22] There is, he finally claims, 'an energy of paralysis'[23] writ large throughout Bellow's fiction; unable to realise life-affirming humanism in the reality of their lives, his heroes 'sustain themselves by falling back on their intellects and imaginations'.[24] Bellow's critics have ignored the extent of this paralysis and have stressed a humanism which is desiderated rather than fully achieved in the fiction. Ultimately then, Wilson acknowledges the humanist dimension in that fiction but insists that it is only a safety-valve through which the hero temporarily escapes from reality:

> Submerged in this harsh, unaccommodating world, Bellow's heroes persistently try to imagine a better one ... Denying any objective validity to their own negative experience of the world, the heroes imagine a world of truth, order, harmony, and love to which they aspire, and to which they are sentimentally attached, but in which they never arrive.[25]

Bellow's critics, by this reading, have been seduced by the same humanist never-never land and have accordingly produced a wholly unsound vision of the author's world. Wilson's analysis is, finally, one that trivialises Bellow's response to American reality by maintaining that his heroes do not confront that reality ('denying any objective validity to their own negative experience of the world'); instead, the gratifications are found in their earnest and desperate solipsism. Further, Wilson explicitly links author and hero in this scenario of retreat and evasion, finding that in *The Dean's December* 'what remains to interest Corde and Bellow are not crises on earth nor the "tensions . . . in the living heavens" but the tensions in his head'.[26]

The humanism to which Bellow's worldview has so often been tied has never been adequately defined either in terms of humanism's own ideological traditions as they might apply to Bellow's work, or the historical appeal those ideologies might have made both to Bellow and his critics during the 1940s and 1950s, when his reputation was being made. However, it seems to me that for many of his critics the assumption is that Bellow's humanism owes much to that strain of post-Renaissance thought which has been defined as 'an ethic which places human happiness as its central concern and is sceptical about the supernatural and transcendental'.[27] But Jacques Maritain in his classic work *True Humanism* (1938) reminds us of the historical ambiguities of humanist thought; although modern humanism has tended to be rationalistic and secular, it is still necessary 'to distinguish between two kinds of humanism':

> a humanism which is theocentric or truly Christian; and one which is anthropocentric . . . the first kind of humanism recognises that the centre for man is God; it implies the Christian conception of man as at once a sinner and redeemed . . . the second kind of humanism believes that man is his own centre, and therefore the centre of all things. It implies a naturalistic conception of man and freedom.[28]

The humanism attributed to Bellow has been very much of this latter sort although, as I have said, no critic has attempted to define the term in relation to his work, nor to acknowledge the two traditions identified by Maritain. Had they done so, no doubt some might have preferred to describe Bellow as a writer working within the Judeo-Christian tradition, one whose metaphysic is theist-humanist in complexion.[29] Maritain, however, goes on to accept that the secularisation of the modern world has affected humanist thought. This development has given rise to a lay understanding of the humanist enterprise, an understanding drawn upon (however vaguely) by those critics who praise Bellow as a humanist. Modern humanism 'essentially tends to render man more truly human and

to make his original greatness manifest by causing him to participate in all that can enrich him in nature and in history. It at once
demands that man make use of all the potentialities he holds
within him, his creative powers and the life of the reason, and
labour to make the powers of the physical world the instruments of
his freedom'.[30] Certainly this reading of twentieth-century humanism was the only one considered credible by the contributors to
Erich Fromm's symposium *Socialist Humanism* (1967); for them,
humanism's value as an intellectually respectable component of
contemporary thought could only be perceived in terms of 'the
consistency, vigour and historical adequacy of a rational programme scientifically founded on the knowledge of the human world
... and of a social programme constituting the integration of the
individual with society'.[31]

However, whether Bellow's critics understand him as either a
civil or a theist-humanist, the essential features of humanist
thought are common to both streams. A. James Reichley in his
survey of *Religion in American Public Life* (1985) has conveniently
noted that 'civil humanism and theist-humanism agree in valuing
personal freedom, distributive justice, citizen participation in social
decisionmaking, and social discipline'.[32] The practice of both
humanisms stresses the communitarian and social implications of
individual potentiality. For the theist-humanist this necessity man-
ifests itself in 'attachment to a particular culture that they seek to
transfigure, aesthetically and sometimes morally, not to escape'.[33]
Civil humanism places an even greater emphasis upon mutuality
and the social imperative, for 'under this formulation the freedom
of the individual is achieved through participation in the general
will'.[34] Above all then, humanism finds its strength in the parti-
cipative and interactive, and contends that the dignity of man and
the survival of humane sensibility can only be achieved through
the social contract.

It is this humanism which has so often been perceived as a
fundamental part of the Bellow world. His eminence in the
academy has been due in no small measure to his position as 'the
darling of the Establishment',[35] and this reputation has been based
very largely upon what the humanist critics see as his proper
rejection of pessimistic extremism. Lionel Trilling, for instance,
applauded Bellow's dissociation 'from the company of those
writers who accept the belief that modern society is frightful,
brutal, hostile to whatever is pure in the human spirit, a wasteland

and a horror'.[36] And Bellow's humanist vote for man could also be welcomed – particularly after the publication in 1953 of *The Adventures of Augie March* – as a vote for American man and the American mythos of possibility and regeneration. Trilling was but one powerful member of the group of New York Jewish intellectuals – sometimes called 'the family' – who for political and cultural reasons championed the young Bellow as their great White Hope in fiction. Bellow had begun his writing career in the pages of *Partisan Review*, the New York periodical where his first story, 'Two Morning Monologues', appeared in the summer of 1941. It was quite natural that Bellow should gravitate towards and be embraced by the anti-Stalinist left-wing intelligentsia; he had been actively involved with Trotskyist organisations while a student both at high school and at university in Chicago during the early 1930s, and in 1937 he married Anita Goshkin, herself a Trotskyist.[37] By 1938 the leading editors of *Partisan*, Philip Rahv and William Phillips, in common with the great majority of the radical left in America had recoiled from the Communist Party after the Moscow trials and had become enthusiastic Trotskyists.

After the Moscow trials and the assassination of Trotsky, the ideals of a socialist humanism were in beleaguered condition. Rahv's essay 'Trials of the Mind' expresses the profundity of gathering despair felt by American Marxists:

> We were not prepared for defeat. The future had our confidence, which we granted freely, sustained by the tradition of Marxism. In that tradition we saw the marriage of science and humanism. But now, amidst all these ferocious surprises, who has the strength to reaffirm his beliefs, to transcend the feeling that he had been duped? One is afraid of one's fear. Will it soon become so precise as to exclude hope?[38]

Although Bellow had severed all links with radical political groups by the early 1940s, it is easy to see that in the political climate of the late 1930s and early 1940s, his first works of fiction would have been anxiously read by those New York Jewish intellectuals who supported him. The hope was that the work of this gifted writer, 'their' writer, one of the family's own, would sustain something at least of those humanist affirmations.

But that Bellow should succeed in wringing such affirmation from historical crisis was also important to a Jewish-American culture which was still struggling to find acceptance in the mainstream of American life. That a Jewish-American novelist might produce a fiction which discovered a voice and a vision of acculturation – this would be a bold stroke for the yearned-for social emancipation of the American Jew. The humanist faith in the integration of the individual and society, mankind and nature, was capable of subsuming and lending moral legitimacy to the ideals of Jewish-American acculturation. It was therefore important that Bellow should deliver such goods, for both of the reasons I have pointed to. Indeed, Mark Krupnick in his recent study of Trilling suggests that the New York intellectuals looked to Bellow to resolve 'the conflict' that life in America posed for them:

> It had become clear by the mid-forties that there was a conflict within the first generation of New York intellectuals between their political hope for a socialist society and their commitment to the American ethos of acculturation and success. That conflict – between old European ideals and American actualities, between tradition and modernity, between politics and art – accounts in part for the extraordinary achievement of figures in Trilling's generation like Meyer Schapiro, Harold Rosenberg, Philip Rahv, Clement Greenberg, and Saul Bellow ... For Trilling's generation the price of acculturation – as members of the American intellectual class, as inheritors of the Western humanist tradition, as modernists – was always very high.[39]

Humanism, therefore, in American politics and culture, was under particular stress at the very moment that Saul Bellow began his career as a writer. It was out of this historical period that the consensus view of Bellow as a humanist was born. Norman Podhoretz, a late arrival to the group of New York intellectuals, has written that 'there was a sense in which the validity of a whole phase of American experience was felt to hang on the question of whether or not he would turn out to be a great novelist'.[40] After the publication of *Augie March*, it seemed to many that Bellow had indeed justified all of the hopes and all of the promise. It was greeted with rapturous approval by the likes of Trilling and Delmore Schwartz, who saw it as the inauguration of a distinctive Jewish-American voice in American fiction, yet it was also a voice that seemed to enthuse even more confidently about the inexhaustible vitality of life itself. Amongst the New York intellectuals only Podhoretz felt that there was something amiss with Bellow's novel, and shrewdly identified its weaknesses of tone; 'a whole phase of American experience' could never have been legitimised in its pages. Bellow overreached in the effort to do justice to such great expectations:

> The phase to which I was referring . . . was this turn toward the acceptance of America by the family in the second generation, the turn away from 'alienation' and toward . . . what? The answer was never clear, and from that lack of clarity arose the other trouble with *Augie*: the quality of a willed and empty affirmation which showed itself in the forced spontaneity of the prose (for I was right about that in my review). The family's 'pro-Americanism' – as Philip Rahv called it . . . in the early fifties was beset by too much doubt, hesitation, and uncertainty to yield much more than a willed and empty affirmation; and all this *Augie* reflected; and in reflecting it exposed how long a way the family still had to travel to reach that hoped-for, yearned-for, oh-so-impossible-she of a condition which a critic was to sum up descriptively in the phrase 'beyond alienation'.[41]

My own chapter dealing with *Augie* indicates the extent to which I share Podhoretz's misgivings. In the novel Bellow offered a rhetoric of humanist hope, if not the substance; in doing so he was able to convince all those, like Trilling, Rahv and Schwartz, who so much desired the substance. Of course, the reasons for *Augie*'s success are bound up with its historical moment, its appeal to the liberal left of the 1950s and its challenge to the dangerous reaction of that decade. By abandoning the stylistic conservatism, 'the facsimile-WASP style'[42] of his first two novels, Bellow confected a cultural document of subversive power. Augie's motto might have been *sans peur* and his adventurous spirit endeared him to all who knew the clammy cowardice which fuelled the Cold War shutdown mentality. Three decades on, the novel can more truly be assessed as one of large weaknesses. In a recent interview Bellow admitted some of these failings, though his most revealing remark – especially with relevance to Podhoretz's views – is an admission of the fundamental disingenuousness of the novel's vision. 'I really knew much more about darkness than I let on . . . I had no excuse for being such an ingenu. I felt like doing the ingenu, that's all'.[43]
The darkness Bellow knew about received its most concentrated

expression in that extremely rigorous and extremely moving novella, *Seize the Day*, a fiction that has always seemed chronologically misplaced, wedged as it is between *Augie* and *Henderson the Rain King*, both of which are infected by a spurious and shallow casting after situational effects. Both novels now seem quixotic curiosities in Bellow's development, though in them we might discern crucial stages in that development, a temperament in search of a situation, a style in search of a resting place. The ending of *Henderson*, in particular, is marked by giddiness and hysteria as Bellow and his disjunct hero prepare to return to an American darkness confronted so much more honestly in *Herzog* and the great novels that succeeded it.

I shall be arguing that a major part of that honest confrontation involved Bellow's rejection of the humanist ethic. His heroes are humanists *manqué*, rejected and defeated by an American ethos so inimical to their basic human needs that they are forced to adopt various strategies of withdrawal. Beginning with Herzog, we find them involved in an honourable, increasingly desperate effort to achieve release from the salient iniquities of American reality, from its human meanness and spiritual vapidity. Excepted from this typology are Asa Leventhal of *The Victim* and Augie March. The former is distinguished by his complete servitude to the reality of meanness and spiritual cowardice of which he is himself both victim and contributor. In this portrait of the city-dweller as neurotic, morally feeble, and humanly impoverished, Bellow provides his most detailed psychological drama of what he elsewhere describes as 'an unconscious collaboration of all souls spreading madness and poison'.[44] Leventhal is a kind of pathological case-study of the enervation which inevitably ensues from capitulation to such forces. His acrimonious, often violent struggle to stave off Allbee's interference is in some elemental way a struggle between light and darkness. It calls to mind a passage from *To Jerusalem and Back*, in which Bellow describes the hatred felt by those whose better impulses, deeply buried, have been stung suddenly into a briefly flaring exposure:

> I have been told often . . . that Russian, the language itself, is one of the strongholds of the human heart . . . even if you condemn people to death you are obliged by the genius of the language to frame the death sentence in loving words. There would seem to be a struggle between light and darkness within the mother

tongue, and perhaps Russian history is in part a rebellion against these loving expressions by which 'realistic' people feel themselves betrayed. They speak loving words and they may feel that a mind stirred by love is dangerous. Peril mobilizes your defenses, and then you murder because your soul has been moved.[45]

Allbee surprises Leventhal into such a betrayal, a betrayal into light. Leventhal's pathos, however, is that he has been conditioned – living among 'realistic' people – to fear, like Joseph of *Dangling Man*, 'the least penetrable part' of his being, 'the seldom disturbed thickets around the heart'.[46] I see Augie March as close kin to Leventhal, as one whose adventures ultimately speak of negation not affirmation, as one whose approach to truth is short-lived. He is another whose life describes 'the American denial of real reality'.

I believe the time has come for a frank revaluation of Bellow's vision. He has for too long been represented as a humanist evangelist, as one whose art demands 'the rediscovery of a moral humanism'.[47] Such a view may have been possible until the appearance of *Herzog*, though my initial chapters call this into question. But with *Herzog* and in each of the succeeding novels, Bellow's representation of post-1960 America has proposed a culture of moral and spiritual collapse, a materially-driven and deeply philistine reality from which his heroes are forced to retreat in dismay. He has described his most recent novel *More Die of Heartbreak* (1987) as 'a lamentation – for all parties'.[48] And certainly there is both lamentation and jeremiad in all his fiction since *Herzog*, addressed to all those characters who have 'shut off access to their own souls'.[49] The humanist effort simply cannot survive such moral and spiritual impoverishment in the culture where 'the greatest things, the things most necessary for life, have recoiled and retreated . . . under pressure of public crisis the private sphere is being surrendered'.[50]

The study that follows offers chapters devoted to Bellow's fiction on a decade-by-decade division. Although I regard *Herzog* as the novel in which we finally see the author acknowledge that dissociative crisis referred to above, the chapters dealing with the earlier novels will argue that they are themselves far from unequivocal consolations, and that especially in the case of *The Victim* and *Augie March* there has been widespread critical misunderstanding of their meanings. The final chapters include a section on the short stories, with particular reference to Bellow's recent return to that form with *Him With His Foot in His Mouth and Other Stories* (1984), and the study concludes with an assessment of the author's most recent work, the novella *A Theft* (1989).

2

The Costs of Surrender: *Dangling Man* and *The Victim*

DANGLING MAN

The opening paragraphs of Bellow's first novel disclose several dispositions which would become characteristic of his fiction throughout the next 40 years of his life as a novelist. There is, firstly, the annunciation of his intention to depart from that school of writing that had Hemingway as its founding father. 'For this is an era of hardboiled-dom. Today, the code of the athlete, the tough boy . . . that curious mixture of striving, asceticism, and rigor . . . is stronger than ever.'[1] For a writer of Bellow's intellectual complexion, the disadvantages of this response to the stresses of modernity were all too obvious and Joseph, the diarist-narrator, points them out – 'most serious matters are closed to the hard-boiled. They are unpracticed in introspection, and therefore badly equipped to deal with opponents whom they cannot shoot like big game or outdo in daring'.[2] As *Dangling Man* was to demonstrate, and as Bellow's subsequent career confirmed, the essential strategy of evasion of the inner self, so much a part of the Hemingway code, could not be maintained in the face of the century's accumulation of those 'opponents' of the self which refused to die the death. Hemingway's heroes had fashioned a style out of inarticulacy and many of the most memorable moments of his fiction were ones that explored and exploited silences between people, between man and the world of sensation. On the contrary Joseph demands articulacy, of himself (thus his conversational foil, the Spirit of Alternatives) and of others. One of the many arguments he has is caused by the refusal of a former colleague to speak to him. Though they had once been 'Comrade Joe and Comrade Jim'[3] in their days as Communist Party members, Joseph has since left the

14

Party, hence the snub. However, he sees it as one that penetrates beyond manners and social custom to threaten the very basis of human identity:

> 'I have a right to be spoken to. It's the most elementary thing in the world. Simply that. I insist on it.'
> 'Oh, Joseph,' said Myron. 'No, really, listen to me. Forbid one man to talk to another, forbid him to communicate with someone else, and you've forbidden him to think, because . . . thought is a kind of communication.'[4]

The imperative to thought in Bellow's fiction is primary, but the Bellow hero comes increasingly to doubt that his particular kind of thought – humane, spiritually cognoscent, emotionally charged – can find a sympathetic audience in the culture in which he exists. Joseph's determination to defy the prevalent model of reality and 'talk about' his inner self, is shared by one of Bellow's most recent heroes, Albert Corde of *The Dean's December*, though both he and Joseph are, effectively, silenced at the close of their narratives.

If one scans any recent bibliography of Bellow criticism,[5] it becomes immediately clear that his first novel has received proportionately very little of that critical attention. It can be claimed that the novel is a short one compared to the likes of *Herzog* or *Mr Sammler*, though wordage alone would seem a frail explanation. As a character, Joseph hardly compels our respect in his dealings with others, and he may make even fewer demands upon our sympathy; he appears to be emotionally wizened, can be querulous and is given to ill-considered outbursts. The novel in which he appears is also aesthetically cramped and hesitant in some ways. The conventional view sees in it an all-too-modish likeness to the Sartrean existential type of fiction. Bellow has himself referred to the 'timidity' and formal restraint of the novel. But looking back on *Dangling Man* it appears assured compared to the likes of *The Adventures of Augie March*. Though this latter is the book that fixed Bellow's reputation in American letters, it is, in my opinion, weaker in terms of coherence of vision and in its guise as a first-person narrative. So, though it may be possible to argue that *Dangling Man* is the weakest of its author's novels and therefore does not merit a high degree of critical attention, I would suggest that there may be other, less obvious, more disturbing grounds for its neglect. The novel ends on what is for Bellow an uncharacteristic note of apparently clear defeat for its central character. Andrew Waterman is one of the few critics who attempt to assess the extent to which such a conclusion can be seen as, in any way, representative of Bellow's fiction as a whole. In what is one of the best survey essays on the author's work, he concludes that 'in his aspirations and difficulties Joseph is an archetype for Bellow's subsequent protagonists. But never again is total failure so nakedly acknowledged as in the ironic exuberance of that last journal entry'.[6] Writing in 1971 Waterman had not the opportunity to include *Humboldt's Gift* or *The Dean's December* in his survey, though both are novels which I would read as more complex, but no less conclusive in their status as narratives that dramatise the strategic withdrawal of the hero from environing forces that threaten to overwhelm him. Though one might still agree that the nature of failure in these later works is not a 'naked' one, I would suggest that this has more to do with the complexity both of character and of confronting environment than with the extent to which they have been defeated by that environment. Yet the vast majority of critics who esteem Bellow do so through praise of his humanism, his struggle 'to wring final affirmations from life's stoniness',[7] through what they regard as his willingness to hold out against the trite responses of alienation and absurdity. *Dangling Man* seems to finish with no such affirmation and thereby becomes a source of discomfiture to critics bent on such a reading of Bellow's work as a whole, to be dismissed as 'a flourish of the conventional literary pessimism Bellow later disavowed'[8] or simply ignored altogether. There is, of course, no reason for critics to seek a reading of a novelist's work which includes all of it; yet as the fundamental argument of this study indicates, those critics who regarded Bellow as the last humanist battler were similarly confounded by *Herzog* and each of the novels that succeeded it. Even *Augie March*, commonly regarded as his most famous novel, has in my view been entirely misunderstood. So *Dangling Man's* comparatively slender coverage in the critical range may be indicative of a more extensive misjudgement of Bellow as one typecast as an affirmer.

The opening paragraph of *Dangling Man* offers another important prefiguration of Bellow's work as a continuity. Joseph is concerned about the constrictions imposed upon those living in the 'era of hardboiled-dom':

Do you have feelings? There are correct and incorrect ways of indicating them. Do you have an inner life? It is nobody's business but your own. Do you have emotions? Strangle them. To a degree, everyone obeys this code . . . If you have difficulties, grapple with them silently, goes one of their commandments. To hell with that![9]

So often has he been dubbed 'the novelist of the intellectuals'[10] it is often overlooked that Bellow makes strong claims for the emotional capacity throughout his work. In *The Dean's December* these claims are elevated to become the sole means of a genuine human intercourse, offering man a way out of the impasse created by the contamination or exhaustion of other modes of intelligibility and communication. 'We no longer confide in each other,' says Joseph of his marital relationship, 'in fact, there are many things I could not mention to her.'[11] The same is true of many of the spouses and siblings in Bellow's fiction; those who ought to be most able to communicate on the level of deep feeling are unable to do so, largely because one party, he or she reflecting and being encouraged by the normative reality, refuses, or is unable to so communicate. Thus Herzog and Madeleine, Citrine and his brother Julius, Tommy Wilhelm and his father Dr Adler, Augie and Simon March, and many others are forced to withhold their deepest feelings and finer ideas because the latter half of these pairings affect to despise their utterance.

Utilitarian, pragmatic, positivistic, materialistic, scientifically ordered and spiritually vapid – these are the conditions that govern American reality and that Bellow's heroes refuse to be governed by. Their refusals are quiet, sometimes wearied, sometimes concealed ones; unlike Joseph most of them cannot trade on a fund of future years but must take whatever final comfort they can from the exigencies of their failures. Joseph's ironic embrace of collectivity at the end of the novel is still a youthful and provisional one; he still has options to keep open, like his creator, who was of a similar age at the time of writing Joseph's story. Whereas Joseph withdraws from self into collectivity, subsequent novels concern central characters like Artur Sammler, in retreat from that latter state. Andrew Waterman ends his survey by looking back from *Mr Sammler's Planet* to *Dangling Man*:

Bellow's fiction has in a way come full circle from *Dangling Man*, also set at a disintegration-point of civilization, and the circle seems to have scored defeat deeper. Where Joseph was young and eager for life, Sammler is old, about to depart it, despite his vital concern wearied by struggle. Where Joseph ended boxed solitary into his room by the world's dense immediacies, the latest of Bellow's long line of ineffectual angels is forced out almost into an extra-terrestrial void.[12]

Indeed, inasmuch as Sammler's experiences have been the hateful ones of pogrom and war, there are grounds for seeing him as a latter-day Joseph, one whose misanthropy and recoil from the insensibilities of mass culture have if anything been increased through youth to age. But Sammler has since been succeeded by Citrine and Corde, both of whom are no less affected by those insensibilities but are much more exemplary in their determination to find transcendent compensations through their forced withdrawal from such 'dense immediacies'.

Dangling Man is, then, a novel that declares its author's intent to face squarely in fiction the intellectual and emotional categories as vital constituents of the fully lived life. Whatever one may make of the novel's conclusion, Joseph has an intense and assiduous awareness of that life and how far he falls short of it. His intolerance of others is largely due to the same awareness, to his knowledge of the compromises man makes with himself in order to cheat that self:

> But then, I may be expecting too much from Myron. He has the pride of what he has become: a successful young man, comfortable, respected, safe for the present from those craters of the spirit which I have lately looked into. Worst of all, Myron has learned, like so many others, to prize convenience. He has learned to be accommodating. That is not a private vice; it has ramified consequences – terrible ones.[13]

Bellow's fiction is full of characters who have learned the art of accommodation to a reality that constricts spiritual and emotional utterance while allowing them to be successful, comfortable, safe – for the present. Joseph's angry denunciation above can in many ways be regarded as that which fuels Bellow throughout the rest of his fiction. It is there, unabated, in Corde's fierce *Harper's* diatribes against an American culture depicted as prizing convenience above all other decision-making criteria. Corde rocks the boat

badly and so is disposed of by being himself expelled from it.
Though Joseph is both too young and socially unimportant to
cause any similar disturbances at the cultural centre, his vision is
true enough to see into the falsities of that reality and the extent of
his own and others' complicity with it.

                    *   *   *

Dangling Man offers a portrait of a man of thought though its
drama arises from the revelation that thought and reason are
insufficient guards against those 'opponents' which well up inside
the consciousness and threaten to overwhelm the character's sense
of reality. The novel's major dialectic is that between reason and
emotion and this debate is sustained, to varying degrees, throughout the rest of Bellow's fiction. Joseph's rationalism is severely
tested by his lonely sequestration, and one of his justifications for
restoring himself to the world at the end is an emotional one,
through his understanding that 'goodness is achieved not in a
vacuum, but in the company of other men, attended by love'.[14] His
self-enquiries lead to what he calls 'the least penetrable part of me,
the seldom disturbed thickets around the heart'.[15] But if these
emotional centres are almost invulnerable, the same cannot be said
for those products of reason and thought, his beliefs, which 'are
inadequate, they do not guard me'. These give him little protection
from 'the chaos I am forced to face'.[16]

It is this battle between reason and emotion that rages within
him, as demonstrated by conversations such as this with his alter
ego, the Spirit of Alternatives:

> 'You want me to trust Unreason?'
> 'I want nothing; I suggest . . .'
> 'Feelings?'
> 'You have them, Joseph.'
> 'Instincts?'
> 'And instincts.'
> 'I know the argument. I see what you're after.'
> 'What?'
> 'That human might is too small to pit against the unsolvables.
> Our nature, mind's nature, is weak, and only the heart can be
> relied on.'[17]

Joseph attempts to construct his reality upon the reason and the fruits of dispassionate thought, but his recorded experience is an account of just how boggy and unreliable such a basis can be. His penultimate diary entry shows he has discovered the insubstantiality of a reality founded upon the reason alone. And yet, paradoxically, one of the truths his experience reveals to him is that this rather solipsistic reality is in many ways more authentic than that reality subscribed to by 'wide agreement'.[18] What he lacks is free access to those 'seldom disturbed' provinces of the heart.

John J. Clayton, in an essay on Robbe-Grillet, concludes with a passage that could serve equally well as an introduction to Bellow's contribution to the representation of reality in fiction:

> The writer as liberator of consciousness? How should the writer help in our liberation? First, by establishing, largely by means of style, a realm of grace and power that offers us a model for life lived in its spirit. Beyond this, the writer has a responsibility to return to us the reality of our experience – not 'objective' reality but the reality of our ongoing lives, reality we are made to deny and forget. Insofar as that reality is drenched in destructive fantasy the writer must not simply pander to our enslavement but undermine the fantasies we secretly live by as well as those we are told to live by. The writer may create a world, but that world must encounter the one we share – either to challenge it or to plumb its depths.[19]

In *Dangling Man* Bellow was already at work realising this responsibility. Joseph, by the end of his narrative, is in full possession of that 'reality we are made to deny and forget' but he lacks the courage to resist further 'enslavement'. In his penultimate diary entry Joseph records a vision he had had, what he describes as 'one of those consummating glimpses'.[20] It is a vision that penetrates into the very marrow of what he had formerly been happy to call the 'facts of simple existence'[21]; it is one of such uncommon clarity that Joseph worries for his sanity:

> The room, delusively, dwindled and became a tiny square, swiftly drawn back, myself and all the objects in it growing smaller. This was not a mere visual trick. I understood it to be a revelation of the ephemeral agreements by which we live and pace ourselves ... this place ... had great personal significance for me. But it was not here thirty years ago. Birds flew through

this space. It may be gone fifty years hence. Such reality, I thought, is actually dangerous, very treacherous. It should not be trusted. And I rose rather unsteadily from the rocker, feeling that there was an element of treason to common sense in the very objects of common sense.[22]

According to Joseph's reasoning, the only basis for trusting the phenomenal world is through the membership of a community of persons; through such collaboration one can partake of 'the necessary trust, auxiliary to all sanity'.[23] But Bellow has here allowed Joseph to stumble into a very ironic piece of casuistry; that there is good reason to doubt common sense perceptions when the ephemerality of the 'agreements' has worn thin is more an argument against this process of mystification, those 'fantasies we are told to live by', than it is a validation of it. And in a dialogue with his Spirit of Alternatives, Joseph touches upon a conception of freedom that becomes ironically pertinent to an understanding of his final epiphany. He tells the Spirit that humanity cannot bear the burden of freedom and that in any case 'it is not even real freedom, because it is not accompanied by comprehension'.[24] With his vision at the novel's close he is in possession of all the ontological knowledge necessary to approach this comprehension but rejects it as being treasonable, a force of self-destruction.

Joseph's conundrum that 'the worlds we sought were never those we saw; the worlds we bargained for were never the worlds we got'[25] adequately sums up the nature of reality for many Bellow protagonists. We think of Asa Leventhal's tidy but strained existence crumbling beneath Allbee's intimidating presence, of Tommy Wilhelm's anguish at the hands of the charlatan Tamkin, of Henderson's entry into the mythic and fabulous world of King Dahfu. All these characters come to realise the necessary pains of withdrawal from the reality subscribed to by collective assent. Like Joseph, they are exposed to 'the diversified splendors, the shifts, excitements, and also the common, neutral matter of an existence'.[26] The nature of reality is continually problematical for such characters as it discloses itself both variously and obscurely. Joseph's most characteristic trait, a confounding lassitude, is described by him in terms which suggest his confused sense of what is real and what is hallucinatory – 'I have begun to notice that the more active the rest of the world becomes, the more slowly I move, and that my solitude increases in the same proportion as its racket and frenzy . . . it is a real, a bodily feeling . . . this will pass if I ignore it. I have always been subject to such hallucinations . . . it can be carried too far, perhaps, and damage the sense of reality'.[27]

The sense of reality is often an embattled one in *Dangling Man* as it has to be, given Joseph's intention to subject it to his unremitting gaze. In his book *City of Words*, Tony Tanner persuades us that 'the true act of recognition is more profound than any act of invention, and the greatest achievement of any invention or art work is when it frees you into a recognition of reality . . . the art which frees you into a true recognition of what is already there'.[28] One of Bellow's strengths as a writer is his ability to perceive and dramatise that most fundamental of recognitions, the pure recognition of an authentic and immarcescible reality, a state of experience untouched by the conventionally diluted and wholly disingenuous ways of seeing and behaving. Joseph has access to this reality, but he rarely achieves the captivating lyricism of a Corde or a Herzog in his descriptions of this state. This is largely due to his rebarbative nature, one result of which is his captious dealings with relatives and friends. One senses that this side of him, that emotionally 'least penetrable' part has at least been leavened by his experience alone and it might be argued that in this case his narrative cannot be wholly regarded as a record of defeat. For though we are forced to share in the privations and the gathering claustrophobia of his life, this closure is still infrequently relieved by brief, though satisfying glimpses of a physical world experienced as if for the first time. The contrast between these rare moments and the dulled state they briefly usurp is extraordinarily effective – and shocking, in the sense of being sensually arresting and euphoric:

> The air had a brackish smell of wet twigs and moldering brown seed pods, but it was soft, and through it rose, with indistinct but thrilling reality, meadows and masses of trees, blue and rufous stone and reflecting puddles. After dark, as I was returning, a warm, thick rain began falling with no more warning than a gasp. I ran.[29]

In this strangely sensitive state, the environment becomes abnormally expressive and the *frisson* that Joseph experiences as a subtle 'thrilling reality' is given its evocative power because it is *not* apprehended as a mere simple fact of existence, but rather as a manifestation of life's extraordinary beauty. This ability to reach behind manufactured and jaded responses to experience and to arrive at a virginal apprehension is an aptitude often possessed by Bellow's heroes.

So Joseph has not been wholly diminished by his extreme introspection. Indeed, his eventual inability to detach himself from a reality validated by 'wide agreement' but, nevertheless, spurious is as much Bellow's indictment of such institutionalised indoctrination as of Joseph's personal flaws. In his essay of 1963, 'Where Do We Go From Here', Bellow condemned the vitiating infantilism at the heart of modern American society, an immaturity of energy and spirit:

> Almost nothing of a spiritual, ennobling character is brought into the internal life of a modern American by his social institutions. He must discover it in his own experience, by his own luck as an explorer, or not at all. Society feeds him, clothes him, to an extent protects him, and he is its infant. If he accepts this state of infancy, contentment can be his. But if the idea of higher functions comes to him, he is profoundly unsettled.[30]

We can distinguish in all this the ideological foundation of many Bellow situations: the bursting of Henderson's 'spiritual sleep', his profound unsettlement being vaguely articulated through his inner voice complaining 'I want, I want' and more recently Charlie Citrine's view of himself as a modern-day Rip Van Winkle who had been 'asleep in spirit' for most of his life. And Bellow includes in *Dangling Man* descriptions that objectify Joseph's impaired sense of reality. The controlling metaphors and images are those of the jungle and a spiritually somnolescent race; these were tropes that Bellow was to return to again and again throughout his later fiction in an effort to suggest the teeming squalor, moral and physical, of urban civilisation in all its effeteness and latent depravity:

> I moved toward the corner, inhaling the odors of wet clothes and of wet coal, wet paper, wet earth, drifting with the puffs of fog. Low, far out, a horn uttered a dull cry, subsided ... I heard behind me the clicking of a feminine stride and, for a moment, thought that Iva had come after me, but it was a stranger who passed at the awning of the corner store, her face made bleary by the woolly light and the shadowy fur-piece at her throat. The

awning heaved; twists of water ran through its rents. Once more the horn bawled over the water, warning the lake tugs from the headlands. It was not hard to imagine that there was no city here at all, and not even a lake but, instead, a swamp and that despairing bawl crossing it; wasting trees instead of dwellings, and runners of vine instead of telephone wires.[31]

Similarly, the opening paragraph of *The Victim*, with its suggested picture of New York teeming with 'barbaric fellahin'[32] amidst a jungle-like landscape, is intended to underline the extent to which an accepted reality can quickly lose its contours and be replaced by an apparition more chimeric, more primitive. Joseph's vision above of the modern wasteland with its plangent, funereal sounds is a reflection of his own troubled relationship with reality. It contains the ghostly figure of the 'stranger . . . her face made bleary by the woolly light'; the image suggests somnambulism and lack of identity but also, significantly, it is suggested that the bleariness is caused by external atmospherics and the 'shadowy fur-piece'. This image-complex is commensurate with Bellow's critique of those citizens who allow themselves to be made spiritually bleary by the 'woolly light' of their society's institutional vapidity. And the figure of the jungle inevitably calls to mind that of its explorers, its adventurers (a metaphor which is itself repeatedly used by Bellow in *Dangling Man*); Joseph savours the irony of his inertia, or at least his physical inertia, comparing himself to those who 'seem to know exactly where their opportunities lie; they break prisons and cross whole Siberias to pursue them. One room holds me'.[33] He is an adventurer of spiritual and existential terrain who nevertheless has one eye on the ones who 'fly planes or fight bulls or catch tarpon' and there is, perhaps, a sense in which his joining the army can be seen as delayed induction into such an adventurer-corps. In this metaphorical jungle, however, the explorer bent upon finding a more spiritually advanced reality must make his discoveries outside ('in his own experience, by his own luck') rather than inside the wilderness.

Finally, however, Joseph draws back from the fruits of his unflagging quest to 'know what I myself am'.[34] He has been 'the earnest huntsman of himself'[35] and has found he lacks the stamina and the valour to sustain himself in the face of unpalatable truths. But though the cruel irony of the novel's conclusion appears to signal Joseph's absolute renegation of that freedom he had formerly prized so highly, the pessimism of all this is mitigated by certain factors. Joseph himself is not convinced he is taking the right path, only the inevitable one and his speculations about his future are accordingly tentative:

> I had not done well alone. I doubted whether anyone could. To be pushed upon oneself entirely put the very facts of simple existence in doubt. Perhaps the war could teach me, by violence, what I had been unable to learn during those months in the room. Perhaps I could sound creation through other means. Perhaps.[36]

Joseph will not become a sleepwalker. He has made a studied decision, aware of its implications if not its consequences, and is likely to remain a man 'keenly intent on knowing what is happening to him'.[37] And if, as I suggested above, the novel is seen as an argument between the competing claims of reason and emotion, then it would appear that Joseph has conceded the insufficiency of his earlier adherence to reason as the predominating principle of his existence. Earlier in the narrative he strives to find an answer to the ultimate questions of existence, an answer which would incorporate reason and avoid the necessity of 'sacrificing the mind' to religious faith. Interestingly, reason is seen as a kind of antithesis to, or even a defence against the importunate stirrings of the heart:

> was there no way to attain that answer except to sacrifice the mind that sought to be satisfied? From the antidote itself another disease would spring. It was not a new matter, it was one I had frequently considered. But not with such a desperate emotion or such a crucial need for an answer. Or such a feeling of loneliness. Out of my own strength it was necessary for me to return the verdict for reason, in its partial inadequacy, and against the advantages of its surrender.[38]

Joseph's final decision in the narrative may be regarded, then, as a revision of this earlier 'verdict'. He does not throw over his respect for the rational, but rejects it as a lonely sustaining principle. His decision to seek out that 'necessary trust'[39] derived from community, as a defence against the potential mania provoked by absolute rationalism, suggests a new openness to emotional intercourse as a vital ingredient of reality. To deny his emotional nature in pursuit of an even greater philosophic asceticism would be, he sees, perverse. The characters in Bellow's subsequent fiction who make such denials are invariably the villains of the piece; for example, one thinks of Madeleine Herzog, Tommy Wilhelm's father and Dewey Spangler; these are all characters who see emotional articulation as a self-indulgence, a weakness. In this way, then, *Dangling Man* establishes the terms of Bellow's debate, to be pursued throughout all his subsequent fiction.

Robert Scholes has offered the astute observation that 'all fiction contributes to cognition by providing us with models that reveal the nature of reality by their very failure to coincide with it'.[40] In *Dangling Man* the nature of reality is revealed by a discrepancy of this kind. Throughout the narrative Joseph has been on the margins of the normative, a fractious, often violent man in his reactions to the orthodox codes of conduct and that model of reality he finds so anathematic – Myron's 'convenient' and 'accommodating' world. It may be argued that Joseph's rejection of the 'hardboiled' is short-lived and that life in the army would appear to offer a very hardboiled existence. Yet, as I have suggested, one of the hoped-for features of the life ahead which attracts him to it is the opportunity to extricate himself from the lonely and enfeebled silence which has increasingly come to be his condition. And, ironically, almost imperceptibly, his dangling days have begun to incorporate some of the very features he had disparaged in the hardboiled – unwillingness to accept the succour of others in favour of 'a close-mouthed straightforwardness' (Joseph is continually rejecting the help of friends and family), a rather grim stoicism, and above all an environing silence which is the token of his self-imposed estrangement. In the end he has become as hardboiled as those he sought to condemn. In all these ways, the conclusion can be regarded as much less than a defeat for Joseph's development as a human being. Significantly, the specific moment of his decision to end his dangling is marked by his inspiring the warm spring air, 'and I recognized that the breath of warm air was simultaneously a breath of relief at my decision to surrender'.[41] His life had truly become an asphyxiating one, without reward and, eventually, without justification.

THE VICTIM

Bellow is fond of telling interviewers that *Dangling Man* he considers to be his B.A. and *The Victim* his Ph.D.[42] As a doctoral presentation *The Victim* perhaps lacks something in originality for, as many have noted, its plotting and characterisation owe a good deal to Dostoyevsky's *The Double* and *The Eternal Husband*. Yet the influence of the great Russian writer, one of Bellow's acknowledged mentors, does not seriously diminish the striking dramatic achievement of this novel of moral and psychological forces made actual. It is for me the finest of Bellow's shorter novels, a work which gives us his most subtle use of point of view, a novel that combines comic irony with a setting in which New York is made to express Asa Leventhal's predisposition towards the neurasthenic and impalpably hostile. He is in many ways the least likeable of all the author's major characters, querulous, ill-mannered and humanly meagre, a Jew without any of the fine Jewish qualities, certainly with none of the sound exegetical facility so often found in the Jewish male. He is, as one of this novel's other Jewish characters says, the product of a 'ghetto psychology'.[43]

Whereas Joseph was one 'keenly intent on knowing what was happening to him', Leventhal possesses an 'intelligence not greatly interested in its own powers'.[44] He prizes the existential safety provided by such cognitive sloth and the novel can be understood as a series of incidents throughout which Leventhal strives to remain protected behind a *cordon sanitaire* of the mind. Though Kirby Allbee penetrates those defences, the breach is momentary and is repaired by the return of Leventhal's wife who re-imposes the routine, the specious reality of Leventhal's life. In a recently published interview Bellow appears to confirm my own reading of the novel *Seize the Day*, giving us the proper terms with which to describe Tommy Wilhelm's conclusive act when he, 'the *bon enfant* making his last hopeless stand, cheated by Tamkin, rejected by his father, enters a funeral parlor to have a good cry over the death of his cherished ideals. You can get took. You can die of it, lie in a coffin. So much for Tommy Wilhelm, who trustingly (or lazily) surrendered his soul to the milder, vaguer view'.[45] An apt description, too, I believe, of Leventhal's surrender. In this sense he is a precursor of Augie March as well as Wilhelm, as my subsequent discussion of *The Adventures of Augie March* will show. But whereas Wilhelm is ultimately confronted by disabling forces which release the grim honesty of his tears, both Augie and Leventhal are allowed to relapse into states of continuing evasion and indifference. If Wilhelm is, in Bellow's phrase, 'a sufferer by vocation',[46] Leventhal, like Joseph's friend Myron Adler, has come to appreciate the tepid rewards accompanying 'the milder, vaguer view'. *The Victim* shows Bellow dealing with a major character who, alone amongst the principal actors in the rest of his fiction (with the probable exception of Augie March) experiences no durable enlightenment, embodies no regenerate promises, enshrines no authorial confidence. Where Joseph has fought the good fight and Wilhelm has lost it, Leventhal would prefer to remain in the dressing-room.

Overall, Bellow's fiction has been distinguished by large and heroic characters, their names giving title to the narratives they dominate. But Asa Leventhal is given no such eponymous status. There may even be a fault in too easily associating his predicament with the condition denoted by the novel's title. At the very least he is forced to share victim status with a good many others in the book. And because I cannot follow the argument of those critics who regard this novel as centrally concerned with anti-Semitism,[47] I would suggest that Leventhal is further undermined by having his Jewishness travestied (by other characters and by Bellow's third-person narrator) as well as being seen to travesty that Jewishness himself in various public ways. Leventhal and Allbee exchange racial platitudes – Allbee, for example, jabs Leventhal with this:

> you people take care of yourselves before everything. You keep your spirit under lock and key. That's the way you're brought up. . . . Nothing ever tempts you to dissolve yourself. What for? What's in it? No percentage.[48]

Leventhal, as usual, is confounded and outraged, his 'expression was uncomprehending and horrified. His forehead was wrinkled. His heart beat agonisingly, and he faltered out, "I don't see how you can talk that way. That's just talk. Millions of us have been killed. What about that?"'.[49] The description of his 'uncomprehending and horrified' features is important. Allbee's assault has been formulaic, his charge of spiritual parsimony an anti-Semitic slur made hoary through history. Yet Leventhal 'uncomprehending' is felled by it even while he seems to understand it, correctly, as 'just talk'. The shuddering glibness of his reply, served up with the childish taunt 'what about that' is also, more chillingly, 'just talk'. In a scene like this Bellow shows a brilliant, scoring wit, with Leventhal the target even as he utters the statement of final, awful defence. The fact that he does not wait for Allbee's reply to that statement, even though 'he seemed to be waiting for a reply', is damning. Indeed, at the start of the next chapter he is angry with himself for 'he felt he had answered stupidly'.[50] We are told that before Allbee's reply could be given (an important point this, implying as it does that there *is* a way of responding to what would seem the Gentile's irreducible guilt) Leventhal 'turned and walked away rapidly . . . his stout body shaken by the unaccustomed gait' – and shaken, too, the reader might suppose, by the pain of having just shot himself in the foot.

Earlier in the narrative Leventhal's touchiness about anti-Semitism spills over into a conversation he is having with Stan Williston. His imputation that Williston is unwittingly a party to the perpetuation of racist sentiment is clearly an unwarranted piece of ugly thinking, and one that rather shows the extent to which Leventhal himself is afflicted by the stereotypes of racial slanging:

> You think that he burned me up and I wanted to get him in bad. Why? Because I'm a Jew; Jews are touchy, and if you hurt them they won't forgive you. That's the pound of flesh. Oh, I know you think there isn't any room in you for that; it's superstition. But you don't change anything by calling it superstition.[51]

Williston responds with remarkable self-control to what is by any standards a highly offensive slander, telling Leventhal that 'the Jewish part of it is your own invention'. And the narrative as a whole shows how fully Leventhal is, in point of fact, touchy, unforgiving, how he himself reinforces the very 'superstitions' he mistakenly finds in Williston. This irony is further stressed in the three-cornered discussion Leventhal has in the café. Here the criticism of Leventhal is carried through by fellow Jews Harkavy and Goldstone. Leventhal has argued that Disraeli has no claim to greatness since he rose to power 'in spite of the fact that he was a Jew, not because he cared about empires so much'. Disraeli he believes had seen his Jewishness as 'a weakness' and had tried to efface it – 'people laughed at his nose, so he took up boxing; they

laughed at his poetic silk clothes, so he put on black'. He will not
allow that Disraeli achieved more than passing the 'test' posed by
overcoming the impediments faced by the Jew wishing to succeed
in Anglo-Saxon public life. Instead of expunging his Jewish identity, Leventhal argues that Disraeli would have done better to
proclaim it. Apart from the validity or otherwise of the argument
itself (both Harkavy and Goldstone take issue with its soundness.
Harkavy believes Disraeli was 'a credit to them [the English] and to
us' and Goldstone thinks that he 'showed Europe that a Jew could
be a national leader'),[52] Leventhal's attitude to the matter once
again reveals his touchiness, his mean-mindedness ('Why should
we admire people like that? Things that are life and death to others
are only a test to them. What's the good of such greatness?'),[53] and
his tendency to reinforce the stereotypes of Jewish behaviour. So
Harkavy rebukes him on just this score – 'why, you're succumbing
yourself to all the things that are said against us'.[54] And towards
the end of the narrative Harkavy has cause to remember the
discussion, telling Leventhal that he had 'never seen such an
exhibition of ghetto psychology. The attitude you took towards
Disraeli amazed me'.[55]

As far as I am aware, no critic has noticed the extent to which
Bellow undermines Leventhal's sense of his Jewishness; most
assume rather that because Leventhal is a Jew he is Bellow's
spokesman. Nothing could be further from the truth. Leventhal is
the worst kind of Jew who uses his identity in an irresponsible,
churlish and damaging way. Because he is weak as an individual
he tries to aggrandise himself by hiding behind the powerful
stereotypes of persecution. In a late conversation with Harkavy we
see an example of this sort of cowardice as Leventhal calumniates
Allbee in order to defend his decision to intercede on Allbee's
behalf with Shifcart, the actors' agent. Given the way he has
previously represented (or, more properly, misrepresented) the
history of his affairs with Allbee, he needs to defend what appears
to be a weakness in acceding to Allbee's request:

'And where does he get the idea that Shifcart can help him?'
Though he knew he was making a mistake, Leventhal said,
and to some extent it was involuntary, 'I think he believes it's all
a Jewish setup and Shifcart can pull strings for him . . . Jews have
influence with other Jews.'
'No!' Harkavy cried. 'No!' His hands flew to his head. 'And

you're trying to do something for him? . . . Boy, do you know
what this does to my opinion of you? Are you in your right
mind?'
   His horror shook Leventhal. . . . Leventhal silently reproached
himself. 'That was a real mistake. I shouldn't have said that. Why
did I let it slip out? I'm not even sure Allbee means that.'[56]

There are two important points to remark here. Harkavy's response shows how Bellow again uses other Jewish characters in
order to condemn Leventhal's irresponsibility with regard to
matters of race. But also, most significantly, Leventhal's final
reflection above would appear to come very close to exonerating
Allbee of anti-Semitism in his eyes. At the very least he is
beginning to doubt Allbee's malevolence in this respect. An
attentive reading of *The Victim* at any rate shows how wide of the
mark critics have been in their treatment of the Jewish issues raised
by Bellow. Maxwell Geismar offers a view which comes close to the
truth, noting that 'Leventhal seems to have inherited all the pain
and suffering of his moral tradition with none of its resources . . .
the whole "Jewish" concept in this hero . . . is so close to paranoia
and madness . . . that it is no longer, in the historic sense, Jewish'.[57]
Robert Alter, in a fine essay in his book on modern Jewish writing
After the Tradition, also sees through the smoke-screen of point-of-
view, remarking that though '*The Victim* gives the appearance of
being a rather conventional novel – a story by a Jewish writer about
a Jew and an anti-Semite, with familiar social or social-
psychological implications . . . there is something patently odd
about Asa Leventhal's Jewishness. Compare it to the Jewishness of
Herzog and it seems almost an abstraction'.[58]
   In many ways then, Leventhal would seem an unsympathetic
case for treatment. Yet if he lacks even a minimal nobility of being,
if we can discover in him only trite neuroses and puerile ways,
what did Bellow hope to achieve through the characterisation of
one so ignoble?
   I should here draw attention to the extent to which my own
understanding of Leventhal's characterisation differs from the
consensus reading of it. The great majority of critics would see
Leventhal at the close of the narrative as one restored to normative
reality, having been spiritually and morally replenished by his
testing experiences at Allbee's hands. There are shades of disagree-
ment over the measure of his rehabilitation, focussing (as is so

often the case with Bellow's fiction) on the novel's epilogue and the reprise meeting with Allbee. Whereas some regard Allbee as at best an ambivalent creature who provokes Leventhal into confronting unwelcome truths, others think of him in wholly negative terms, as embodying a principle of depravity and failure which Leventhal is right to resist at all costs. Thus Gabriel Josipovici, giving us Leventhal as humanist battler:

> he doesn't let Allbee drag him down. . . he retains his sanity and his sense of responsibility, though not by growing hard-boiled and ceasing to care. And in this he is like Augie and Wilhelm and Henderson and Herzog. They all have reason, and more, to give up, break down, despair, or grow hard, callous, indifferent to the claims of others. Yet they do neither but weather the blows and trust their initial instincts.[59]

Others argue that Leventhal and Allbee do drag each other down, and that the novel records Leventhal's struggle to overcome the threats to sanity and sense represented by Allbee and his troubled relationship with him. Tony Tanner, for example, would have us believe that Leventhal has been 'exposed to an anarchic threat and survived, enhanced by a deeper wisdom'.[60] And Richard Lehan claims that:

> Leventhal is Allbee's victim so long as he admits that he is responsible for Allbee, he is simply weighed down by what is base in the human nature. Each character becomes locked in the bad faith of the other, becomes fixed by a relationship which prevents the possibility of change . . . becomes the absurd victim of the other's distorted view, until each begins grotesquely to resemble the other.[61]

Both of the above critics believe that Leventhal has in the end come to accept 'what existence is'.[62] John Clayton, too, swells the consensus interpretation of the Allbee-Leventhal relationship as one giving rise to a 'danger wrought by the closeness between them'.[63] Clayton also finds cause to differ from Norman Podhoretz, with whose views I essentially agree. Podhoretz can see no great sea-change in Leventhal's orientation at the end of the novel; instead he considers that he 'has merely (like a successfully analysed patient) learned something about himself that has helped him come to terms with the world and make a settlement'.[64] But, for Clayton, Leventhal 'has changed permanently' and the reader of the epilogue finds him 'healthier, happier, and a father-to-be'.[65] And although Clayton has the discrimination to see that 'Asa's change is partial', he concludes that 'Asa goes much farther than Joseph in joining humanity without surrendering to society. His success heralds the overeager affirmation of Bellow's next novel, *The Adventures of Augie March*'.[66] The comparison with Joseph is unsound, and though the mention of Augie has a comparative validity this does not as I pointed out previously, reflect credit on Leventhal.

At the other end of the spectrum are those critics who are disappointed by Bellow's handling of the epilogue. Andrew Waterman, for instance, is concerned that 'the less troubled "softened" state of relative maturity in which we leave Leventhal seems unearned, as if shutting the door on Allbee's body he has partly shut his mind to the issues it brought alive to him. As in *Dangling Man*, a final flourish covers unresolved complexities'.[67] Marvin Mudrick similarly complains that Bellow fails to 'regain our confidence at the end by losing his own, when he shrugs off the whole plot as a bad season through which Leventhal has safely passed'.[68] These critics fail to see that it was very much a part of Bellow's purpose to suggest that Leventhal's maturity is a bogus state, that it is in fact Leventhal, rather than Bellow, who is seen to shrug off the 'plot' of his relationship with Allbee as 'a bad season' through which he passes. The epilogue is meant to show Leventhal not 'born again, into a truer version of reality'[69] but as benighted as ever. Marcus Klein comes closest to my own view of the matter, though I believe he understates the opportunities for enlightenment proffered to Leventhal:

nature as transcendent reality brushes Leventhal lightly once – for a brief moment of half-sleep he feels the whole world present to him and about to offer him a mysterious, it would seem redeeming, discovery. But the discovery blows by him and at the end of his action, having abandoned ultimate questioning and now re-entering a darkened theatre with his wife, he is no closer to a notion of reality.[70]

To return to my question above concerning the possible grounds for Bellow's interest in one so unprepossessing, I would suggest that the answer is to be found in the developing representation of reality as we find it in Bellow's fiction as a whole. I argue in subsequent chapters of this study that characters such as Herzog and Corde have had to adopt strategies of withdrawal from the dominant reality of American life. Leventhal is a study of one who succumbs to that reality, who capitulates to its management. He is a forerunner, in large-scale, of numerous more minor characters in the later novels, of men such as Willie Herzog, of those who subside into the bland and the licit. Moses Herzog can 'remember a time when Willie, too, had been demonstrative, passionate, explosive, given to bursts of rage, flinging objects on the ground . . . and where had it gone, the wrath of Willie Herzog? . . . Into a certain poise and quiet humor, part decorousness, part (possibly) slavery. The explosions had become implosions, and where light once was darkness came, bit by bit'.[71] *This* is the state – the slavery and the darkness, modified by something like relief at having, as he would say, 'got away with it' – that we find Leventhal in at the close of *The Victim*. It is a sign of Allbee's acute discernment that he compares Leventhal to Caliban; Caliban is not only enslaved, but deservedly so – only he proves ineducable, resisting Prospero's efforts to enlighten him and at the end of *The Tempest* he is restored to his proper place at the foot of the hierarchy. Like Caliban, Leventhal is *infirma species*; he has refused enlightenment and has been restored to the debased reality of his life.

*   *   *

Bellow's opening descriptions of Leventhal emphasise his normal condition of apathetic vision. The description concentrates on the eyes 'under their intergrown brows'. These were 'intensely black and of a size unusual in adult faces. But though childishly large they were not childlike in expression. They seemed to disclose an intelligence not greatly interested in its own powers, as if preferring not to be bothered by them, indifferent; and this indifference appeared to be extended to others. He did not look sullen but rather unaccommodating, impassive'.[72] This description prepares us for the stress Bellow will place upon Leventhal's perceptive and judgemental failures throughout the narrative. In a recent interview Bellow points out that one of the themes of *The Dean's December* 'is the American denial of real reality, our devices for evading it, our refusal to face what is all too obvious and palpable'.[73] Throughout *The Victim* it becomes clear that Leventhal's 'indifference' is just such a strategy of defence, a means of denying known truths concerning the affiliations between himself and others. His reality is distorted precisely because of 'this indifference . . . to others'. He seeks to cultivate the sinister naivety of his 'childishly large' eyes; but so much of the world is inimical to that project, so much of life threatens to overwhelm Leventhal's indifference. But as long as he can maintain the fundamentals supporting his identity – his marriage, his job, his apartment (with its 'heavy folds of curtain' which give him 'a feeling of suspension and quietness')[74] far above the teeming crowds on the pavement below – he can maintain his psychic equilibrium.

But Bellow strongly implies that Leventhal is a generic New Yorker. The lonely, the anxious, the world-beaten – these are the types who have become the victims of the reality system. Among them, as M. Gilbert Porter reminds us, we see in *The Victim*:

> The furious husband assaulting his unfaithful wife in the street below Leventhal's window, the men sleeping off their whisky on Third Avenue, lying in doorways or on the cellar hatches, the dead Mickey, the Yiddish pedlar bitterly grubbing out a meagre living as a hustler, the dishwasher with 'raw hands and white nails' in the restroom of the movie house, whose taste for horror movies perhaps reflects the conditions of his life, the elderly Filipino busboy who moves in a daily world of dirty dishes and steam tables, the man bleeding to death in the subway, denied aid by a policeman who insists on 'policy'.[75]

These are some of the human faces presaged by the epigraph from De Quincey, in a sea full of 'innumerable faces, upturned to the heavens; faces, imploring, wrathful, despairing faces that surged upward by thousands, by myriads, by generations'. To all of these faces Leventhal would wish to blind his eyes, fearful of the contact that might bind him to them forever. One of the reasons he gives up attending night school is that the atmosphere attaching to the place, 'especially on blue winter nights' together with 'the grimness of some of the students, many of them over fifty, world-beaten but persistent . . . disturbed him'.[76] Though he is, we're told, 'frequently mindful' of that part of humanity 'that did not get away with it – the lost, the outcast, the overcome, the effaced, the ruined',[77] his mindfulness is a state of fear not compassion.

Allbee is an emissary from this constituency of the baleful and woebegone. Yet his appearance gives Leventhal the chance to assert his humanity, by accepting the existence of the ties that bind him to this wider world. Just before Leventhal sees Allbee in the park for the first time, Bellow's narrator appears to signal a new climate of hope, one in which even Leventhal might overcome his habitual indifference to others. In this climate 'eyes seemed softer than by day, and larger, and gazed at one longer, as though in the dark heat some interspace of reserve had been crossed and strangers might approach one another with a kind of recognition'.[78] Leventhal, however, fails to discover any such liberating viewpoint. Since a very large part of Leventhal's failure to come close to what Klein calls 'a notion of reality' is his inability to find a point of view which takes account of what Bellow would call 'real reality', it is crucial that the reader is gradually given access to a viewpoint which can authoritatively call Leventhal's into question. And the deftness with which Bellow controls point of view in this novel is marvellously accomplished. In part Leventhal is undermined in those scenes in which we see his views – of Allbee, for example – being seriously questioned by other observers such as Williston and Harkavy and Leventhal's brother, Max. Leventhal, too, often has cause to revise his own points of view as in his comments about his sister-in-law's madness or his mother-in-law's hostility towards him. More subtly, there are many scenes wherein the reader may see that Leventhal's criticisms of others are ironically more pertinent as criticisms of Leventhal himself.[79] But perhaps the most direct and damning indictment of Leventhal's distorted judgement derives from having that judgement exposed to Allbee's more profound and authoritative vision. As I commented in my introduction to this chapter, most critics have assumed that there can be little identification between Bellow and his 'anti-Semitic' protagonist. However, I would argue that Allbee is invested with certain privileges and advantages, both intellectually and morally, which make his point of view capable of carrying the weight of Bellow's own.

Like Prospero in *The Tempest*, Allbee in many respects plays the role of a providence in this novel. One of his most obvious advantages is his ability to hold Leventhal for crucial moments in a state of thrall, to create (or, at the very least, to augment and sustain) the plot within which Leventhal becomes embroiled. Allbee, moreover, has a power of insight into Leventhal which the latter finds uncanny and disturbing. Allbee also is in the mould of his creator in his effortless ability to switch from a colloquial to a metaphysical idiom. On several occasions Leventhal remarks upon this ability, as Allbee begins to fall 'into that tone of speculative earnestness that Leventhal detested'.[80] Often, we are directed by this 'speculative earnestness' to consider subjects which are recurring ones in Bellow's work. When Allbee deprecates the declining ethical standards of New York life, his lament sounds very like that of Artur Sammler, and Bellow himself has often gone on record with similar judgements[81] – 'Oh, boy! – New York. Honour sure got started before New York did. You won't see it at night, hereabouts, in letters of fire up in the sky. You'll see other words. Such things just get swallowed up in these conditions – modern life'.[82]

Yet the majority of critics who have discussed the novel persist in seeing Allbee as at best a maladjusted neurotic, at worst a drunken bum. Malcolm Bradbury, for instance, tells us that 'throughout the larger part of the book Leventhal is pursued by the repulsive Allbee'.[83] In what sense is Allbee 'repulsive'? Bradbury doesn't elaborate, but one may surmise that this is not just a reference to his physical appearance. But if it is partly Allbee's personal slovenliness that offends Bradbury, the first description of Leventhal convinces us that he is himself no paragon of sartorial taste for he appears 'dishevelled, and he was even ordinarily not neat. His tie was pulled to the side and did not close with the collar; his shirt cuffs came out beyond his coat-sleeves and covered his thick brown wrists; his trousers sagged loose at the knees'.[84] Tony Tanner also contributes to Allbee's bad press by describing him as an 'anti-Semitic degenerate failure'.[85] But Ihab Hassan is most splenetic of all in his references to 'this mad and repulsive intruder' who strikes him as not only an 'anti-Semite', but 'a suffering and insufferable creep'.[86] I would suggest that these critics have accepted Leventhal's derisive terms in describing Allbee and that by so doing they have shown how partial is their understanding of the novel. It is Leventhal who early in his reacquaintance with Allbee refers to him as 'a bum and a drunk'.[87] As in many other instances, Leventhal later has cause to revise this opinion. Williston tells him that 'Allbee had stayed on the wagon' at *Dill's*, that 'he wasn't fired because he drank',[88] and Allbee later proves Leventhal wrong when he returns to the apartment in sober condition. Leventhal had loaned him five dollars, expecting him to drink it away – 'if he takes one shot . . . he'll take two and then a dozen. That's the way they are'.[89] Again and again one discovers critics using Leventhal's judgements of other characters as though these judgements were sound and valid. So Robert Gorham Davis describes Leventhal's sister-in-law as 'an excitable Italian woman dominated by her mother'.[90] Even Leventhal himself is forced to accept how badly he has misjudged his brother's family. Perhaps the most charitable response to such precipitant criticism is to see it as a case of the critics being misled by appearances. Yet inasmuch as *The Victim* is precisely to do with the kinds of damage that can be done by judging on the basis of mere appearances, it would seem that many critics may be taken to task by a true reading of the novel they claim to understand.

From the very start of their meeting, Allbee is given status as one of penetrating and true vision. Though Leventhal sneeringly describes him as 'one of those guys who want you to think they can see to the bottom of your soul',[91] this is an accurate description. Allbee tells Leventhal that he 'wanted to see but not be seen, and you're mad because you got caught'.[92] But any attempt to escape from Allbee's gaze is futile. That gaze is steadfast. At first Leventhal had used a sideways glance in order to escape from Allbee, but he is soon caused to regard him candidly and Allbee 'returned his look, examining him as he was examined, in concentration and seriousness'.[93] This is *the* Bellovian vision. It is the way Bellow himself examines his subjects and it is the way all of those major characters most closely to be identified with Bellow have seen into themselves and others. But while this is Allbee's most natural form of seeing, it is not Leventhal's. It is only while 'caught' in Allbee's orbit that he can sustain and return such a stare. As the third-person narrator puts it, Allbee has better 'balance' than Leventhal. This poise is variously revealed. In contrast to Leventhal's volatile and frequently belligerent personality (he twice considers doing violence to Allbee in this first scene, once before Allbee has even spoken to him and once after he has left him; later he considers murdering Allbee on two separate occasions, and twice makes impulsive physical assaults on him) Allbee displays a calm control. Leventhal's mental equilibrium is precarious. He knows that 'in his present state of mind he was . . . easily carried away by things'.[94] In the company of others he meets socially, such as the Harkavys, he has to put himself through 'a bracing process' before he can appear composed – 'he was fond of them, they were kind, but he had never been able to work out a satisfactory balance with them'.[95] And when he most needs such composure, as when Allbee accuses him of being responsible for his dismissal by Rudiger, his efforts 'to keep a clear head came to nothing; he felt himself slipping into confusion'.[96]

In contrast, Allbee (that mad, repulsive, degenerate creep) comports himself on almost all occasions with courtesy, tact and equanimity. His balance is shown in the superb little scene of conflict which demonstrates his subtle intelligence. Though Leventhal has already thought of doing physical violence to Allbee, it is entirely characteristic that his thoughts on this are comically confused – 'if he starts something . . . I'll grab his right arm and pull him off balance . . . No, his left arm and pull towards my left; that's my stronger side'.[97] Allbee's physical mastery over Leventhal is, however, simple, direct, and effective:

> Leventhal stared into his laughing face and then began to walk away, whereupon Allbee thrust his arm straight before him and held him back. Leventhal grasped it, but he did not jerk according to his plan. He felt no resistance to his grip. It was he rather than Allbee who was off balance, and he removed his hand.[98]

This literal sleight of hand immediately defuses Leventhal's aggression while simultaneously forcing him to take novel account of Allbee. When we try to visualise the above tableau one of its first effects is a comic one derived from Leventhal's momentary paralysis as he stands there holding up Allbee's arm. But if we take it further we might become conscious of the physical sensation experienced by Leventhal as he feels not the expected resistance to his grasp but something more disturbing for one of his particular anxieties, the *weight* of the arm which he has been made responsible for holding. The ball, it might be said, is suddenly in his court. Off balance again though, he fails to return it. Once again 'Allbee had taken him by surprise. It was surprising'.[99] Or, perhaps, not so surprising. In many ways this scene is a miniature of the larger developments in relations between the two men later in the novel. Throughout the narrative Leventhal is forced to realise the weight of Allbee's presence and there are moments when 'in concentration and seriousness' he understands the human importance of being prepared to take that weight.

For the most part, however, Leventhal's errors of judgement and his indifference to others cause in him a falsification of reality. Very often, with comic irony, we hear Leventhal pronouncing upon others in senses more fittingly applied to himself. Here, his comments on Allbee's mental state are a perfect *summa* of his own defects in that department:

> it was questionable whether this queer, beaten, probably suffering Allbee was in control of his actions ... haunted in his mind by wrongs or faults of his own which he turned into wrongs against himself; and that stirring around of the thoughts and feelings, that churning – everybody experienced it, but for a man like that it must be ugly, terrible, those thoughts wheeling around.[100]

All this from Leventhal who, on the night before has to leave the light on as he has 'this feeling that he was threatened by something while he slept. And that was not all. He imagined that he saw mice darting along the walls'.[101] Bellow also offers a subtle running commentary throughout the novel whereby Leventhal's behaviour towards Allbee is seen reflected in his relationships with others. So in his place of work after his nephew's death he notices that while some of his colleagues have the decency to commiserate others 'didn't even have time to nod. It showed the low quality of the people, their inferiority and meanness ... This Millikan, when he finally did get around to ask a personal question, never listened to the answer, only seemed to'.[102] The moral, in the light of his conduct with Allbee, is obvious.

Virtually every episode of the novel gives us another example of Leventhal's judgemental perversity. Of course he suffers from a nervous debility which is strongly connected to his mother's madness. Whether this debility is due to some hereditary disorder or whether, as his wife Mary believes, it is due to 'the fears of hypochondria'[103] is never fully resolved. Yet Bellow uses Leventhal's childhood memories of the maternal image to suggest that his unacknowledged fault – his lack of emotional involvement with others – is indeed a mentally diseased condition:

> He began to consider his own unfortunate mother ... invariably he saw her wearing an abstracted look, but he was not in fact sure that her look was abstracted. Perhaps he attributed it to her.

And when he examined his idea of her more closely he realized that what he really meant by abstracted was mad-looking; a familiar face and yet without anything in it directed towards him. He dreaded it; he dreaded the manifestation of anything resembling it in himself.[104]

The opening description of Leventhal's own features, already quoted above, would seem to offer a confirmation of his worst dread. I do not suggest that Leventhal is in a real sense insane; no doubt his wife's diagnosis of hypochondriacally induced symptoms is correct. But Leventhal's particular type of abstraction, revealed in his face and its 'unaccommodating, impassive' indifference is responsible for his judgemental failures, leading in turn to a distorted view of reality. In my chapter on Bellow's novel of 1982 *The Dean's December* I quote the following passage from that work:

> the advanced modern consciousness was a reduced consciousness inasmuch as it contained only the minimum of furniture that civilization was able to instal (practical judgements, bare outlines of morality, sketches, cartoons instead of human beings); and this consciousness, because its equipment was humanly so meager, so abstract, was basically murderous.[105]

Leventhal is himself seriously affected by an abstraction of this sort. Albert Corde, Bellow's hero in *The Dean's December*, is afraid that Americans 'have lost all capacity for dealing with experience – no capacity to think about it, no language for it, no real words'.[106] Some such inadequacy may explain Leventhal's dismay at Allbee's capacity for thinking and speaking about the reality below the surface. Leventhal's own mannerisms of speech, his conversational idiom, is not only witless and inept, but it shows how his capacity for real communication is being eroded. Attempting to make conversation with his young nephew Philip, for instance, he does not really attend to what the boy has said so that his 'replies' are almost non-correlative statements that appear to have no care for the liaisons so crucial to adult-child discourse:

> 'Is this your whole supper?' he asked. 'When it's hot like this, I never eat a lot'. The boy had a rather precise way of speaking.
>   'You ought to have bread and butter, and so on, and greens,' said Leventhal.

Philip interrupted his eating to look at his uncle briefly. 'We don't cook much during the heat wave,' he said ... His hair had been newly cut, roughly clipped on top and shaved high up the back of his neck to a line above his large but delicately white ears.

'What kind of barber do you have?'

'Philip looked up again. 'Oh, Jack McCaul on the block. We all go to him; Dad too, when he's home. I told him to cut it this way. I asked for a summer haircut.'

'They ought to take away the man's licence for giving you one like that.' He said this too forcefully and overshot his intended joke, and he paused and made an effort to find the right tone.[107]

On closer scrutiny it is clear that Leventhal's second sentence is a response not to Philip's reply but to his own first remark. Similarly, Leventhal ignores Philip's repetition and goes on to make his hurtfully gauche 'joke' which has paid no attention to Philip's foregoing remark about having asked to have his hair cut so short. This scene is another example of Leventhal not being able 'to work out a satisfactory balance' in his dealings with others. But then he doesn't give himself much practice; with this boy who is, after all, his brother's son, he can only feel like an outsider, 'a visitor'.[108]

The catalogue of social ineptitude continues throughout the narrative. Leventhal, it seems, is tone-deaf in his dealings with others. His equivocations when faced with his sister-in-law's mother (whom also he has never met before) are the reactions of one chronically ill-at-ease in company, one so unused to taking account of others, normally, indeed, so indifferent to their existence, that he is at first paralysed in response and finally, in this failure, relapses back into what we may take to be his normal condition – defensive, belligerent, unaccommodating. The 'thin-lipped formality'[109] of Leventhal's face is a mask, though *The Victim*, I would argue, is a novel that strongly suggests the mask is well-nigh irremovable. Witness his preposterous discomfiture as he tries to come to terms with what he imagines to be yet another of life's snubs. Faced by his sister-in-law's mother for the first time, he decides to dispense with his normal mask, though perhaps only to take up another. He 'was conscious of prolonging his nod almost into a bow; he wanted to be prepossessing'.[110] But how lost and inadequate he is without its protective impassivity:

Since she remained silent, Leventhal stood undecided; it seemed inadvisable to say more; to sit down without being answered would embarrass him. But, also, it might be impolite to return to the kitchen. Maybe he misunderstood her taciturnity. However, she seemed to avert her head from him, and he had to struggle with an angry urge to compel her to face him. Nevertheless she had not spoken, and he could not be sure. It was possible that he was mistaken ... He had decided that the grandmother's look was unfriendly, though in the dusty green-tinged light that came through the lampshade it was difficult to get a definite impression. But he felt her antagonism.[111]

All this because an old lady, understandably very distraught at the grave illness of her grandson, has seemed not to take due account of Leventhal's efforts at a prepossessing formality. Never mind the interference to clear vision posed by the bad light, a slight's a slight whatever way he looks at it. Better 'compel' the old lady's attention. But how to do this? Perhaps by some sort of simple physical expedient, such as driving his fist into her head as he had wished to do to a woman in the cinema who was wearing an obstructive hat? ('Woman or no, Leventhal had had a powerful desire to drive his fist into her head, tear the hat off ... Oh, how he sometimes regretted not slapping off that hat').[112] Shortly after the old lady has delivered her 'snub', Leventhal passes her in the hallway and 'was tempted to jostle her'.[113] Personally, this is the kind of thinking and behaviour I would describe as degenerate, bum-like, repulsive and creepy. In any case, by the time Mr Leventhal has to brace himself for his next social summit he has firmly replaced the mask so that the most mobile feature of his face is the drop of sweat that runs down his cheek:

> 'This is my husband's brother,' said Elena.
> 'Yes, sure,' said Villani taking the cigar out of his mouth. Leventhal impassively looked back at him, his eyes solemn and uncommunicative, only a little formally inquiring. A drop of sweat ran down his cheek.[114]

It shouldn't pass notice that Leventhal's rudeness here (he doesn't make any rejoinder to Villani's friendly 'How do?') is every bit as insulting as that he has imagined the old lady to have meted out to him a few moments earlier. And this is par for the course. After responding curtly to the friendly chat of Mr and Mrs Nunez when he meets them on the stairway of his apartment building, he refuses their invitation to 'Come in and have a beer'. A few moments later, 'he set out again, nodding to Mrs Nunez on the stoop as though he saw her for the first time'.[115]

Given that scenes such as the above establish the norms of Leventhal's behaviour with those whose interest in him is confined to a friendly 'how do', we can hardly expect him to welcome Allbee's much more pressing interrogations.

A large part of Leventhal's failure derives from his excessive *amour propre*. This is partly seen in his condescension towards Allbee and others, partly in his unwillingness to consider the validity of others' points of view. Occasionally, however, Allbee is able to cut through the deceptions that guard Leventhal from a true vision of reality. He has, for example, often thought of himself as having first-hand knowledge of human dereliction. He is quick to tell Allbee that he, too, has been 'stony broke, without a nickel for the automat'.[116] Allbee is dismissive and 'with his outstretched arm and open hand he made a gesture of passing the comparison away':

> There rose immediately to Leventhal's mind the most horrible images of men wearily sitting on mission benches waiting for their coffee in a smeared and bleary winter sun; of flophouse sheets and filthy pillows; hideous cardboard cubicles painted to resemble wood, even the tungsten in the bulb like little burning worms that seemed to eat up rather than give light. Better to be in the dark. He had seen such places. He could still smell the carbolic disinfectant. And if it were *his* flesh on those sheets, *his* lips drinking that coffee, *his* back and thighs in that winter sun, *his* eyes looking at the boards of the floor ... ? Allbee was right to smile at him; he had never been in such a plight.[117]

Allbee here is a facilitator of truth. Without explaining further, Bellow appears to hint at Allbee's magical powers over Leventhal. The 'gesture' used by Allbee above is on one level commonplace; yet its resultant effect on Leventhal's imagination is to provoke a rare moment of objectivity. In another context Allbee's gesture is familiar to us as the conjurer's stage mannerism introducing the startling out of the apparently banal. His potency in this regard is very much a part of his charisma. As Ihab Hassan has noted he 'tends to waver uneasily between a fictional character and thematic symbol'[118] and as a number of critics have remarked, his name itself suggests his status as a larger-than-life embodiment of elemental humanity.

The moment Leventhal is out of Allbee's company he is returned to his normal state. So 'alone on the stoop' his 'glance seemed to cover the street; in reality he saw almost nothing but was only aware of the featureless darkness'.[119] Very infrequently he is brought to an awareness of the 'strange things, savage things' which are usually filtered out of his reality. These vignettes of the crudely real he pictures as 'trembling drops, invisible, usually, or seen from a distance. But that did not mean that there was always to be a distance, or that sooner or later one or two of the drops might not fall on him. As a matter of fact he was thinking of Allbee'.[120] Again Allbee is seen – though, importantly, directly by Leventhal this time – as capable of bringing such realities within Leventhal's sight. Waiting for his nephew Philip at the harbour, we find him beginning to come to a philosophical understanding of what the full life really entails. Had this piece of clear thinking appeared earlier in the narrative one might well have questioned Bellow's tact in attributing such a degree of insight to Leventhal. In its place, however, it is a tribute to Allbee's influence upon him:

> The strain of waiting made him almost tremble, yet it was pleasurable, a pleasurable excitement. He wondered why it was that lately he was more susceptible than he had ever been before to certain kinds of feelings. With everybody except Mary he was inclined to be short and neutral, outwardly a little like his father, and this shortness of his was, when you came right down to it, merely neglectfulness. When you didn't want to take trouble with people, you found the means to turn them aside. Well, the world was a busy place ... You couldn't find a place in your feelings for everything ... On the other hand, if you shut yourself up, not wanting to be bothered, then you were like a bear in a winter hole, or like a mirror wrapped in a piece of flannel. And like such a mirror you were in less danger of being broken, but you didn't flash, either. But you had to flash.[121]

Here, as in all of Bellow's later fiction, the rediscovery of the emotional life is the essential prerequisite of the character's assertion of humanity. Herzog it is who wonders at the truth for him of the proverb *'je sens mon coeur et je connais les hommes'*.[122] Unlike Bellow's later heroes, however, Leventhal's discovery does not provide him with a durable intimation. At the end of *The Victim* Leventhal has returned to ground, like the bear in its winter hole. And when Philip arrives and they go out into Manhattan, it isn't long before that 'pleasurable excitement' begins to give way to more familiar emotions as Leventhal began to feel 'empty and unstable', to feel that 'his earlier confidence in the understanding between them was fading'.[123]

Allbee's particular kind of presence and importunacy no doubt plays its part in having him cast as one who 'plagues Leventhal with his drunkenness, his filth, his insidious anti-Semitism and his claims of victimization',[124] but it is only while being so 'plagued' that Leventhal shows any sign of being able to break free of his imprisoning self-directedness:

> Leventhal . . . was so conscious of Allbee, so certain he was being scrutinized, that he was able to see himself as if through a strange pair of eyes: the side of his face, the palpitation in his throat, the seams of his skin, the shape of his body and of his feet in their white shoes. Changed in this way into his own observer, he was able to see Allbee, too, and imagined himself standing so near behind him that he could see the weave of his coat, his raggedly overgrown neck, the bulge of his cheek, the colour of the blood in his ear; he could even evoke the odour of his hair and skin. The acuteness and intimacy of it astounded him.[125]

Allbee, it might be said, is the sun that strikes against Leventhal's mirror causing it to flash, causing him to be 'deprived . . . for a moment of his sense of the usual look of things'.[126] It is worth remarking that the kind of meticulous intimacy experienced by Leventhal above is very similar to Albert Corde's search for what he would call 'the depth-level' in those around him. The urgency with which Corde pursues this factor is due to his belief that 'this organic, sensory oddity . . . must be grasped as knowledge. He wondered what reality was if it wasn't this . . . Reality didn't exist "out there." It began to be real only when the soul found its underlying truth'.[127] The 'sensory oddity' he refers to is remarkably similar to Leventhal's unwonted microscopic survey of his own and Allbee's features:

What, for example, did he know about Dewey Spangler? Well, he knew his eyes, his teeth, his arms, the form of his body, its doughnut odor ... That vividness of beard, nostrils, breath, tone was real knowledge ... In the same way he knew his sister Elfrida, the narrow dark head, the estuary hips, the feminized fragrance of tobacco mixed with skin odors ... With Minna the reality was even more intimate – fingernails, cheeks, breasts, even the imprint of stockings and of shoe straps on the insteps of her dear feet when she was undressing. Himself, too, he knew with a variant of the same oddity – as, for instance, the eyes and other holes and openings of his head.[128]

Of course the difference between Albert Corde and his early predecessor in Bellow's fiction is that the former has the philosophical sense to welcome such knowledge for its existential worth. But the fact that this kind of awareness is given such philosophical authority in *The Dean's December* is in itself another validation of Allbee's status in *The Victim*, for it is he who gives Leventhal the gift of 'a strange pair of eyes' which enables him to see with such extraordinary lucidity.

At the literal centre of *The Victim* is the scene dominated by the sage Schlossberg. His much-quoted speech about the modes of the human is brilliantly used by Bellow not only as a value-stating passage, but as a means of exposing Leventhal's lack of such values. Schlossberg insists that humanity is measured by its capacity for genuine feeling, just as the good actor is he who can command the emotional response of the audience without 'hoking it up'. Schlossberg's criticisms of the declining standards of mass taste look forward to Bellow's much more sustained castigation of a puerile public consciousness in later novels such as *Herzog*, *Mr Sammler's Planet* and *The Dean's December*. The old man is worried that these days 'everything comes in packages. If it's in a package, you can bring the devil in the house. People rely on packages. If you will wrap it up, they will take it'.[129] People become vulnerable to mountebanks like Herzog's cuckolder Valentine Gersbach; he knows how to package emotionality like any other commodity – 'emotional plasma which can circulate in any system'.[130] 'Good acting', says Schlossberg, 'is what is exactly human':

This girl Livia in *The Tigress*. What's the matter with her? She commits a murder. What are her feelings? No love, no hate, no fear, no lungs, no heart . . . A blank . . . But I don't know if she's too pretty or what to have feelings.[131]

The attack serves to further condemn Leventhal for his own emotional neutrality.

By the thirteenth chapter of *The Victim* the assault upon his reality reaches a critical point, reaches what he calls 'the show-down'. By this time he is as sharply aware as he will ever be of the compromises he has had to make with his moral, emotional and social life in order to preserve his existential security:

Illness, madness, and death were forcing him to confront his fault. He had used every means, and principally indifference and neglect, to avoid acknowledging it and he still did not know what it was. But that was owing to the way he had arranged not to know. He had done a great deal to make things easier for himself, toning down, softening, looking aside. But the more he tried to subdue whatever it was that he resisted, the more it raged, and the moment was coming when his strength to resist would be at an end.[132]

His fault is, of course, his fear of emotional expenditure. This is made clear enough in the second of those moments of sensory intensity when he sees into the heart of himself and his nominal adversary:

suddenly he had a strange, close consciousness of Allbee, of his face and body, a feeling of intimate nearness . . . he could nearly feel the weight of his body and the contact of his clothes. Even more the actuality of his face, loose in the cheeks, firm in the forehead and jaws, struck him, the distinctness of it; and the look of recognition Allbee bent on him duplicated the look in his own. He was sure of that. Nevertheless he kept alive in his mind the thought that Allbee hated him, and his judgement, although it was numbed by his curious emotion of closeness – for it was an emotion – did not desert him.[133]

The crucial sentence in the above is the final one. Leventhal's judgement has been at fault throughout: he misjudges Allbee on a number of counts, ends up misjudging his brother's family, and is generally proved to be a man of singularly maladroit perception.

That perception is still very much at fault above. Allbee in no way 'hates' him; I could not find one objective description of Allbee's disposition which could in any sense be construed in such a way. As I noted previously, Allbee's behaviour, certainly in comparison to Leventhal's, is courteous and pacific (Phoebe Williston remembers Allbee as having been 'intelligent and charming' and 'brilliant' – a judgement which Leventhal typically and scornfully dismisses).[134] The significant clause in the above, however, concerns the 'numbing' of that wrong judgement by the 'curious emotion of closeness' he feels for Allbee. The strong implication here is that such an emotional connection – so rare in Leventhal – has the power to act as a corrective to reason gone wrong. A reality which is not capable of taking account of the emotional as much as the rational area of consciousness will always, Bellow's fiction maintains, be a debased reality tending to inhumanity, to intellect unleavened by the heart. In a recent interview Bellow, apropos *The Dean's December*, clarifies this point, suggesting that this emotional haemorrhage is responsible for the chilly climate of our times, for 'the brutalized city and the psyche of its citizens':[135]

> The estrangement of human beings from one another is a fact of life, no longer a hypothetical matter. The price you pay for the development of consciousness is the withering of the heart. Therefore one must *will* the recovery of feeling, and one must use one's intelligence, too . . . *How* is one to educate oneself to feeling? . . . Corde recognizes the necessity of ennobling reckoning. He comes to understand that we carry about, within, an iceberg which has to be melted. Intellect, itself a source of coldness, must become involved in the melting project. To have intellect devoid of feeling is to be crippled.[136]

In Bellow's later fiction this estrangement is often manifested in the breakdown of familial relations, particularly fraternal relations. Thus, Tommy Wilhelm and his father, Augie and Simon March, Henderson and his family, Moses and Willie Herzog, and in *The Victim*, Asa and his brother Max are all poignant manifestations of such estrangement. Both Asa and Max are aware of their mutual guilt in this regard. When Max visits Leventhal after the funeral he is described as addressing him 'diffidently, a little formally, feeling his way with a queer politeness, almost the politeness of a stranger'[137] and Leventhal notices that Max never refers to Mary,

Leventhal's wife, by name – 'like Elena, he probably did not know what her name was'.[138] Once again, Bellow shows how such estrangement issues forth in Leventhal's painfully inept efforts at conversation with Max. 'How should they talk when they had never, since childhood, spent an hour together?'[139] The following dialogue with Max (who, it's important to remember – for Leventhal clearly doesn't – is in the early stages of the grief of bereavement) establishes Leventhal's gross insensitivity, his only concern being to do with his fantastic belief that Max's wife Elena holds him responsible for Mickey's death:

> 'So how are things going?' he said. He thought Max would speak about Elena. He was in fact certain that the main object of his visit was to discuss her with him.
> 'I guess as good as I can expect.'
> 'Phil all right?'
> 'Well, when one kid passes on it's pretty hard on the other one.'
> 'He'll come around.'
> Max said nothing to this, and Leventhal began to think he was debating whether to mention Elena at all, undecided at the last moment, and struggling with himself.
> 'Yes, kids come around,' Leventhal repeated.[140]

The entire scene continues in this vein and begins to have overtones of bizarre comedy as Leventhal's ludicrous charges against his in-laws are finally understood by an astounded Max:

> 'Tell me, is the old woman around much – her mother?'
> 'Oh, she's in and out all the time.'
> 'For God's sake, throw her out!'
> His vehemence astonished Max.
> 'She doesn't have anything to do with it.'
> 'Don't let her get a hold. Protect yourself against her.'
> Max for the first time began to smile . . .
> 'What kind of talk is that!' he said. 'I never heard anything so peculiar in all my life. First you've got ideas about Elena and now the old woman . . .
> 'She's full of hate,' Leventhal insisted.
> 'Go on, she's a harmless old woman.'
> If he were wrong about Elena, thought Leventhal, if he had

overshot the mark and misinterpreted that last look of hers in the chapel, the mistake was a terrible and damaging one ... But he was right about the old woman, he was sure. 'You must get rid of your mother-in-law, Max!' he said with savage earnestness.[141]

This scene with Max provides the final discrediting of Leventhal's judgement and has, incredibly, been almost completely overlooked by the critics. It shows how thoroughly his regard is self-directed and how humanly damaging are the consequences. The reality concocted by such judgement is consequently inimical to truth and friendship. Leventhal shows himself to have refused to undertake 'the melting project' offered by Allbee.

Eventually he succumbs to a total seizure of intellectual and emotional energy which comes just as Allbee is reaching a position of utter surety. Wearing a new set of clothes and having 'a new aspect', appearing 'more solid' with his haircut and newly shaven face, he tells Leventhal of his conviction that 'a man can be born again. – I'll take a rain check on the kingdom of heaven, but if I'm tired of being this way I can become a new man'.[142] Against this exuberant faith Leventhal is a figure of slumped exhaustion and at this point one might well take the opportunity to ask the critics which of the men is the real down-and-out. Against Allbee's bold triumphalist declaration of human potential and freedom, Leventhal takes refuge in a profound despair:

> At this moment Leventhal felt Allbee's presence, all that concerned him, like a great tiring weight, and looked at him with dead fatigue, his fingers motionless on his thighs ... He was played out ... he was unable to clarify his thoughts or bring them into focus and he lacked the energy to continue the effort ... His dark, poring face with its full cheeks and high-rising dull hair was hung towards his chest. He drew a deep, irregular breath and raised his hands from his lap in a gesture of exorcism against the spell of confusion and despair. 'God will help me out,' passed through his mind, and he did not stop to ask himself exactly what he meant by this.[143]

It is difficult for me to understand how one so pathetically moribund can be seen at the end as 'born again', for after this his moments of illumination are partial at best. At Harkavy's he again feels an 'opportunity to discover something of great importance' about the nature of his life, but the moment passes unachieved and 'it came into his head that he was like a man in a mine who could smell smoke and feel heat but never see the flames'.[144] Even as he walks up to his final meeting with Allbee in the flat, he is still confounded, not knowing 'how to deal with Allbee . . . too agitated to make any plans' and still denying he knows what Allbee 'had hoped for in the first place'.[145]

The epilogue itself shows no significant alteration in his habitual mode of thought and behaviour. He continues to show he is no friend of truth as, looking back on his dealings with Allbee, he asks himself, incredibly, 'hadn't he tried to be fair? Didn't he intend to help him?'[146] He also continues to display that indifference which, throughout the novel, has been his particular trait. Before he meets Allbee in the theatre he supposes that 'by now he was in an institution, perhaps, in some hospital, or even already lying in Potter's Field. Leventhal did not care to think too much or too literally about it';[147] and when he finally does have to confront the living fact of Allbee again, when he is finally 'aware that Allbee was coming up to him . . . he did not raise his eyes until he heard him speak'.[148]

*   *   *

Bellow's fiction as a whole is brimful of those characters – some minor, some major, like Leventhal and Augie March – who 'did not care to think too much or too literally' about the nature of reality. And in *The Victim* it is the much-maligned Allbee who is given the brilliant insight into what he calls 'the real trimmers', the ones who are 'not for God and they're not for the Old Scratch. They think they're for themselves but they're not that either'.[149] Leventhal is a *bona fide* trimmer who resents Allbee because he resents the bottom line from which the latter refuses to budge:

I know what really goes on inside me. I'll let you in on something. There isn't a man living who doesn't. All this business, 'Know thyself'! Everybody knows but nobody wants to admit. That's the thing. Some swimmers can hold their breath a long time – those Greek sponge divers – and that's interesting. But the way we keep our eyes shut is a stunt too, because they're made to be open.[150]

Earlier in the narrative Leventhal had seen a workmate as one whose indifference to others made him 'like a shellfish down in the wet sand, and you were the noise of the water to him'.[151] Typically, he cannot see how he, too, scuttles across the same wet floor. But Bellow's narrator, and the story he tells, leave us in no doubt that this is Leventhal's territory, that 'the imperfections of the pane through which Leventhal gazed suggested the thickening of water at a great depth when one looks up towards the surface'.[152] But Allbee knows the stunts, knows Leventhal can hold his breath only for so long until he resurfaces. Then, having momentarily to face the 'real reality', 'his terror, like a cold fluid, like brine, seemed to have been released by the breaking open of something within him'.[153] But Leventhal will scuttle back down to the wet sand, like Augie March in search of whatever 'would give . . . cover from this mighty free-running terror'.[154] Augie, however, has more style than Leventhal. He, at least, knows better than to stay in one place for too long, and certainly knows better than to ask anybody but himself Leventhal's final, flailing question to Allbee – 'Wait a minute, what's your idea of who runs things?'.

The Victim, then, is a wonderfully well-made novel which provides a critique of its central character through the exploitation of point of view. Though Leventhal is so decisively undermined by the range of more authoritative viewpoints I have drawn attention to, the mark of Bellow's human compassion (as well as of his subtle manipulation of viewpoint) can be detected in the extent to which we may still sympathise with this protagonist. This may be due to our recognition that, for all his faults, Leventhal's fears, his bridling personality, his psychic insecurity are all manifestations of the ties which bind him to that sea full of 'imploring, wrathful, despairing faces'; the more he struggles against Allbee the more does he become wrathful and, finally, full of despair, imploring God to deliver him from his crisis. He is, in the end, a pathetic rather than a detestable figure. We can sympathise with him partly because we are caught up in Bellow's finely-wrought narrative design which allows us to observe the gathering crisis and, perhaps, to feel the panic of Leventhal's increasingly desperate resistance to it. But the larger measure of our sympathy may be derived from a deeper and darker identification, a knowledge of our own salt memories of that Dantesque sea full of faces, of the distance we have put between ourselves and that sea, of the steps we have had to take in order to create and sustain that distance.

3

A Fugitive Style: *The Adventures of Augie March, Seize the Day, Henderson the Rain King*

THE ADVENTURES OF AUGIE MARCH

Although *The Adventures of Augie March* (1953) was highly praised by the majority of contemporary reviewers, succeeding generations of critics have been less impassioned in their estimations of its worth. Though literary historians can continue to find a convenient niche for it as a work of protest against the tranquillised 1950s, an activist novel in Eisenhower's decade of inertia, it is more properly seen as a work that conceals its protagonist's existential despair beneath a rhetoric of affirmation and a posture of hope. Still, as one more recent critic put it, 'despite its initial success, the novel has not worn well',[1] and many critics now see it as at most a daring innovation on the part of a writer indulging himself stylistically at the expense of his readers' patience and his character's plausibility. Bellow's aim may well have been to give, through a stylistic *laissez-allez*, the necessary sense of swiftness and truth, spontaneity and artlessness which might have made his picaro's adventures read like the very stuff of lived experience. But what he achieved was a great deal less, and many readers may well agree that in the end Bellow trades unjustifiably on their tolerance. Those who are able to warm to the earlier chapters (though even these have not been exempt from harsh criticism; the acerbic Maxwell Geismar describes these as 'the weakest part of the book' in which the prose for 'almost the only time in Bellow's work, is turgid and wooden'[2]) go on to find themselves defeated by the later parts where, in Leslie Fiedler's view, the novel becomes 'shriller and shriller, wilder and wilder' until 'it finally whirls apart in a frenzy

54

of fake euphoria and exclamatory prose'.[3] Given Bellow's picaresque structure there can be little continuity in the novel's episodes apart from that offered by Augie's narrative presence, and like Augie's thoughts themselves (in Grandma Lausch's vernacular these 'are about as steady as the way a drunkard pees'[4]) the novel is profligate with its energies in a dizzy pursuit of randomness.

Even Bellow himself, talking in a 1979 interview, disowned a character he had endowed with an excess of vitality, on the grounds of excess – '*such* a blue-eyed *ingenu* and leads such a charmed life. Too much the Sherwood Anderson sort of thing: "Gee whiz, what wonderful people, what a mysterious world!" All wrong'.[5] Like many new fictional voices that strive to be distinct, Bellow was on the one hand rewarded by a sudden popularity and on the other punished for creating a voice loud enough and obvious enough to be an easy target for ridicule. So Norman Mailer in *Advertisements for Myself* saw Bellow's almost overnight success as a result of 'the flaccid taste of these years' and Augie as 'an impossible character' whose adventures 'could never have happened, for he is too timid a man ever to have moused into more than one or two cruel corners of the world'. *Augie March* suffers from 'narrative disproportions ... elephantiastical in their anomaly'.[6]

Perhaps more damage was done by ostensibly friendly reviewers such as Richard Chase who contributed to the overvaluations of this novel. Chase was able to speak of *Augie*'s plot as like that 'of Whitman's *Song of Myself*.[7] And Delmore Schwartz furthered the headlong flight into critical exaggeration when he wrote of *Augie March* as 'superior to *Huckleberry Finn* by virtue of the complexity of its subject matter and to *U.S.A.* by virtue of a realized unity of composition'.[8] But though such contemporary responses seem well off the mark as literary judgements, they tell us much about their cultural context, about the welcome given by intellectuals of the 1950s to a rhetoric of defiance and affirmation. In a time of cultural stagnation Bellow's yea-saying narrator struck a bold note; that it was a note originating in deep self-doubt and denial was obvious only later, and only to a few discerning critics, but while it reverberated it guaranteed its author's place in American letters.

In *Augie March* Bellow seemed to celebrate America in a wild way he had not done before and would not do again, and Americans saw the novel as a challenge to an age of conformity. As one critic remembered in support of the novel's tone, 'it's nice' as Holden

Caulfield once remarked, 'when somebody gets excited about something'.[9] It was a big American booster of a book which, according to Albert J. Guerard 'soon had a great influence – possibly the greatest influence exerted by any one book – on other novelists espousing activist attitudes'.[10] And though he does not mention the connection explicitly, Guerard goes on to suggest that *Augie March* has about it that fiery dissent more usually associated with the Beats. Through its linguistic posture it confirmed that 'one way or another (it seemed in the 1950s) language had to be awakened, enriched, intensified. Prose must, like the sensibility, burn'.[11] As Bellow himself described it, 'I felt there was something delirious about the writing of *Augie March*. It over-ran its borders'.[12] Such stylistic spillage endeared him to a dull and parched time and Augie's repudiation of exacting ideologies seemed an heroic disposition in an age of coercive conformity and organisation-man good manners.

Yet, as I have suggested, the immediate response to the novel was an essentially flawed one. By far the most perceptive of the later, more considered treatments of it came from Norman Podhoretz. Written only five years after publication, his assessment is balanced, historically acute, and deflationary:

> Both in its attempt to create a new idiom that could express the intellectual's joyous sense of connection with the common grain of American life and in its assertion that individual fulfillment is still possible in this fluid and rootless society of ours ... Augie speaks for that period, roughly between 1948 and 1955, that some have called the age of conformity and neo-Conservatism and others the era of 'intellectual revisionism'. But in its failures as a novel – the willed spontaneity of the writing, the abstractness of the hero – we can also detect the uncertainty and emotional strain that lurked on the underside of the new optimism. The elation in the discovery of America was indisputably sincere, but it was a temporary mood, as deceptive an indication of the feelings within as the surface texture of Mr. Bellow's prose. Not nearly enough conviction stood behind this mood to sustain against the slow inexorable grinding of the years of atomic stalemate, the grinding and anxiety which would not be denied.[13]

Podhoretz's identification of the concealed nature of the novel's truth, and of the ersatz in its style, has been noted by only a very few critics since J. J. Clayton does sound a similar note, attending to the 'sinister undercurrents' that lie beneath Augie's 'larkiness'. 'Underneath the "yea" is a deep, persuasive, "nay" – underneath belief in the individual and in the possibility of communion is alienation, masochism, despair.'[14] I would like to develop the brief notice given by these critics to this novel's 'sinister undercurrents', to suggest that Augie's affirmative voice is in many ways a darkly ironic one, and that the novel ought to be seen as Bellow's subtle modification of the picaresque mode so that it can express the inauthentic nature of reality in modern times.

*　　　*　　　*

Himself 'the by-blow of a travelling man',[15] Augie exemplifies the process of becoming part of an adventitious culture. Though his narration is retrospective (I shall discuss the importance of this later in the chapter), Augie is still unable or unwilling ('I'm not going to try to unravel all the causes'[16]) to distinguish between the causal and the contingent among the formative elements of his life. He prefers instead to consider himself a product of Chicago's proliferating but inscrutable human energies, out of the ethnic melting-pot, unruly, clamouring, varietistic:

> In the mixture there was beauty – a good proportion – and pimple-insolence, and parricide faces, gum-chew innocence, labor fodder and secretarial forces, Danish stability, Dago inspiration, catarrh-hampered mathematical genius; there were waxed-eared shovellers' children, sex-promising businessmen's daughters – an immense sampling of a tremendous host, the multitudes of holy writ, begotten by West-moving, factor-shoved parents.[17]

And throughout the narrative Augie will continue to find various kinds of refuge in seeing himself as 'democratic in temperament',[18] as one of America's crowd, 'a crowd that yields results with much more difficulty and reluctance'.[19] There is, as will become clear, a good deal of self-justifying logic in the elder Augie's choice of this particular indifference to social analysis. The important thing to realise, however, is the extent to which this older narrator is his own image-maker, the extent to which his narrative posture eschews in particular that kind of analysis which would reveal him as anything other than one of the multitude, acted on by implacable and unidentifiable powers. His distrust of closed systems of belief which so often provokes, and provides the rationale for his restless movement in the novel, can at times lead to an embrace of the pseudo-mystical. He may give the impression of attempting to assess the environment and his own place within it but, doomed to be 'a picaro for whom the world is always dissolving because it is of his own creation',[20] his search continually takes him away from rigorous findings towards an illusory freedom in a world of possibilities.

Augie tells us that he was 'born under the sign of the recruit' and most critics have seen his being adopted by others as a fundamentally positive thing, a willingness to entertain the competing claims of others while at the same time retaining that very American sense of life's manifold possibilities. Yet if space can suggest possibility, a movement towards a positive expansion of experience, it can also suggest escape, a movement away from unpalatable truths. It is my view that this latter meaning informs Augie's mode of motion, so that his various withdrawals from the different societies he mixes with signify a retreat from moral and spiritual sincerity. Einhorn, his early mentor and role model, is granted such stature because Augie sees him as defiantly uncircumscribed, and in this passage Bellow exploits metaphors of space and restriction in a description of Einhorn:

But when you believed you had tracked Einhorn through his acts and doings and were about to capture him, you found yourself not in the center of a labyrinth but on a wide boulevard; and here he came from a new direction – a governor in a limousine, with state troopers around him, dominant and necessary, everybody's lover, whose death was only one element, and a remote one, of his privacy.[21]

In a book that emphasises the actions and material gains of power, Augie willingly surrenders himself to those who can in some way augment his romantic view of life as possibility. Exercises in hero-worship such as the above tell us much about his need to romanticise and mythologise relationships until finally he can come to refer to himself as his own hero, a 'Columbus of those near-at-hand'.[22]

There is in *Augie March* an ironic parallel to Bellow's later, more bitter acknowledgement that an authentic existence may necessitate withdrawal from an America terminally contaminated by a materialist ethos. For Augie, too, is in withdrawal, but not from the corruptions of public life, as in the case of Herzog, Corde or Crader; Augie's withdrawal is from his own profound awareness of the claims of the spirit. Often, his recognition is mediated through his common man persona, as in the following passage:

> Well, now, who can really expect the daily facts to go, toil or prisons to go, oatmeal and laundry tickets and all the rest, and insist that all moments be raised to the greatest importance, demand that everyone breathe the pointy, star-furnished air at its highest difficulty, abolish all brick, vaultlike rooms, all dreariness, and live like prophets or gods? Why, everyone knows this triumphant life can only be periodic. So there's a schism about it, some saying only this triumphant life is real and others that only the daily facts are. For me there was no debate, and I made speed into the former.[23]

It is significant that the final statement should use the metaphor of speed. Yet the glibness of the assertion is appropriate, for speed, together with space, is often Augie's refuge from a prolonged and serious consideration of the issues he raises above. Not for him Herzog's metaphysical *longeurs* or Citrine's rigorous mysticism. Augie sniffs space with a fugitive's desperation; his awareness of and attraction to 'a world of great size beyond . . . of abstraction, a tremendous Canada of light'[24] comes to seem more and more expedient. It is difficult to be persuaded by one whose life is given to passing enthusiasms, who was careful not to be vexed by 'what didn't come easy. After all, I wasn't yet in any special business, but merely trying various things on'.[25]

It might be thought that I am being harsh on Augie, that it is wrong to expect too much of one so young. But Augie's adventures are being penned by his elder version and they are inescapably filtered through an experienced, not an innocent eye. In this sense the entire narration becomes an extended apologia for whatever failures or inadequacies are felt most strongly by Augie as narrator. Only rarely does this older narrator break in, or more accurately break down to tell us squarely, and penitently, about his bad faith. Augie knows of the darkness common to all ('there is a darkness. It is for everyone'[26]), knows he is part of 'the mud-sprung, famine-knifed, street-pounding, war-rattled, difficult, painstaking, kicked in the belly, grief and cartilage mankind, the multitude',[27] but his acknowledgement strives to be tolerant, pragmatic and indulgent of human weakness, and, of course, his own weakness. In *Augie March* Bellow had not yet (at least not explicitly) begun that move away from the democratic cast of humanism towards his later castigations of mass inanity. Augie's acceptance of human limitation will become increasingly impossible for later heroes, the more so as the weakness and limitation begin to transgress the bounds of tolerance and begin to hurt, coerce, and even, in Humboldt's case, kill their victims. Whereas these later heroes are in varying degrees outraged by their cultural habitat, Augie on the contrary sees himself as an exponent of social process, representative of its dynamic. The 'plundering of reality' which is treated with desperate concern by Sammler, Citrine and Corde, is viewed by the elder Augie as just another facet of that process, an inevitable deterioration, the spirit shot along with the body:

> In the peculiar fate of people that makes them fat and rich, when this happens very swiftly there is the menace of the dreamy state that plunders their reality. Let's say that anyway old age and death would come, so why shouldn't the passage be comfortable? But this proposal doesn't make a firm mind, in the strange area where things swim too fast. Against this trouble thought may be a remedy; force of person is another one, and money and big-scale lavishness, unpierceable concreteness, organisational deeds. So there are these various remedies and many more, older ones . . . . most people make do with what they have, and labor in their given visible world, and this has its own stubborn merit.[28]

This kind of statement, ostensibly common-sensical (and Augie's colloquial idiom is particularly irritating in a passage like this, giving us the kind of wise paternalism that sits on the stoop resting its bones) is in fact, as Podhoretz noted with concern, impossibly abstract, its glibness showing through the rhetorical veneer. Perhaps again we must make allowances for the novel's historical moment and acknowledge that in 1953 such a representation was less facile than it now appears. Spoiled for choice, the number of possible roads back to an authentic, unplundered reality even included shoring oneself up with dollars and big-scale spending.

If the mind was wronged by the affluent age, by the depredations of the fat and rich bourgeois gods, then, so Augie's argument runs, it might also be cured by the same energies acting as a paregoric. Back in his world of infinite possibilities, Augie relishes the glow of societal excess, and asks us to accept that whatever the suffering at the borders, there is still a divine average which will make life tolerable for the many, the world of 'most people' who 'make do with what they have'. If the darkness is endemic so too is the fund of hope, Augie's *animal ridens* forever buoyant. The spectacle of 'mud-sprung, famine-knifed' humanity is for Augie just that, a spectacle, just one more facet of life's grand display:

> I had to wait for his calls in the police station ... moving from dark to lighter inside the great social protoplasm. But the dark of this West Side station! It was very dark. It was spoiled, diseased, sore and running. And as the mis-minted and wrong-struck figures and faces stooped, shambled, strode, gazed, dreaded, surrendered, didn't care – unfailing, the surplus and superabundance of human material – you wondered that all was stuff that was born human and shaped human, and over the indiscriminateness and lack of choice. And don't forget the dirt-hardness, the doughfats and raw meats, of those on the official side. And this wasn't even the big Newgate of headquarters downtown but merely a neighborhood tributary.[29]

As a good example of Augie's image-making, this passage demonstrates how glibly ethics are surrendered to exclamatory rhetoric throughout his narrative. The *New York Post* called *Augie March* 'this vast swarm of a book' in its review, and Augie's range of metaphors in the above suggests the aptness of that description. Lional Trilling found a moral centre to this novel in its 'demonstration of how to achieve and celebrate human richness'.[30] My reservations, however, bear down precisely on the way this 'richness' is celebrated. The perils lie in Augie's assertion that the richness is all, that against the vast human aggregate no infirmity, no malevolence can possibly gain ascendancy. In plenitude, 'surplus and superabundance of human material', the swarm of mankind, there will, says Augie, be mistakes – 'mis-minted and wrong-struck' – but in the ultimate this may just be surplus 'stuff', not harmful to the racial colossus which will contain it and move forward regardless. Augie bypasses meaningful reflection on the causes or the consequences of this human misery and instead asks us to join him in celebration and wonderment ('but the dark of this West Side station!') in the presence of 'the great social protoplasm' of which such misery is but a small part.

There may well be as Trilling says 'a demonstration of how to achieve and celebrate human richness' in Augie's picture, but we are at liberty severely to question the methods he employs and the moral suppressions behind them. As we near this century's close we have learnt enough to suspect a language that sees individuals as so many coins wrong-struck or well-struck, that is familiar with the 'dough-fats and raw meats' of mankind, that little cares for the maladjusted and broken in spirit because they are part of an 'unfailing' system. Chicago had its stockyards and the century its Dresdens and Belsens. *The Dean's December* sees Albert Corde involved with more bitter and truer metaphors of human mass; with Chicago's slums and its inhabitants who live in 'endless regions of the stunned city – many, many square miles of civil Passchendaele or Somme'.[31] For Corde, the only immutable element in the human constitution 30 years after *Augie* is that there are 'endless regions' of the 'spoiled, diseased, sore and running'. These reflect no connection with the vivacity of the social process, but only reveal 'the slums we carry around inside us. Every man's *inner* inner city'.[32]

There are surely occasions when optimism can strike us as shallow, as a manifestation of weakness rather than strength or mettle. As one of Augie's friends puts it, 'A train could hit you and you'd think it was just swell and get up with smiles, like knee-deep in June'.[33] According to Alfred Kazin 'the Augie March way is the longing to embrace in life itself, in its most commonplace texture, the actual miracle of existence, the great gift itself, conferred and confirmed and to be praised in every breath, richer than any words for it'.[34] But Kazin's comment is a hallelujah from the 1950s too, written perhaps at the last moment at which it was possible to pen such a flourish. And yet Kazin was right; there is indeed a longing in Augie for an affirmation of all life, but, as we shall see, that longing is both fear-ridden and fraudulent on Augie's part. Reading *Augie March* does not release us from, but rather emphasises what John Aldridge has called 'the force of the fall from innocence, of the failure of an heroic design'. The effect of the novel is to provoke yet another 'surly spasm of futility'[35] at the impossibility of recovering the fever of optimism which affects to be 'the Augie March way'.

The further Augie moves from his family in Chicago, and from the extended family we are given portraits of in the early chapters, the less firm does his grasp upon 'the Augie March way' become. More frequently we hear a voice of despair, despair based upon his long-denied knowledge of the true reality behind his nostalgic, doctored vision of the past:

> For should I look into any air, I could recall the bees and gnats of dust in the heavily divided heat of a street of El pillars – such as Lake Street, where the junk and old bottleyards are – like a terribly conceived church of madmen, and its stations, endless, where worshipers crawl their carts of rags and bones. And sometimes misery came over me to feel that I myself was the creation of such places. How is it that human beings will submit to the gyps of previous history while mere creatures look with their original eyes?[36]

Augie's preoccupation with the superiority of the non-human, creaturely domain ('I could look out like a creature'[37]) is thus related to his unwillingness to admit his implication in the world of human degradation. His responses to the animal universe are based on a form of hubris, a distancing of himself from the 'rags and bones' of his fellow man. Though susceptible to pangs of misery directly related to the consanguinity he feels with others, he refuses to examine the true provenance of these feelings, preferring instead to ascribe them to 'the gyps' of imperfect memory. Kazin suggested that *Augie March* offered 'the deepest commentary I know on the social utopianism of a generation which always presumed that it could pacify life, that it could control and guide it to an innocuous social end'.[38] Perhaps this is the most charitable way to regard Augie's disaffected vision of human suffering, as a natural response to punctured idealism.

Most commentaries are agreed that the Mexican interlude is the most unsatisfactory part of the book as a whole. The style of writing appears increasingly inadequate, and there are notable discrepancies between this bloated style and the thinness of the events. My own view is similar to that of John Aldridge who feels that 'the style is forced to compensate for the insufficiency of the experience on which it is intended to comment'.[39] The one consolation is that in this section we are finally allowed access to what is, in my view, the philosophical heart of Augie's adventures and their meaning in terms of Bellow's development as a novelist of ideas.

In a passage that calls to mind Bellow's confession that there was a deceit involved in his creation of Augie's innocent and naive persona, we face the most sincere of all Augie's utterances, his self-contempt issuing forth a painful truth:

> to arrive at the chosen thing needs courage, because it's intense, and intensity is what the feeble humanity of us can't take for long. And also the chosen thing can't be one that we already have, since what we already have there isn't much use or respect for. Oh, this made me feel terrible contempt, the way I felt, riled and savage. The f— — — slaves! I thought. The lousy cowards!
>
> As for me personally, not much better than some of the worst, my invention and special thing was simplicity. I wanted simplicity and denied complexity, and in this I was guileful and suppressed many patents in my secret heart, and was as devising as anybody else. Or why would I long for simplicity?[40]

At a stroke this confession forces us to regard Augie's narration as wilfully rhetorical, a thing of guileful posturing. It explains his reluctance to do more than cheerfully wave banners in front of 'the great social protoplasm' and also his irritating ingenuousness. The mindlessness which to many readers seemed to mark Augie's incoherent adventures is here owned up to as a deliberate holding off of complexity for simplicity's sake. Marvin Mudrick, in a very acute essay, regrets the novel 'is very sad in its pretense of joy, the pretense of a self-reforming but unregenerate misanthrope', but though aware of the sham behind Augie's optimistic mien, and of the peculiar parvanimity which his attitudes occasionally reveal ('Augie March is a Jew almost fortuitously and without consequence . . . who recollects the anti-Semitic brutalities inflicted upon him in his childhood only to disclaim their influence upon him',[41]) Mudrick misses the existential rationale behind the pretense.

His 'democratic temperament' can now be seen as another refuge from existential truth and the fidelity to a reality he finds too 'intense' to countenance for long. Indeed, in moments of searing truth he is far more likely to vilify the multitude ('f— — — slaves') for its worship of false images than he is to identify himself with it.

The entire narration, as given to us by the older Augie, now has an ironic, rather pathetic look to it. It tells the story of a half-life, a life undertaken with the lowest expectations of personal fulfillment, in the debased conviction that 'this way he can't get justice and he can't give justice, but he can live'. The adventures of Augie March are provoked not by an exploratory spirit but rather by the fear-driven, craven need to deny his own being. The self-defamation continues:

> Personality is unsafe in the first place. It's the types that are safe. So almost all make deformations of themselves so that the great terror will let them be. It isn't new. The timid tribespeople, they flatten down heads or pierce lips or noses, or hack off thumbs, or make themselves masks as terrible as the terror itself, or paint or tattoo. It's all to anticipate the terror which does not welcome your being.
>
> Tell me, how many Jacobs are there who sleep on the stone and force it to be their pillow, or go to the mat with angels and wrestle the great fear to win a right to exist? These brave are so few that they are made the fathers of a whole people.
>
> While as for me, whoever would give me cover from this mighty free-running terror and wild cold of chaos I went to, and therefore to temporary embraces. It wasn't very courageous.[42]

Even in moments of candour like this, Augie still makes his exonerative efforts, attempting to take refuge in the lowest common denominator of humanity, in the world populated by 'almost all'. But his admissions still have far-reaching implications for a proper interpretation of the novel. The evaluative terms through which the novel's meaning have formerly been understood have, in effect, to be transposed. The conviction that 'personality is unsafe . . . it's the types that are safe' goes far to explain why many readers have found *Augie March* to be a pretentious narrative, one in which fakery can be found in voice and tone. The voice can now be recognised as belonging to a guileful and self-estranged rather than naive protagonist, whose wanderings through a series of 'temporary embraces' are undertaken as a way of avoiding the pains of that reality he calls a 'wild cold of chaos'. The famous boldness of the pose ('I am an American, Chicago born . . . and go at things free-style') is in direct opposition to the shrinking figure beneath. No wonder then that readers have found Augie lacking in personality and depth of being; he would forego such luxuries for the surer, safer domain that belongs to the human 'types'. Knowing the 'mighty free-running terror' of living in a full awareness of self, he instead chooses neither absurd laughter nor sober nihilism, nor even that heroic 'Augie March way' which is the novel's surface. Instead he chooses to embrace a stereotypical reality and by so doing becomes Bellow's saddest creation, more cowardly than Joseph, more futile than Corde or Crader. His *gaminerie* is his part of the 'deformation' which he sees the multitude inflicting on itself 'so that the great terror will let them be'.

Augie can now be seen as a character concealed from himself and, for most of the narrative, from his readers. The centrality of the passages under discussion here makes those views comprising the consensus reading of *Augie March* seem dubious. Keith Opdahl, for instance, writes of 'Augie's happy acceptance of his time and place'.[43] He, and the critic who confidently describes Augie as one 'determined to live fully in an unpredictable and unrolling present'[44] misses the unhappy sight of his faint-hearted escape into 'temporary embraces'. So wide is the discrepancy between the rhetoric and the reality of Augie's existence that such judgements, founded as they are upon an acceptance of that rhetoric, are quite mistaken. The alternative to my reading of *Augie March* might be one that places his confessional remarks in a developing context, seeing them as some sort of nadir statement in a life which eventually matures. But the reader who goes in search of such a rehabilitation will be disappointed. The concluding episodes of the novel only confirm that Augie will continue to treat life as a kind of *pis aller*. He relapses into his characteristic guise, refusing to admit complexities for fear of where they may lead, saying 'Oh, but why get too earnest? Seriousness is only for a few, a gift or grace, and though all have it rough only the favorites can speak of it plain and sober'.[45]

He returns to quoting with conviction Padilla's slogan of 'easy or not at all'.[46] Slowly, but it seems inevitably, Augie begins to take the line of least resistance once again:

> I went along whiffing a cigar and lacking any air of steady application to tasks, forgetful, elliptical, gleeful sometimes, but ah, more larky formerly than now. While I mused I often picked up objects off the street because they looked to me like coins . . . thus obviously hoping for a lucky break. Also I wished somebody would die and leave me everything.[47]

'Nevertheless', protests Augie, 'I was getting somewhere, you mustn't go entirely by appearances. I was coming to some particularly important conclusions.'[48] What follows is the often-quoted 'axial lines' passage, in essence a reiteration of the less well-known passage to which I have referred earlier. There is, though, a significant modification in this restatement of what it takes for man to grasp an authentic reality, and this concerns the ease with which such a reality can be reached and sustained. In the earlier passage Augie had spoken of the hard road to this kind of fulfillment, of the 'courage' and 'intensity' needed to overcome cigar-whiffing distraction. Against this, the idea of exploiting one's axial lines reads like a piece of pseudo-mysticism, a dark night of the soul as written by Padilla. Augie gives us a mysticism for loafers and suggests that access to the higher realms of being can be had as easily as the objects he picked off the street:

'I have a feeling,' I said, 'about the axial lines of life with respect to which you must be straight or else your existence is merely clownery, hiding tragedy. I must have had a feeling since I was a kid about these axial lines which made me want to have my existence on them, and so I have said 'no' like a stubborn fellow to all my persuaders, just on the obstinacy of my memory of these lines, never entirely clear. But lately I have felt these thrilling lines again. When striving stops, there they are as a gift. I was lying on the couch here before and they suddenly went quivering right straight through me. Truth, love, peace, bounty, usefulness, harmony! And all noise and grates, distortion, chatter, distraction, effort, superfluity, passed off like something unreal. And I believe that any man at any time can come back to these axial lines, even if an unfortunate bastard, if he will be quiet and wait it out. The ambition of something special and outstanding I have always had is only a boast that distorts this knowledge from its origin, which is the oldest knowledge, older than the Euphrates, older than the Ganges. At any time life can come together again and man be regenerated ... He will be brought into focus. He will live with true joy.'[49]

This is the passage regarded as the most concise statement of Augie's philosophy by most critics, a shining vision of the transcendent possibilities available to man. If my argument in this chapter has been at all persuasive, it should be clear that the above is at most an effort to reconcile Augie's serious desire for transcendence with his constitutional faults of lethargy and caprice. Certainly there is nothing in the preceding narrative that could persuade us to share his millenial faith in the possibility of regeneration for himself and all who merely have to 'be quiet and wait it out'. If anything, the succeeding parts of his adventures refute this faith and reveal it to be simplistically discovered and experientially discredited, wishful thinking masquerading as mystical wisdom.

The Adventures of Augie March is Bellow's portrait of capitulation to the forces of unreality. And Augie, in his friend Mimi's nice phrase, is one of those who digs for unreality 'more than for treasure, unreality being their last great hope because then they could doubt that what they knew about themselves was true'.[50] The structure of the novel is one that conveys 'a dominant pattern of defeat'[51] for Augie March, that illustrates Bellow's appreciation of human fallibility (to be increasingly explored in later novels) and the blandishments that man has created for himself so that he need not face up to himself. The war puts an end to Augie's impossible plans to put his axial lines to work ('I aim to get myself a piece of property and settle down on it',[52]) probably as well considering his track-record in seeing things through. And he, too, seems to recognise with self-contempt that his sudden burst of patriotism has its roots in a craven need to evade deeper responsibilities:

> I got carried away immediately. Overnight I had no personal notions at all. Where had they gone to? They were on the bottom somewhere. It was just the war I cared about and I was on fire . . . After a while, if I thought of my great idea, I told myself that after the war I'd get a real start, but I couldn't do it while the whole earth was busy in this hell-making project . . . I went around and made a speech to my pals, much to the amazement of people, about the universal ant heap the enemy would establish if they won . . . Oh yes, I got up on my hindlegs like an orator and sounded off to everyone.[53]

In response to that last confession we may well say, so what's new? And we can't help but recall Joseph's similar welcome of military life as an end to the burdens of being true to the intensities of self-knowledge in *Dangling Man*. The picaresque mode in this novel is an escape from rather than a movement to, and Augie's quixotism a replacement of true by false ideals. That Augie can occasionally admit his weaknesses more than many of this novel's critics have seemed able to is a tribute to Bellow's subtle and ironic modification of the picaresque hero. It is an original and witty reaccommodation of the mode to modern times, allowing it to express, in ironic camouflage, many of the damages and compromises inflicted upon man as spiritual aspirant in this age.

Towards the end of the narrative, Augie, in Florence as a tourist, is accosted by an importunate old lady wishing to peddle her services as a guide. This incident forces home the point that Augie has all but succeeded in eradicating the idea of 'personality' from his life. The old lady is suddenly angered by his irritable dismissal of her as just another of those people who insist on bothering him and she explodes:

'People! But I am not other people. You should realize that. I am – ' and she was voice-stopped, she was so angry. 'This is happening to *me!*' she said . . . What was the matter, hadn't this thing taken long enough, wasn't it gradual enough? I mean, the wrinkles coming, the gray choking out the black, the skin slackening and the sinews getting stringy? . . . What was the matter that she still was as if in the first pain of a deep fall?

Later Augie comes to realise the meaning of the old lady's outburst:

This ancient lady was right too, and there always is a *me* it happens to. Death is going to take the boundaries away from us, that we should no more be persons. That's what death is about. When that is what life also wants to be about, how can you feel except rebellious?[54]

The point is that it is this 'me' that Augie is in flight from. Unlike the old lady, whose insistent claim to self he at first mistakes for pathetic vanity, Augie desires the anonymity of type rather than the significance of personality.

In the end he is riddled with the puerile ways of the feeble humanity he is so much a part of. When he returns to Stella after the war he returns also to the implementation of his scheme for realising his axial lines. He knows then, as he did even at the time when he first conceived this 'project' that he 'didn't have the least idea of how to go about it. And of course it was only one of those bubble-headed dreams of people who haven't yet realized what they're like nor what they're intended for'.[55] This conception of the axial lines is, as Augie plainly says, just 'one of those featherhead millenarian notions'.[56]

The novel finally has more significance as an indicator of what Mailer called the flaccid taste of an indiscriminate decade than as the great American novel it was originally thought to be. The reviewer who saw in *The Adventures of Augie March* a transfiguration of American literary convention so that 'for the first time in fiction America's social mobility has been transformed into a spiritual energy which is not doomed to flight, renunciation, exile, denunciation'[57] has the distinction of being comprehensively wrong. Augie's energy is precisely one which is given over to the flight, renunciation, exile and denunciation of his spirit and his being. As a fugitive from the only reality worth the name, Augie is a medal-winner, urging himself on to new heights of evasion, buckling himself fast to whatever fancy will dissolve his terror of self-confrontation. So the last glimpse we have of Augie sees him aptly engaged in the struggle to outpace a newly gathering storm:

> Then on the long sand the waves crashed white; they spit themselves into pieces. I saw this specter of white anger coming from the savage gray and meanwhile shot northward, in a great hurry to get to Bruges and out of this line of white which was like eternity opening up right beside destructions of the modern world, hoary and grumbling. I thought if I could beat the dark to Bruges I'd see the green canals and ancient palaces. On a day like this I could use the comfort of it, when it was so raw.[58]

This, too, is that existential ferment from which Augie will continue to run, besieged by his dark modern consciousness of the 'wild cold of chaos', a spiritual vagrant in search of the powers of distraction, 'the green canals and ancient palaces' wherein he might seek an always temporary refuge. At the end of his first novel, Bellow's character surrenders his self-determination to external governance. With no regret Joseph agrees that 'the next move was the world's'.[59] Perhaps Augie's adventures are best seen as an example of the dangers of surrendering oneself to such a random agency. Bellow's succeeding novels will show an increasing determination to revise this capitulation.

SEIZE THE DAY

Wedged between the stylistic extroversions of *The Adventures of Augie March* and *Henderson the Rain King, Seize the Day* is still 'the real pastrami between two thick slices of American store bread'.[60] The members of the Royal Swedish Academy evidently shared the taste for pastrami, as they singled out the novel for special mention in the Nobel Prize citation. Even the Bellow-baiting Mailer grudgingly throws a bouquet in the direction of the 'surprisingly beautiful ending' of the novel, 'the first indication for me that Bellow is not altogether hopeless on the highest level'.[61] Hopelessness is, however, very much Bellow's theme here, a profound hopelessness which seems to me deepened by the novel's much discussed final scene. Because of Bellow's immaculately rendered linear plot, the reader is led to anticipate a climactic ending, a resolution to suspenseful elements of the narrative – 'he was aware that his routine was about to break up and he sensed that a huge trouble long presaged but till now formless was due. Before evening, he'd know'.[62] Many critics, lured on by the false signals of *Augie March*, were determined to extract a humanist affirmation from the concluding paragraph of the book, with Tommy's copious tears being seen as expiatory and sanative, the waters of rebirth and baptism.[63] Others are altogether dissatisfied with the conclusion, seeing it as unclear in its meanings or artistically misjudged.[64] My own belief is that the language used by Bellow in the concluding paragraph cannot possibly uphold the range of affirmative meanings so often thought to reside there. The point is that such meanings cannot be discovered elsewhere in the unrelentingly miserable sequence of events that make up Tommy's day; critics are therefore driven to distort the modest meanings and perfectly lucid language of the final paragraph so that it takes the shape of a polarising rhetoric persuasive enough to act as a countermand to the accumulated logic of the novel as a whole. But such interpretations only succeed in muddying waters which would otherwise be unacceptably clear in what they disclose about the depth of Tommy's despair and, more worrying to such critics, about Bellow's attitude towards the humanist possibility. 'Does Tommy weep for himself, or the dead stranger and the ultimate human state embodied within him?'[65] asks one exasperated party in an effort to interrogate the obvious. He joins the ranks of those who find that the 'final burst of lyricism is disguising irresolution'[66] which gets him off the hook by passing the buck back in Bellow's direction. Malcolm Bradbury, in attempting to answer the same question, 'why does Tommy weep', offers this multiple response:

> His final release may thus be supposed to be his restoration, his atonement, his discovery of his own mortality but also of its potential. Tommy weeps for the body of another, and his own insufficient and debased body; he weeps, too, to find that 'killing' to which he has devoted his day has a meaning, being part of the compromised struggle that life makes with lifelessness. He weeps also to find himself a part of the city's moving crowd, a crowd to which he has been helplessly trying to reach; and he weeps to discover the mortality that makes the living and the dead into one community, making life senseless but making living activity into a value, because it is simply all there is.[67]

I doubt whether there is either the sense or the suggestion in that final paragraph to justify such a plurality of interpretation. There is, however, plenty of sense in the paragraph. It is lyrically beautiful in its evocation of Tommy's convulsive *cri de coeur* and it is also, as I wish to argue in this discussion, a resolution which does not shrink from its ultimate condemnation of the inhumanity of American reality. There is neither ambiguity nor irresolution in that condemnation, but instead Bellow's bleakest disavowal of the normative conditions that prevail there.

Coming after the apparent affirmations of *Augie March*, critics perhaps expected more of the same. Yet as I argued in my response to that novel Augie is properly seen as a character in flight from self-knowledge, well-practiced in the ways of distraction and the art of concealment. Given this it is no surprise to find the first sentence of *Seize the Day* telling us that 'when it came to concealing his troubles, Tommy Wilhelm was not less capable than the next fellow'. Or 'so at least he thought'[68] adds the narrator, an important qualifier and one that distinguishes Tommy from Augie straightaway. Augie has both the energy and the style to accomplish his self-deceptions; Tommy, on the contrary, has no style and precious little energy left. Bellow's narrator stresses throughout the horrific price Tommy pays for his *gaucherie*, his styleless bearing ('fair-haired hippopotamus'), his failure in the material world, and his lack of emotional reserve. Unlike Augie, Tommy has no notion of how to dissemble successfully. The narrator slightly mocks his efforts to keep up appearances, telling us that Tommy 'had once been an actor – no, not quite, an extra – and he knew what acting should be. Also, he was smoking a cigar, and when a man is smoking a cigar, wearing a hat, he has an advantage; it is harder to find out how he feels'.[69]

Tommy knows the groundrules, knows how he is expected to behave, having learnt from his father how, despite 'bad luck, weariness, weakness, and failure' he must still affect a low-key tone, must 'sound gentlemanly, low-voiced, tasteful'.[70] Tommy knows the rules, but always loses the game. 'I am an idiot. I have no reserve . . . I talk. I must ask for it. Everybody wants to have intimate conversations, but the smart fellows don't give out, only the fools'.[71] By many standards, Dr Adler's repudiation of his son is justified and Bellow has carefully prepared a case for the doctor's perception of Tommy as a slob, a miscreant, a maladroit bungler with an unerring talent for taking the wrong road. And yet, as one critic has noted, though Dr Adler 'is right, when his slovenly, failure-ridden son comes on his knees, begging, to both feel and articulate his disgust. He is right but not human'.[72] And this is, of course, Bellow's subject here: not Tommy's pathos but all those, such as Tamkin and his father, by whose example he seems such a misfit. But this is the final irony of the novel – that the one person who clings to the reality of what it means to be human is, in the eyes of the world, a misfit. Whereas Joseph of *Dangling Man* set out in knowledgeable defiance of a 'commandment' of American reality – 'if you have difficulties grapple with them silently',[73] Tommy's pathos derives from his unexamined acceptance of this axiom. His tears are an expression of his inability to live within a reality that is contemptuous of their shedding. Years after the publication of *Seize the Day*, Bellow spoke in an interview of his belief in the vitality and seriousness of emotional display and of the harsh protocol of contemporary life that rules against such display:

Is feeling nothing but self-indulgence? What about William Blake's belief that a tear is 'an intellectual thing'? . . . When people release emotion, they so often feel like imposters. By restraining themselves, they claim credit for a barren kind of honesty. In modern literature, there are not many clean and beautiful bursts of emotion or moral power . . . In *Humboldt's Gift*, when Citrine is beaten and abused in court, he has an impulse to speak out indignantly . . . but he checks himself because he realizes that it would only make matters worse for him. Nothing is gained by letting yourself go among people who hate such letting go.[74]

The conclusion to *Seize the Day* contains one 'beautiful burst of emotion' and, in the context of the novel's critique of cultural norms, the conclusion also has great moral power.

What Tommy painfully learns is just the truth that 'nothing is gained by letting yourself go among people who hate such letting go'. Whereas Citrine, and Herzog and Corde too have realised the prudence of closing the valves of feeling in public, Tommy has neither the intelligence nor the guile to develop such sophisticated strategies of concealment. Though many critics believe that the final scene sees a 'possibility of communion'[75] for him 'in the centre of a crowd', this, like all the other affirmative readings, ignores important, clarifying elements of the language of the text. Bellow's stress is upon Tommy 'hidden' in the centre of the crowd. And that Tommy eventually unburdens his heart while among strangers and that the final image provoking this release is that of a dead man strongly suggests, as one critic has put it, that Tommy's 'unshared life looms permanent' and that 'true feeling can only be generated within one's own self, and only *toward* one's own self'.[76] Though he cries openly he is in a crucial way as concealed as ever, 'protected by the occasion'[77] of the funeral so that the onlookers are never aware of the truly shocking nature of his isolated suffering. Instead of being outraged, embarrassed, or in other ways strongly affected by that grief, these onlookers are merely curious, or even envious – ' "It must be somebody real close to carry on so". "Oh my, oh my! To be mourned like that", said one man . . . with wide, glinting, jealous eyes'.[78] Ironically, too, Tommy comes to seem a dramatic embodiment of Bellow's idea that 'when people release emotion, they so often feel like imposters'. One mourner wonders whether he was 'perhaps the cousin from New Orleans they were expecting'.[79] So not only the language but also the context of this final scene appears to demonstrate not 'the possibility of communion', not a movement 'up, up, up into the firmament of wishful allegory'[80] not, as Bradbury would have it, Tommy's newly found connexions with the city's crowd, but rather his awful isolation within the crowd, his emotional release figured as a sinking downwards towards extravagant oblivion.

*   *   *

In the same interview already quoted from above, Bellow goes on to remark, *apropos* his short story 'The Old System', that 'in a family situation such as the one in "The Old System", people do sound off' in an emotional way. Yet at the centre of Tommy's life is his father's refusal to accept such an 'old system' of family responsibility which could countenance such a discourse. Bellow's belief in the moral necessity of such a discourse has been reaffirmed most recently in *The Dean's December*, though there, perhaps significantly, family coherence is sustained through the supervision of a matriarchy. In *Seize the Day* Dr Adler seems to have abdicated paternal responsibility, leaving Tommy to mourn that 'his own son, his one and only son, could not speak his mind or ease his heart to him'.[81] Dr Adler is in fact 'one of those people . . . who hate such letting go', one who 'felt that his son was indulging himself too much in his emotions'.[82] Ironically, one of the two people Tommy meets who encourages emotional expression is Maurice Venice, the Hollywood agent who, priming Tommy for his screen test, urges him to let himself go, 'don't be afraid to make faces and be emotional. Shoot the works. Because when you start to act you're no more an ordinary person'.[83] Again, this seems to express Bellow's idea that people 'feel like imposters' when releasing emotional energy. Only actors cry, pull faces. Ordinary people, doing so, feel like actors. So 'one fellow smiles, a billion people also smile. One fellow cries, the other billion sob with him'.[84] Ordinary people, however, are restrained by the emotionally repressive reality of their culture, are conditioned by the average 'to behave the same way as the average'.[85] Only movie stars can depart from the leaden rule of the average, and in impersonating emotion their audiences are allowed to impersonate them. The reality, embodied so successfully by Dr Adler, 'a master of social behaviour',[86] is founded upon the law of reason for reason is what one needs if one is truly to seize the day and reason is what Dr Adler personifies, as surely as Tamkin preaches it. Love, emotionalism, feeling are all utter anathema to the likes of Wilhelm senior. Dr Adler, like his namesake, Myron, of *Dangling Man*, has learned to prize convenience above all else and this is the sense behind his credo, his advice to his son, 'carry nobody on your back'.[87] To have feelings is to be vulnerable; moreover, feelings are a positive disadvantage in the world of business. Feelings belong to immature types. Perhaps, Wilhelm thinks, his father 'may be trying to teach me that a grown man should be cured of such feeling.

Feeling got me in dutch at Rojax. I had the *feeling* that I belonged to the firm, and my *feelings* were hurt when they put Gerber in over me'.[88]

There is at least a cold candour about Tommy's father's refusal to entertain the feelings of his son. Apart from the minor characterisation of Maurice Venice, the other figure that encourages Tommy's self-expression is the charlatan Tamkin. Tamkin is really the major character of the novel,[89] the prototype of many in Bellow's fiction, a particularly American characterisation (he bears a resemblance to the likes of Rinehart of Ellison's *Invisible Man*, Milo Minderbinder of *Catch-22*, and the numerous protean figures of Thomas Pynchon's fiction), 'this model of the contemporary mind, ragbag of public and private facts and fancies lavishly scattered like farts in a windstorm, as miscellaneous and unassemblable as amputated legs and arms, tumbling outward toward horizons of meaninglessness'.[90] He is certainly the forerunner of Valentine Gersbach of *Herzog* and Dewey Spangler of *The Dean's December*. Like the former Tamkin is a self-proclaimed poet who 'put himself forward as the keen mental scientist'.[91] Both Dr Adler (described as 'a fine old scientist') and Tamkin, who gambled 'scientifically', are associated with a kind of anti-humanistic scientism which will reappear in Bellow's fiction in increasingly nasty forms until it is given its baleful apotheosis in *The Dean's December*. Like Spangler, Tamkin may have 'no purpose except to talk'.[92] In a world such as Tommy's, wherein even casual contacts are bounded by prohibitions of communication and expression (witness Tommy's relationship with the hotel newsvendor, Rubin, 'the kind of man who knew, and knew and knew. Wilhelm also knew many things about Rubin, for that matter, about Rubin's wife and Rubin's business, Rubin's health. None of these could be mentioned, and the great weight of the unspoken left them little to talk about'),[93] it was a relief to find one such as Tamkin who 'spoke of things that mattered'.[94] So, just as Corde fatally unburdens himself to Spangler in Budapest, Tamkin finds Tommy willing prey. Following his rejection by his father, Tommy stumbles into Tamkin's orbit, feeling that there at least he would find one who could 'sympathise with me' and try 'to give me a hand'.[95] It is, of course, Tamkin who voices the novel's *carpe diem* motto. Like Madeleine Herzog, Gersbach, Spangler and Kirby Allbee, Tamkin is the successful predator, perfectly adapted to the jungle that is the American metropolis, 'the end of the world, with its complexity and machinery; bricks and tubes, wires and stones, holes and heights'.[96] But as one critic has noted, Dr Tamkin's adjustment to these conditions is a mechanically frightening one:

> He is a man who had learned the weaknesses of the human condition and who puts his knowledge to practical use. He is presented as not only devoid of sympathetic understanding but as one for whom the possibility of it has ceased to exist. Bellow's image of Dr. Tamkin is one of the most singular condemnations in contemporary literature of what modern man has become. From his voice come some of the most profound and incisive insights of the novel ... yet for him insight is not a moral achievement but a tool.[97]

Just as Gersbach's audiences, deprived of 'good sense, clarity, truth'[98] come to attend a man who will pump them with 'emotional plasma',[99] so Tommy prays that Tamkin 'would give him some useful advice and transform his life'.[100] And again, like the confused types of Herzog's acquaintance who crave 'something real to carry home when day is done',[101] so Tommy knows that he is 'a sucker for people who talk about the deeper things of life, even the way he does'.[102]. Tamkin's major trick (not difficult to apply successfully in Tommy's case) is to jargonise psychological experience, to mystify, to 'deepen' the banal, to appear both scientific and spiritual, and to present the whole case as impossibly complex so that 'you can't understand without first spending years on the study of the ultimates of human and animal behaviour, the deep chemical, organismic, and spiritual secrets of life. I am a psychological poet'.[103] Gersbach is termed 'a poet in mass communications' and his technique of exploitation is similar to Tamkin's:

> A man like Gersbach can be gay. Innocent. Sadistic. Dancing around. Instinctive. Heartless. Hugging his friends. Feeble-minded. Laughing at jokes. Deep, too. Exclaiming 'I love you!' or 'This I believe!' And while moved by these 'beliefs' he steals you blind. He makes realities nobody can understand.[104]

With Tamkin, the problem was also one of intelligibility. Like Gersbach, he has no being beyond his acquisitive drives, his desires for significance. He succeeds because of his protean nature ('Funny but unfunny. True but false. Casual but laborious, Tamkin was')[105] and because of his fake profundities which, too, comprise realities beyond comprehension, so that 'listening to the doctor when he was so strangely factual, Wilhelm had to translate his words into his own language, and he could not translate fast enough or find terms to fit what he had heard'.[106]

But this confusion of language and meaning is one that, for Tommy, extends to the entire gamut of knowledge, and knowledgeability, to lead the individual towards the nightmare reality of absolute unintelligibility where solipsism has its perpetual ascendancy:

And was everybody crazy here? What sort of people did you see? Every other man spoke a language entirely his own, which he had figured out by private thinking; he had his own ideas and peculiar ways. If you wanted to talk about a glass of water, you had to start back with God creating the heavens and earth; the apple; Abraham; Moses and Jesus; Rome; the Middle Ages; gunpowder; the Revolution; back to Newton; up to Einstein; then war and Lenin and Hitler ... You were lucky even then to make yourself understood. And this happened over and over and over with everyone you met. You had to translate and translate, explain and explain, back and forth, and it was the punishment of hell itself not to understand or be understood, not to know the crazy from the sane, the wise from the fools, the young from the old or the sick from the well. The fathers were no fathers and the sons no sons. You had to talk with yourself in the daytime and reason with yourself at night. Who else was there to talk to in a city like New York?[107]

This is one of the great pieces of writing in Bellow's fiction and persuasively expresses this novel's concern with the breakdown of community. In its sombre realisation of a total disjunction even between like-minded people, the above passage is one that prepares us for that final passage that confirms Tommy's fears about the futility of attempting to find empathy outside the self.

Tamkin is both a creator and a beneficiary of the state of affairs described above. He feeds on its victims with utter impartiality. Bellow's physical description of Tamkin appears to emphasise the animal in him as well as the deceiver; and there are insinuations too of Mephistophelian grossness and carnality:

What a creature Tamkin was when he took off his hat! The indirect light showed the many complexities of his bald skull, his gull's nose, his rather handsome eyebrows, his vain moustache, his deceiver's brown eyes. His figure was stocky, rigid, short in the neck, so that the large ball of the occiput touched his collar. His bones were peculiarly formed, as though twisted twice where the ordinary human bone was turned only once, and his shoulders rose in two pagoda-like points. At mid-body he was thick. He stood pigeon-toed, a sign perhaps that he was devious or had much to hide. The skin of his hands was ageing, and his nails were moonless, concave, clawlike, and they appeared loose. His eyes were as brown as beaver fur and full of strange lines ... There was a hypnotic power in his eyes, but this was not always of the same strength, nor was Wilhelm convinced that it was completely natural. He felt that Tamkin tried to make his eyes deliberately conspicuous, with studied art, and that he brought forth his hypnotic effect by an exertion. Occasionally it failed or drooped, and when this happened the sense of his face passed downward to his heavy (possibly foolish?) red underlip.[108]

Interestingly Gersbach, too, is malformed, has a pegleg, and is also depicted as carnally gross, 'with a head like a flaming furnace'.[109] He is associated in Herzog's consciousness with a lurid vulgarity – 'when I think of Valentine ... I see the mobs breaking into the palaces and churches and sacking Versailles, wallowing in cream desserts or pouring wine over their dicks'.[110] The image of Tamkin's twisted anatomy is, of course, the analogue of the perversion of the natural which is his stock-in-trade. 'If you were to believe Tamkin ... everybody in the hotel had a mental disorder, a secret history, a concealed disease ... like the faces on a playing card, upside down either way. Every public figure had a character-neurosis.'[111] And commensurate with the suggestion that Tamkin embodies a kind of barely concealed, devilish bestiality, is his view of the world as an infernal place of pain and suffering:

Wilhelm said, 'But this means that the world is full of murderers. So it's not the world. It's a kind of hell.'

'Sure,' the doctor said. 'At least a kind of purgatory. You walk on the bodies. They are all around. I can hear them cry *de profundis* and wring their hands. I hear them, poor human beasts.

I can't help hearing. And my eyes are open to it. I have to cry, too. This is the human tragedy-comedy'.[112]

But it is Tamkin who walks on the bodies of his suffering victims, transferring the legitimate terms of description from himself to them, the 'human beasts'.

Tamkin himself is not a complex being. Bellow's narrator allows us (in a way similar to that scene in *Herzog* where we peer through Gersbach's bathroom window to see him bathing Herzog's little girl; in such a context Herzog can realise Gersbach for that which he truly is, 'not an individual but a fragment, a piece broken off from the mob'[113]) to feel the terror that buoys up Tamkin's masquerade, to feel too the slightest bit of sympathy for the sense in which Tamkin is as much the prey of 'the world's business'[114] as Tommy:

his face did not have much variety. Talking always about spontaneous emotion and open receptors and free impulses he was about as expressive as a pincushion. When his hypnotic spell failed, his big underlip made him look weak-minded. Fear stared from his eyes, sometimes, so humble as to make you sorry for him. Once or twice Wilhelm had seen that look. Like a dog, he thought.[115]

While Bellow's descriptions of Tamkin emphasise his malformations, his crudity, there is another suggestion, too, that he is a puppet, a doll, most obvious at those moments when his eyes 'drooped' and 'the sense of his face passed downward to his heavy (possibly foolish?) red underlip'. His inscrutability, so disturbing at times to Tommy, guards no sage complexity, only barren-mindedness and the humble furtiveness of a frightened animal.

Seize the Day cancels out the false optimism of *Augie March* and in its depiction of dissociation and dissolution, of Dr Adler's well-dressed affability ('he bought his clothes in a college shop farther uptown')[116] triumphing over his son's despair, of Dr Tamkin's high-powered mountebankery, it is a novel that ought to have done more to dispel the widely held view of its author as one committed to humanism.

HENDERSON THE RAIN KING

There are clear reasons for seeing *Henderson the Rain King* (1959) as a natural successor to *The Adventures of Augie March*. *Seize the Day* with its formal rigour and thematic bleakness has always seemed a chronological peculiarity, and in his reply to this interviewer's query Bellow appears to confirm that chronological displacement:

> I have always had trouble 'placing' *Seize the Day*. Although chronologically it appears in 1956, between *The Adventures of Augie March* (1953) and *Henderson the Rain King* (1959), I have been more inclined to group it with *Dangling Man* (1944) and *The Victim* (1946) . . . My own feeling was that the novel was written earlier and held over, but I had no way of proving that.
>
> Well, it was written over a period of years and I don't remember now when it was begun. You may be right about it.[117]

Though in recent years Bellow has subjected *Augie March* to his own critical reappraisal, he has been as yet unwilling to do the same with *Henderson*, a novel which is damaged by similar failings:

> There were two things wrong with *Augie March* as I see it now. It got away from me, for one thing. I had found a new way to write a book. It was my very own. But I had no control over it. I couldn't say no to any of the excesses . . . Up to a point it was effective. Americans who read it felt liberated by its excesses, but I don't think *The Adventures of Augie March* is going to wear well. Its other fault was disingenuousness. I really knew much more about darkness than I let on. I knew perfectly well what nihilism was. I had no excuse for being such an ingenu. I felt like doing the ingenu, that's all.[118]

I agree with those critics who see *Henderson* as a novel that 'starts where Augie leaves off',[119] though I do not regard that as a recommendation. *Henderson*, too, is weakened by a lack of authorial control which is particularly evident in the articulation of theme, in the ill-management of certain central images, and in many passages where Bellow's gift for potent comedy degenerates into the trivialisation of issues and concepts which deserved less clownish treatment.

Positive responses to the novel range from those which regard it as a triumphant *jeu d'esprit*, as the most satisfying expression of the author's comic voice, to those which are based on traditionalist lines, seeing Henderson as a successful reincarnation of an American archetype. According to this view Henderson takes his place alongside the likes of Hank Morgan, Connecticut Yankee, and, inevitably, Huck Finn. Bellow himself looks back on the novel as a liberating influence, telling an interviewer in 1979 that he'd 'got a stupendous break with *Henderson the Rain King*. That man was talking through his hat, and therefore could say what he pleased. And he turned out to be a considerable rhetorician'.[120] We might well ask why we should spend any time listening to such a character, especially if we disagree with Bellow's estimate of his rhetorical powers. Still, there are those who would argue that *Henderson* is a work of parodic intent, with Hemingway's African stories one of the targets. Tony Tanner is one critic who gives Bellow the benefit of many doubts:

> Yet when the book reaches away from negation towards celebration, when we feel the full force of Bellow's refusal to accept despair, then it takes hold of us in a positive way beyond the scope of mere parody. Something important, we feel, is brewing up even if we cannot quite identify it through the tangled exuberance of the novel's surface.[121]

But Marvin Mudrick is much less tolerant. His views are accurate in every respect:

> By the time of *Henderson the Rain King*, the pretense of joy has become grotesque in its frantic didacticism and lack of conviction. Bellow is reduced to having his hero converse with Africans whose level of English is 'I no know' or 'I no bothah you' or 'Me Horko'; and even when the Me-Tarzan-You-Jane dialogue is expanded for the King's quasi-Oxonian ditherings about lions, Henderson continues to associate himself with such quaint locutions as 'strong gift of life' . . . Bellow would like Henderson to be *truly* American, purebred old-stock Anglo-Saxon (of all things!), Paul Bunyan in an age of bad nerves; but Henderson in the pages of the book is half Augie, half catcher in the rye. One wonders whether Bellow has any notion of how much he is borrowing in postures and phony wistfulness from a writer so

far inferior to him as Salinger; especially at the embarrassing conclusion, when Henderson races round the plane with the child in his arms, that Salinger child ... who will redeem us all.[122]

In connection with the question of compositional honesty Bellow has referred to the difficulty he had in preparing 'a suitable ground' for his muse or, as he puts it, his 'prompter'. He told an interviewer that:

> he won't talk until the situation's right ... I must be terribly given to fraud and deceit because I sometimes have great difficulty preparing a suitable ground. This is why I've had so much trouble with my last two novels [if as I've already suggested *Seize the Day* in fact precedes *Augie March* in order of composition, then Bellow would be referring here to *Augie March* and *Henderson*].[123]

The fact that Bellow experienced such 'difficulty' with *Augie March* would square with his comments, already quoted, about the 'disingenuousness' of that novel. That he admits to similar difficulties with *Henderson* perhaps explains my own sense that Henderson was indeed 'talking through his hat'. Yet Bellow asks us to accept the fundamental seriousness of Henderson's quest; as he said, 'I felt that my fooling [in *Henderson*] was fairly serious'.[124]

It is noteworthy that Bellow should have gone on record at the time with the comments above about his being 'terribly given to fraud and deceit' since most adverse criticism of *Henderson* concerns an element of fakery and posturing, especially with regard to its conclusion. Robert Boyers can claim that he does not know 'any serious commentator who has found that ... conclusion satisfactory'.[125] He joins ranks with the likes of Ihab Hassan who, in a felicitous phrase, tells us that Henderson's quest lacks 'the reticence of struggle', that 'it seems a little faked ... his final reconciliation to life appears self-induced'.[126] And Boyers too complains that 'a decision is made at the end of *Henderson the Rain King*, but it does not emerge from the novel itself ... the decision is willed rather than achieved, and it is asserted largely at the expense of fundamental realities the novel has resolutely impressed upon us'.[127] Keith Opdahl makes a similar point, noting that while 'Henderson boasts of a large thematic victory ... his difficulty in delivering on these claims – the qualification and ambiguity which he finally insists on – sustains the comic spirit of the novel but creates thematic confusion'.[128] Dan Jacobsen believes too that because 'we never see Henderson back in the United States . . . his transformation is finally no more than a matter of assertion on his part'.[129] And Norman Podhoretz, reviewing the novel for the *New York Herald Tribune*, found that 'the note of affirmation on which Mr. Bellow closes is not in the least convincing'.[130] Of course, if one assumes that Bellow's aim in this novel is essentially comic, then such criticisms might seem unjustified. Perhaps Henderson is indeed 'a caricature of all Bellow's characters who seek salvation', one through whom 'Bellow can laugh at his own questing spirit'.[131] My own view of the novel's conclusion is that in its giddiness and desperate intensity we admire it for what it is, what Bellow once termed 'a beautiful burst of emotion'; but its lyricism is finally unpalatable, its uplift leaves us feeling queasy rather than secure. One wonders about the nature of Henderson's euphoria, about its origin and its durability. There is, as Marvin Mudrick says, something grotesque about this joy and it is difficult to imagine its survival. The novel, in truth, fails to deliver the ending its readers had been primed to expect: would Henderson have found America any more hospitable on his return? Deprived of the answer to this question, our experience of this novel can only register frustration at Bellow's refusal to complete its logic of design.

*   *   *

Throughout this study of Bellow's fiction I am suggesting that one of its major complaints is directed at the atrophy of man's emotional potential. In the absence of an authentic emotional life, the individual's experience of reality is crippled. Eugene Henderson has a superabundance of vicarious feeling, so much so that one critic at least has been led to see Henderson's adventures as ones that teach him the value of subjecting those feelings to an intellectual discipline. 'Too much feeling has contributed to Henderson's belated understanding of what reality is.'[132] Yet we have only to turn to the novel's conclusion to be persuaded that such a view is not fully valid. There we see that Henderson remains endowed with a huge emotional vitality; he is, after all, not satisfied with a token single lap around the body of the plane but we remember him as the embodiment of energy and kinetic ebullience. And the novel as a whole seems to insist that his particular emotional life requires its contact with reality to be sustained by extreme or violent experiences. He remembers stepping on a land mine while doing military service and presents the memory in positive terms as an experience which 'gave my heart a large and real emotion. Which I continually require'.[133] The kind of reality that he seeks is simply not on offer in 1950s America and in this sense the narrative as a whole can be read as one which attempts to justify, and then explore the fruits of secession from American society. In this sense *Henderson* is related to Bellow's other novels which portray heroes in justified dissent and withdrawal. Henderson is given to quoting Daniel's prophecy to Nebuchadnezzar, 'they shall drive thee from among men, and thy dwelling shall be with the beasts of the field'.[134] The first 40 pages of the novel, much admired by critics, are ones given over to Henderson's strangely halting efforts to explain why he and America have fallen out, why he ends up as a modern Daniel forging literal links with the lions of the Wariri.

The urgent dissatisfaction inside him that cries 'I want, I want' is a plea in no sense assuaged by the conditions of life described in those first 40 pages. These pages strongly suggest the extreme incompatibility between Henderson and his culture. Yet many critics were unwilling to concede that Bellow might have created in Henderson an unAmerican defector who ends up having more in common with the pagan *gens de couleur* than the New England brahmin stock from which he derives. Perish the thought that Henderson could have been anything less than an American flag-waver gone in search of his nation's true destiny:

Henderson wants the dominant national consciousness to arouse itself and awaken to its true greatness of soul. He does not know how to arrive at this greatness, but he is convinced that the experts are wrong. The 'experts' are those advocates of doom, wastelanders who predict the downfall of the West and the collapse of industrial America. Bellow does not accept such a vision of apocalyptic despair based on a facile rejection of technology. His faith in contemporary civilization and his belief that mankind will ultimately make it come through forcefully in *Herzog*.[135]

Of course, this is a facile generalisation of the popularly held view of Bellow's position. As this whole study argues against such a view I shall not offer a particular rebuttal here. But the point is that by the time of *Henderson*'s publication, Bellow had come to be seen as an author whose work expressed a conservative mythology, his humanism seen as a faith in American progressivism, a rebuke to all those detractors who doubted America's manifest destiny as the leaven in the lump of nihilism and despair:

> Henderson projects an image which America, or the United States, to be precise, does, or could, or should present to the rest of the world. The effect is quite different from that made by Uncle Sam of an earlier period or by the Ugly American, who had appeared prominently in the fiction of more recent times. This latter is the negating image which enemies, detractors and despairing friends of the United States have conjured up. Bellow's Henderson is a counterimage – an affirmative one. He appears as an awakening giant, on the verge of a new consciousness, representing the hopes and determination of those who still share the American dream and see the United States as the leaven which will eventually bring freedom and love to our world.[136]

As my introductory chapter suggests, the view persists that Bellow still enshrines such orthodoxies in his fiction, and certainly explains why commentators reacted so unfavourably to a novel like *Humboldt's Gift*. Still regarding him as the spokesman of the kind of establishment ideology we see luridly outlined in the above quotation, they were surprised by that 'most renunciatory of Bellow's novels'.[137] And with both *The Dean's December* and *More Die of Heartbreak*, the former a novel which suggests an equivalence in many respects between American and Eastern European decadence, he must have seemed to many who still regarded him as 'the darling of the Establishment',[138] as a quisling voice.

In Henderson, Bellow created an American aristo whose forbears have included a Secretary of State, ambassadors to England and France, and whose father was 'a friend of William James and Henry Adams'.[139] But Henderson's riches only serve to aggravate his disaffection. America's commodity culture generates and rewards the utilitarian species and Henderson feels his uselessness in the capitalist dynamic:

So what do you do with yourself? More than three million bucks. After taxes, after alimony and all expenses I still have one hundred and ten thousand dollars in income absolutely clear . . . Taxwise, even the pigs were profitable. I couldn't lose money. But they were killed and they were eaten. They made ham and gloves and gelatine and fertilizer. What did I make? Why, I made a sort of trophy, I suppose. A man like me may become something like a trophy. Washed, clean, and dressed in expensive garments. Under the roof is insulation; on the windows thermopane; on the floors carpeting; and on the carpets furniture, and on the furniture covers, and on the cloth covers plastic covers; and wallpapers and drapes! All is swept and garnished. And who is in the midst of this? Who is sitting there? Man![140]

He feels himself to be a leisure-class layabout, his affluence bearing down on him like an obliterating pall. Mid-twentieth-century America forces the materialist imperative and Henderson's sole function is to symbolise success, to advertise reward. The final provocation that sends Henderson off to Idlewild to catch a plane for Africa is the death of old Miss Lenox, the Henderson's home-help. And again Bellow's attack is upon the destructive burden of materialism. Entering Miss Lenox's house, Henderson is confronted by room upon room of junk, a profusion of useless objects that becomes for him a galvanising *memento mori*. Miss Lenox's mania for hoarding the obsolete and thrown-away suggests again the earlier indictment of America's commodity-culture:

In the cottage I had to climb from room to room over the boxes and baby buggies and crates she had collected. The buggies went back to the last century, so that mine might have been there too, for she got her rubbish all over the countryside. Bottles, lamps, old butter dishes, and chandeliers were on the floor, shopping bags filled with string and rags, and pronged openers that the dairies used to give away . . . and bushel baskets full of buttons and china door knobs. And on the walls, calendars and pennants and ancient photographs.[141]

Henderson suddenly understands the full significance of all the human waste which goes unnoticed in an American reality which tells people they are 'nothing but instruments of this world's processes'.[142] He realises that this profusion of rubbish points up, poignantly, the contrasting emptiness of Miss Lenox's life, a spinster who collects baby buggies:

> And I thought, 'Oh, shame, shame! Oh, crying shame! How can we? Why do we allow ourselves? What are we doing? The last little room of dirt is waiting. Without windows. So for God's sake make a move, Henderson, put forth effort. You, too, will die of this pestilence. Death will annihilate you and nothing will remain, and there will be nothing left but junk. Because nothing will have been and so nothing will be left. While something still *is – now*! For the sake of all, get out'.[143]

Henderson thus becomes the first of Bellow's heroes to unequivocally cut and run, to get, as he puts it, 'clean away from everything'.[144] He leaves not because he is 'unfit to live among men',[145] but because he realises that America has created normative conditions which are unfit for men to live in. As he says just before he goes, 'there is a curse on this land. There is something bad going on. Something is wrong. There is a curse on this land!'[146] The emphasis is not on the rotten in Henderson but on the evil within America. It is thus the beginning of the novel, that part dealing with the reasons behind Henderson's journey, which makes the novel's conclusion so unconvincing. For he may have benefitted from his African experiences, but we have no reason to suppose that the 'curse' has been lifted from his native land. It is therefore difficult to accept the appeal to the future at the conclusion of the narrative.

Although some critics have taken Henderson to be a symbol representing America as a whole,[147] a large part of the edification afforded him in Africa seems to be concerned with establishing the rightness of his individualism. He approaches a sort of joyful solipsism based upon a new awareness of reality as a relative condition:

> Travel is mental travel ... What we call reality is nothing but pedantry ... The world of facts is real, all right, and not to be altered. The physical is all there, and it belongs to science. But then there is the noumenal department, and there we create and create.[148]

Yet when we begin to try to make sense of his African experience we soon discover the kind of muddled thinking which makes such a task impossible. We are aware that he is on a quest for spiritual fulfillment, in search of a reality which can accommodate his spiritual as well as his sensual nature. However, by the time we reach the end of the novel, we are not certain that his search has provided him with this new orientation, or whether he is willing or able to accept any new knowledge which has been made available to him. Inasmuch as King Dahfu's brand of wisdom (an unlikely and singularly ill-matched *potpourri* of primitive and civilised theories, the latter deriving in the main from Wilhelm Reich, whose psychotherapy emphasised the interrelatedness of flesh and mind) is coherent, it urges Henderson towards a recognition of the inherently real. He urges Henderson to 'move from the states of mind which I myself make to the states which are of themselves'; and in his very Herzog-like letter he writes to his wife, Henderson shows Dahfu's influence in a remark such as this – 'we don't see the stars as they are, so why do we love them? They are not small gold objects but endless fire'.[149] Yet in the same letter he appears to accept the inevitability of failure, the futility of aspiring – 'I don't think the struggles of desire can ever be won. Ages of longing and willing, willing and longing, and how have they ended? In a draw, dust and dust'.[150] And though like so many of Herzog's letters this one never gets posted, Henderson's final memory of its contents consists of a single axiomatic affirmation – 'it's love that makes reality reality. The opposite makes the opposite',[151] the elemental truth of which one is glad to put against so much of the pretentious verbiage one has been subjected to along the narrative way, against what one critic has termed the 'Bellafrikanisch' of Dahfu's idiom and against Henderson's own cracker-barrel philosophising which has him sounding like 'Daddy Warbucks trying to explain Spinoza'.[152]

The novel is full of contradictions and inconsistencies which undermine reader comprehension. For instance, in a climactic passage, facing the enraged lion he and Dahfu are trying to cage Henderson tells us that he 'had boasted to my dear Lily how I loved reality ... but oh, unreality! Unreality, unreality! That has been my scheme for a troubled but eternal life. But now I was blasted away from this practice by the throat of the lion. His voice was like a blow at the back of my head'.[153] This comes from a character who has often impressed upon us that 'when you come right down to it, there aren't many guys who have stuck with real life through thick and thin, like me. It's my most basic loyalty'.[154] Are we to assume that faced by the furious roar of the lion Henderson is shocked into an absolute, if fleeting self-revelation? That the entire preceding narrative must now be viewed as a lengthy demonstration of his 'practice' of living a life of 'unreality'? And that 'blasted away from this practice' he will henceforth be more capable of living life authentically?

That an answer to such questions is difficult to achieve is partly due to Bellow's insecure management of theme and image. Throughout the novel we have been made familiar with Henderson's belief that 'truth comes with blows' and so his use of this metaphor in the climactic passage quoted above might appear consistent enough. In the third chapter, this idea of pain as a facilitator of truth is first presented, as Henderson tells us that 'beside my cellar door last winter I was chopping wood . . . and a chunk of wood flew up from the block and hit me in the nose . . . as I felt the blow my only thought was *truth*. Does truth come in blows?'.[155] The image is used again during his ritual wrestling bout with Itelo where 'it took a different form; not "Truth comes with blows" but other words, and these words could not easily have been stranger. They went like this: "I do remember well the hour which burst my spirit's sleep" '.[156] And at other points in the narrative Henderson reaffirms the real and truthful messages communicated by 'blows' of different kinds. So the climax to the quest for reality, that end to 'unreality' provided by the lion's roar 'like a blow at the back of my head' has to struggle against Bellow's previous uses of this image. If truth does come presaged by blows, the reader is entitled to ask which of Henderson's history of blows has carried most 'truth'? Are we to understand that all his previous moments of revelation are undermined by the force of this final stunning discovery? If so, then Bellow's repeated use of the 'truth as blows' trope is confusing, tending as it does to suggest an equivalence between the moments, all of which have been associated with truth.

The confusion surrounding Henderson's final intimation is compounded when he tells his companion, Romilayu, that though King Dahfu 'thought he could change me . . . I met him too late in life . . . I was too gross. Too far gone'.[157] This suggests that the climactic revelation was partial or fleeting. Dahfu represented an ideal, but the ideal has not been internalised in Henderson's being. 'I wish I could have opened my heart entirely to that poor guy',[158] says Henderson of Dahfu. At the end of the novel, then, we are faced with this kind of equivocatory prose at a point when we had every right to expect a clarifying perspective.

The last pages of the novel do not suggest that Henderson regards his return to America as anything more than an opportunity to see his wife and children again. He explains his desire to return as 'a bad case of homesickness', a need to 'get back to Lily and the children'.[159] Bellow offers no evidence of any reconciliation between his hero and the conditioning values of the America he is returning to:

> We're supposed to think that nobility is unreal. But that's just it. The illusion is on the other foot. They make us think we crave more and more illusions. Why, I don't crave illusions at all. They say, Think big. Well, that's boloney of course, another business slogan.[160]

And his recollection of his relationship with Smolak the bear also seems to suggest a continuing disaffection with the community. As he and Smolak share the car of a circus roller coaster, 'while the Canadian hicks were rejoicing underneath with red faces ... we hugged each other, the bear and I, with something greater than terror and flew in those gilded cars'.[161]

Henderson the Rain King, with its thematic uncertainties, its vacillating between a rhetoric of affirmation and despair, its final, desperate lunge towards reconciliation with the American homeland, is Bellow's unsatisfactory farewell to an unsatisfactory phase of his writing career. Both Augie March and Henderson seem in retrospect rhetorical creations; we remember them for their distinctive voices and mannered characteristics rather than for any compelling articulation of truth. With the publication of his next novel, *Herzog*, Bellow reasserted control over rhetorical excess and revealed that he not only 'knew much more about darkness' but was very capable of an honest confrontation with it.

4

Hearts Without Guile: *Herzog* and *Mr Sammler's Planet*

Herzog is a showcase for its author's particular gifts of intelligence and his creative use of that intelligence, his capacity for finding, through characterisation and narrative technique, the felicitous means whereby they can be most trenchantly bodied forth against disturbing cultural norms. Even when measured against *The Dean's December*, a work of very large significance both in terms of Bellow's own development as a writer and in terms of American literature as a whole, *Herzog*'s stature remains. The seriousness of its subject-matter (sustained, indeed enhanced through Bellow's comic strategies) was a timely corrective to the Bantam appearance of *Henderson the Rain King*, and, for most critics, *Herzog* was its author's most considerable novel to date.[1] The most famous dissenting voice was that of Richard Poirier whose essay, 'Bellows to Herzog' presented the novelist as a self-deceived, if not hypocritical poseur who had refused to acknowledge the extent to which he himself peddled 'the Waste Land outlook', a trafficker in fake seriousness, one who could 'replace the "commonplaces" of alienation with even more obvious commonplaces about "the longing to he human"'.[2] Unfortunately, Poirier's essay is weakened by its tendentious presentation, its flushed rhetoric detracting from its usefulness as a critique. But Poirier's complaint that Bellow's vision as a whole fails to give artistic realisation to that 'longing' is in an ironic sense responded to by the likes of Citrine and Corde, both of whom come to recognise that their longing derives from a complex of forces antithetical to the human, a yearning, in fact, for the cancellation of 'everything merely human'.[3]

Poirier's attack may, indeed, have all of its point in its stridency of tone, for its substantive argument – that Bellow is as alienated as 'the disaffected, subversive, radical clique'[4] whom he publicly abuses – is a more *ad hominem* restatement of the widely held view that Bellow's fiction is very often one of paradox,[5] one in which the life-longing affirmations are often weak contestants in the struggle against alienating forces in society. So when Poirier unmasks the figure he has been at considerable pains to present as canting and self-deluded in his 'effort to blind himself to the fact that he is no less "repelled" by such things as "the degradation of the urban crowd"',[6] he is being merely rhetorical about what has been a constant preoccupation in the novelist's attitude since Joseph of *Dangling Man* looked with recoil at the Chicago slums.

But though Poirier's argument declines into polemicism, it does arrive, in a cackhanded fashion, at the critical question which has had to be faced by all serious readers of *Herzog*. Many have seen the novel as 'an attempt to reach beyond mere victim-literature to some more positive ground of hope',[7] but some have gone on to conclude that this aspiration is confounded by the conclusion of the narrative which would seem to stress Herzog's passivity, his posture of indifference towards intruders and to their perception of him ('If I am out of my mind, it's all right with me'),[8] and his retiral from the struggle against such vulgarians as Gersbach.[9] This reaching towards a new orientation of hope for man seemed to be at least impeded by the tenor of the novel's conclusion and markedly deflected by Bellow's next novel, *Mr Sammler's Planet*. There Marcus Klein was able to positively identify that 'repulsion' of which Poirier wrote. Sammler sees 'in the richness of human life cause for revulsion'[10] according to Klein. What Klein called 'those characterizing shiftings between "alienation" and "accommodation"'[11] were beginning to find the latter element in this polarity more difficult to achieve. In my view, *Herzog* fully establishes Bellow's move away from the necessity of such 'accommodation' towards, not alienation (as Poirier would have it) for his heroes, but a condition which, in its dramatised context, comes to seem an idealisation of the remote – of secession from society as a new ethic of 'duty' for the sane, for the maintenance of sanity and civility. Brotherhood, the value of community, is given a new and ironic connotation in Bellow's later works. Charlie and Julius Citrine, Moses and Will Herzog, Spangler and Corde (whose early relationship is portrayed as brotherly) are brothers in name only, their sad incommunicability expressing the widening gap between that reality modelled upon the ethos of business and science, the sphere of practical miracles, of those like Julius, Will, and Spangler, the person who 'knows-the-world-for-what-it-is',[12] and that other reality, fully cognisant of heart and spirit, which is the transcendent condition reached, if only momentarily, by Charlie, Moses and Corde. Bellow uses fraternity ironically, to stress all that conspires against consanguinity. As in this passage, where Herzog reflects on all that divides him from his brother, and from what passes for brotherhood in the modern age:

> there's a strange division of functions that I sense, in which I am the specialist in . . . in spiritual self-awareness; or emotionalism; or ideas; or nonsense. Perhaps of no real use or relevance except to keep alive primordial feelings of a certain sort. He mixes grout to pump into these new high-risers all over town. He has to be political, and deal, and wangle and pay off and figure tax angles . . . Will is a quiet man of duty and routine, has his money, position, influence, and is just as glad to be rid of his private or 'personal' side. Sees me spluttering fire in the wilderness of this world, and pities me no doubt for my temperament. Under the old dispensation, as the stumbling, ingenuous, burlap Moses, a heart without guile, in need of protection, a morbid phenomenon, a modern remnant of other-worldliness – under that former dispensation I would need protection. And it would be gladly offered by him – by the person who 'knows-the-world-for-what-it-is'. Whereas a man like me has shown the arbitrary withdrawal of proud subjectivity from the collective and historical progress of mankind. And that is true of lower-class emotional boys and girls who adopt the aesthetic mode, the mode of rich sensibility. Seeking to sustain their own version of existence under the crushing weight of *mass*.[13]

It is, I think, no exaggeration to assert that in this passage are contained the major themes of Bellow's later fiction: the anxieties about the dissolution of personal (that is, emotionally articulate, spiritually aware) life in the face of the juggernauts of utilitarian ethics and materialist conformities, and the fear (which will consolidate into a conviction in *The Dean's December* and *Humboldt's Gift*) that those who refuse to withdraw from dissension, who instead insist wittingly or unwittingly (as is the case, respectively, with Corde and Humboldt) on challenging the orthodox reality, will be eradicated, discredited as public figures. And though *Herzog* does not contain the sustained attack on the scientific worldview found in both *Humboldt's Gift* and, particularly, *The Dean's December*, there are enough passing references to the matter,[14] to allow us to see the novel as a seedbed for Bellow's developing concern here too. Inasmuch as such anxieties and such responses on the hero's part are unequivocally exhibited in *Herzog*, I would like to regard this novel (rather than the next, *Mr Sammler's Planet*)[15] as the watershed in the line of development I have been following in Bellow's fiction.

*   *   *

That 'orthodox reality' to which I refer above is regarded by Herzog as the external sign of the American malaise, a destructively exclusive interpretation of the real. 'People are dying', he thinks, 'for lack of something real to carry home when day is done',[16] their lives blighted by 'their great need, their hunger . . . for good sense, clarity, truth'.[17] Herzog's arch-persecutors, his ex-wife Madeleine and his ex-friend Gersbach, are both characterised as theatricians, as defacers of the real. Though they appear to others, weaker than themselves, as intelligent and strong-willed creatures, they are in fact empty of personality, and Madeleine particularly is seen as without self-understanding, as much a victim of that 'hunger' for the real as a victimiser. They utterly lack the ability to understand their experience in moral terms, instead regarding their relationships with others as power-plays. Madeleine's intelligence is dissipated by her erratic and obsessive nature, her potential wasted in morbid bouts of self-scrutiny, or headlong flights into self-obliteration accomplished by delivering herself into various mysticisms such as religion (her Catholicism) or personality (Gersbach). In all these general traits and their particular manifestations, both Madeleine and Gersbach are prototypes of that 'advanced modern consciousness' which 'was a reduced consciousness',[18] so brilliantly depicted in *The Dean's December*. In that novel the generic features of this consciousness are that it would contain 'only the minimum of furniture that civilization was able to instal (practical judgements, bare outlines of morality, sketches, cartoons instead of human beings)'.[19] This reduced consciousness is incapable of countenancing experience except in the most abstract way and, as a result, is devoid of a moral reality. Such a dissociation is certainly present in Madeleine, whose effect upon, and reaction to others also adumbrates Bellow's later critique of mass society in *The Dean's December* and *More Die of Heartbreak*, where the individual's craving for significance (for 'something real to carry home when day is done') makes them soft targets for those of strong will and intellect who yet lack the moral responsibility to accompany these attributes. In this particular way, Madeleine and Gersbach father Spangler. Madeleine's primary effect upon others is to make them feel 'exceptional, deeply gifted, brilliant'.[20] Comically, even her psychiatrist, Dr Edvig, falls prey to her influence. In a 'letter' to Edvig, Herzog tells him that Mady 'enriched her record by conning you'.[21]

In many ways (though one thinks particularly of the combative relationship that prevails between Allbee and Leventhal in *The Victim*) Bellow's fiction is an examination of power relations, or rather of the abuse of power both in society at large and in smaller, familial groupings. This is given its fullest treatment in the political dimension of *The Dean's December*, where totalitarianism is displayed as already existing in important sectors of American society as a result of the puerility of mass consciousness in that nation. In *Herzog* there is an allied concern with the dynamics of power relations seen both in Herzog's ruminations and unposted correspondence with national figures and in the machiavellian ploys of people such as Madeleine. Thus, in a letter to Martin Luther King Herzog writes 'the Negroes of Alabama filled me with admiration. White America is in danger of being depoliticalized. Let us hope this example by Negroes will penetrate the hypnotic trance of the majority. The political question in modern democracies is one of the reality of public questions'.[22] Again the source of concern is to be found in the damage being done to the calibre of reality in American culture. Herzog's fear that 'invariably the most dangerous people seek the power'[23] is a generalisation given specific force in the case of Madeleine, whose public status derives from her belligerence and *hauteur* rather than from traditionally moral strengths. To Herzog it seems that the world is much more ready to accept the gross neuroses and coldly applied iniquity of a Madeleine – a patrician of a sort for whom 'the strength to do evil is sovereignty'.[24] Madeleine, a latter-day Margot Macomber, 'has the power to hurt' and knows it. This, then, is 'mental politics'[25] the analogue in private terms of that larger political reality that Bellow will examine so acutely in *The Dean's December*.

In the context of their adversarial relationship with the hero, such characters as Madeleine, Spangler and the negro pickpocket of *Mr Sammler's Planet* – an extension of that type for whom the administering of evil was sovereign strength – are portrayed as, above all, implacable, their ascendancy assured. It is important to mark this since it justifies the hero's retiral from engagement with such an entrenched, consensus reality. In Bellow's view, Madeleine exemplifies the breed of the age which, like Lowell's skunks, 'will not scare'.[26] Lowell's poem posits a conjunction between personal sickness and communal malaise (as does Bellow, taking Madeleine and Gersbach as the prime exhibitors of malaise), a sickness that creeps through the whole community. The skunks of the poem are the only creatures in it with any resolution. They know what they want, and take it. They can march so brazenly up the main street of the community and possess their desire with impunity only because of the puerility of that community. The horror of Lowell's vision is all in its acknowledgement of the abdication of the civilised strain, its brutal recognition that nothing, no one will impede the skunks' progress. Gersbach more than Madeleine is Bellow's skunk (Madeleine's surety of purpose is only apparent; her baselessness is continually revealed, as is the truth that she, too, is in search of 'a savior'[27]) and *his* horror is in the ease with which he can command the attention of a mass audience. In the face of such a capitulation, Herzog realises the futility of struggling against the new barbarians:

> The warm lake wind drove Moses westward, past the gray gothic buildings. He had had the child at least, while mother and lover were undressing in a bedroom somewhere. And if, even in that embrace of lust and treason, they had life and nature on their side, he would quietly step aside. Yes, he would bow out.[28]

In an age in which 'all higher or moral tendencies lie under suspicion of being rackets'[29] bowing out is a response which may be measured in terms of civility and sense rather than defeat.

Though his letters are, for the most part, addressed to public figures, their ironical effect is to signify the extent of Herzog's remoteness from public reality. For while they convey the nervous fecundity of his thought, their very number prepares us for Herzog's final renunciation of them – 'he had no messages for anyone. Nothing. Not a single word'.[30] Denial of the possibility of containing reality through language is a major part of Citrine and Corde's experience. Herzog's silence at the close of the narrative is a rejection of that negotiation with reality which he had himself described as a humanist responsibility:

> Still, what can thoughtful people and humanists do but struggle toward suitable words? Take me, for instance. I've been writing letters helter-skelter in all directions. More words. I go after reality with language. Perhaps I'd like to change it all into language.[31]

The extent to which *Humboldt's Gift* and *The Dean's December* make this exhaustion of prevailing modes of communication a major theme suggests that *Herzog* is their authentic precursor in Bellow's work as a development. Through the device of the letters, the reader is drawn into Herzog's peculiarly intense consciousness and experiences there the privations and paradoxical loneliness of a man whose pen-friends are as distant, as eloquently speechless as the starry heavens at 'five in the morning'.[32] The letters keep us in touch with the quintessential Herzog, the intellectual for whom language has once had an alchemical power; in combination with the narrative proper we can also see his travails within the plot – the broken marriages, the self-recrimination – that help to justify and explain his eventual withdrawal.

The Dean's December argues for a return to sentiment as an admissible feature of social intercourse, argues, indeed, that without this the prospects of real communication would be minimal, if not non-existent. Madeleine, significantly, though all too plausibly, refuses to acknowledge feeling as a grounds for communication with Herzog – 'don't give me that line of platitudes about feelings. I don't believe in it. I believe in God – sin – death – so don't pull any sentimental crap on me'.[33] In this proscription, Madeleine participates in that reality against which Herzog appears so unhistorical, 'living amid great ideas and concepts, insufficiently relevant to the present, day-by-day, American conditions'.[34] These conditions are inimical to a reality founded upon 'the inner experience of the heart'.[35]

Whereas Gersbach, witheringly termed 'a poet in mass communications'[36] by Herzog, can speak in the language of the masses, the latter is 'handicapped by emotional confusion ...

resisting the argument that scientific thought has put into disorder all considerations based on value'.[37] That latter argument is one that will reappear more centrally in *Humboldt's Gift* and *The Dean's December* as one that influences Corde and Citrine in their fulminations against contemporary American reality. The devaluation of that reality is largely attributed to the corrosive effect (both physiological and ideological) of science upon the human mind. In the grip of that devalued reality, Herzog also realises its coercions, the most insidious of which concerns the diminution of feeling in human affairs. Like his successors in Bellow's fiction, he exercises a caution with regard to emotional display, recognising the potential dangers of emotional overspill. In the following passage which looks forward to several similar passages in the later novels,[38] Bellow raises Herzog's tenor of thought to achieve a lyrical insight into the nature of reality both personal and public:

> In the mild end of the afternoon, later, at the waterside in Woods Hole, waiting for the ferry, he looked through the green darkness at the net of bright reflections on the bottom. He loved to think about the power of the sun, about light, about the ocean. The purity of the air moved him. There was no stain in the water, where schools of minnows swam. Herzog sighed and said to himself, 'Praise God – praise God.' His breathing had become freer. His heart was greatly stirred by the open horizon . . . but principally by the green transparency as he looked down to the stony bottom webbed with golden lines . . . If his soul could cast a reflection so brilliant, and so intensely sweet, he might beg God to make such use of him. But that would be too simple. But that would be too childish. The actual sphere is not clear like this, but turbulent, angry. A vast human action is going on. Death watches. So if you have some happiness, conceal it. And when your heart is full, keep your mouth shut also.[39]

The nature of Herzog's vision here is closely tied with Corde's lyrical coda at Mount Palomar and with Citrine's many moments of mystical transportation. In each case the exhilaration for character – and reader – is derived from the audacity of the operative images and metaphors, of freedom, purity, fullblooded expansion of the human spirit. The effect is also generated out of the felt contrast between the provisional nature of the insight ('if his soul could cast a reflection so brilliant') which, despite its power and beauty, cannot hope to prevail against the earnest abrasion of 'the actual sphere'. The exhilaration gathers intensity because both character and reader know it to be, not false, but impossible to sustain. The insight in the above passage has to accept the logic of its dark conclusion which has no room for numinous echoes, but which instead must take account of man's darkening presence, of reality as made by man, not God. The purity and limpidity are replaced by the angry turbulence of muddy water, a sea in which larger and more predatory fish than minnows hunt their prey. This is the reality that Bellow's heroes recoil from, the truth which 'is true only as it brings down more disgrace and dreariness upon human beings, so that if it shows anything except evil it is illusion, and not truth'.[40] In this reality the 'turbulent, angry' types like Madeleine are dominant, the predators for whom 'the strength to do evil is sovereignty', whose *raison d'être* is to find one like Herzog, as yet unreconciled to 'historical necessity' so that they might 'as a collective project ... destroy his vanity and his pretensions to a personal life so that he might disintegrate and suffer and hate, like so many others'.[41] In a universe in which 'death watches' rather than God, it is perhaps to be expected that Bellow, with a nice touch, tells us of Madeleine's 'constant interest' in 'murder mysteries'.[42] Later, at Gersbach's house, contemplating her murder, Herzog knows that 'in spirit she was his murderess'.[43]

His eventual refusal of this murder of revenge is due to his realisation that there is little to kill in Madeleine. Though she is an evil-doer, Herzog understands the extent to which both she and Gersbach exist outside of such morally absolute categories. Since 'the individual is obliged, or put under pressure, to define "power" as it is defined in politics',[44] Madeleine takes her example of strength from the prevailing political model which posits forces in confrontation, balances of terror, duplicity with honour. To be strong one had to be beyond the vulnerability of commitment, to dissemble with conviction, to be armour-plated. Gersbach particularly is seen as one of the modern mountebanks:

Modern consciousness has this great need to explode its own postures ... It throws shit on all pretensions and fictions. A man like Gersbach can be gay. Innocent. Sadistic. Dancing around. Instinctive. Heartless. Hugging his friends. Feeble-minded. Laughing at jokes. Deep, too. Exclaiming 'I *love* you!' or 'This I *believe*.' And while moved by these 'beliefs' he steals you blind. He makes realities nobody can understand.[45]

In the absence of real identity we have 'cartoons instead of human beings'.[46] Power is the ability to be without developed personality. By evolving 'techniques of exploitation and domination'[47] such as Gersbach's trick of inhabiting multiple personalities, one might become a cultural impresario, a manipulator. So Gersbach makes the transition from being 'a one-legged radio announcer' to 'a terrific operator' who hires the hall for his own poetry reading, sells the tickets himself, and then locks the hall so that his audience can't escape from the awfulness of his weeping while 'reading a poem about his grandfather who was a street sweeper'.[48] A large aspect of Augie's cowardice is due to his retreat from self-confrontation, his notion that 'personality is unsafe in the first place. It's the types that are safe'.[49] In an age of types, Gersbach occupies them all:

> He's a ringmaster, popularizer, liaison for the élites. He grabs up celebrities and brings them before the public. And he makes all sorts of people feel that he has exactly what they've been looking for. Subtlety for the subtle. Warmth for the warm. For the crude, crudity. For the crooks, hypocrisy. Atrocity for the atrocious. Whatever your heart desires. Emotional plasma which can circulate in any system.[50]

He is to Herzog the supreme type of contemporary barbarism ('when I think of Valentine . . . I see the mobs breaking into the palaces and churches and sacking Versailles'),[51] dangerous not because of what he is or represents (which is nothing), but because of the power he can exert over mass audiences who are in deep need of 'something real . . . good sense, clarity, truth'. For Gersbach and his kind, such need is the means to self-aggrandisement:

> as soon as he slams the door of his Continental he begins to talk like Karl Marx. I heard him at the Auditorium with an audience of two thousand people. It was a symposium on desegregation, and he let loose a blast against the affluent society . . . And then there was the audience, a comfortable audience of conventional business people and professionals who look after their businesses and specialties well enough, but seem confused about everything else and come to hear a speaker express himself confidently, with emphasis and fire, direction and force. With a head like a flaming furnace, a voice like a bowling alley, and the wooden leg drumming the stage. To me he's a curiosity, like a Mongolian idiot singing *Aida*. But to *them* . . .[52]

The emptiness of subject-matter is taken for granted. What matters is the polish of delivery. That the demagogue mouths quackery is neither here nor there as long as, in good presidential timbre, he delivers his meaningless words with conviction. What one lacks in moral and intellectual terms can be amply compensated by the dynamic performance. Thus 'the sight of James Hoffa' on a television chat show made Herzog realise 'how terrible a force angry single-mindedness can be . . . I'll tell you what I would have said to Hoffa. "What makes you think realism must be brutal?"'.[53] But brutal it is commonly agreed to be; 'facts *are* nasty' says Sandor Himmelstein as if expressing an apodictic remark. To lay claim to another reality, grounded upon humane principles, is politically unsafe ('Mr. Truman calls people Bleeding Hearts when they question his Hiroshima decision')[54]; one risks being brutalised, or, more effectively, patronised or ignored as a curiosity ('Young Jews, brought up on moral principles as Victorian ladies were on pianoforte and needlepoint').[55]

The courtroom scene throws further, more harrowing light upon this desensitised reality and leads to a decisive ephiphany for Herzog. Forced by his inner compulsion to listen to the catalogue of horrors inflicted upon a young child, Herzog again notes the bizarre absence of emotion in the courtroom:

> All this seemed to Herzog exceptionally low-pitched. All – the lawyers, the jury, the mother, her tough friend, the judge – behaved with much restraint, extremely well controlled and quiet-spoken . . . Judge, jury, lawyers and the accused, all looked utterly unemotional. And he himself? He sat in his new madras coat and held his hard straw hat. He gripped his hat strongly and felt sick at heart.[56]

The exaltation of reason at the expense of emotion is all too clear throughout this scene where the bland indifference of the participants to these particularly nasty facts affects Herzog as a confounding of the intellect ('I fail to understand! thought Herzog')[57] and then as a physical revulsion ('he wondered whether he was going to come down with sickness . . . he felt stifled, as if the valves of his heart were not closing and the blood were going back into his lungs').[58] And though the scene culminates in a way that suggests the futility of such an emotional reaction, in the context of the novel as a development its effect is to stress the desperate need for such a reaction. In a world in which 'some kill, then cry. Others, not even that',[59] Herzog's feelings stand against the acquiescence of the many who subscribe to the view that 'the actual sphere' is, inevitably, an angry, turbulent, and hateful one; Herzog is heart-assailed and tormented by the apparent inadequacy of his response:

> With all his might – mind and heart – he tried to obtain something for the murdered child. But what? How? He pressed himself with intensity, but 'all his might' could get nothing for the buried boy. Herzog experienced nothing but his own *human feelings*, in which he found nothing of use. What if he felt moved to cry? Or pray? He pressed hand to hand. And what did he feel? Why he felt himself – his own trembling hands, and eyes that stung.[60]

But this collapse into a grotesque solipsism is only a momentary betrayal of his best self and, as I hope to show, Herzog's withdrawal at the end of the narrative is in no sense a withdrawal into solipsism. The failure of feeling as an agency of human reciprocity is only apparent and the immediate effect – Herzog's intended act of revenge upon Gersbach and Madeleine who had stolen his child from him – is also one of temporary spleen. That he eventually refuses to carry through such an act is testimony to his gathering enlightenment. Gersbach, Herzog finally understands, is not substantial enough as a being to be worth annihilation:

> I apparently believe that if the child does not have a life resembling mine, educated according to the Herzog standards of 'heart', and all the rest of it, she will fail to become a human being. This is sheer irrationality, and yet some part of my mind takes it as self-evident. But what in fact can she learn from them? From Gersbach, when he looks so sugary, repulsive, poisonous, not an individual but a fragment, a piece broken off from the mob. To shoot him! – an absurd thought. As soon as Herzog saw the actual person giving an actual bath, the reality of it, the tenderness of such a buffoon to a little child, his intended violence turned into *theater*, into something ludicrous.[61]

'Not an individual but a fragment, a piece broken off from the mob' – the denunciation is precise, and total. Gersbach's significance is in no sense connected to that which inheres in personality, but rather is to do with his connections with 'the mob', the extent to which his own inner vacuity is typical of man in the mass.

'Dirt enters at the heart' is Herzog's death-threatening acronym to Gersbach. Its significance extends beyond Bellow's concerns in *Herzog* to those of much of his later fiction where the contamination present in the languages of contemporary life has truly entered at the heart. The 'historical process' has generated (if that is the term; Gersbach signals 'the creative depth of modern degeneracy')[62] a reality out of technological efficiencies and scientific reasonings, utilitarian and contingent, transcending the human ethos except as it is materialist in its complexion:

> No wonder 'personal' life is a humiliation, and to be an individual contemptible. The historical process, putting clothes on our backs, shoes on the feet, meat in the mouth, does infinitely more for us by the indifferent method than anyone does by intention . . . And since these good commodities are the gifts of anonymous planning and labor, what international goodness can achieve (when the good are amateurs) becomes the question. Especially if, in the interests of health, our benevolence and love demand exercise, the creature being emotional, passionate, expressive, a relating animal. A creature of deep peculiarities, a web of feeling intricacies and ideas now approaching a level of organization and automatism where he can hope to be free from human dependency. People are practicing their future condition already. My emotional type is archaic. Belongs to the agricultural or pastoral stages.[63]

There is superb irony in Bellow's idea of 'the good' as 'amateurs'. In a culture of specialists the man of sound heart is made to seem a throw-back, an archaism, a joke. Though the creature be 'a relating animal' it is forced into the kinds of relation practiced by Gersbach, approximating to 'a level of organization and automatism' whereby an easily classifiable mutuality between human 'types' can be found and exploited – 'subtlety for the subtle. Warmth for the warm'. Against Herzog's amateurish philanthropy Gersbach can offer the versatility of 'emotional plasma which can circulate in any system'. And as Sammler 'did feel somewhat separated from the rest of his species, if not in some fashion severed – severed not so much by age as by preoccupations too different and remote, disproportionate on the side of the spiritual, Platonic, Augustinian, thirteenth-century',[64] so Herzog too is forced to consider the degree of his severance, as one more properly cast in 'the agricultural or pastoral stages' of man's development. With his tongue not quite in his cheek he goes as far as to suggest that his severance is due in part to the vestiges of 'European pollution' in his affective system so that he is 'infected by the Old World with feelings like Love – Filial Emotion. Old stuporous dreams'.[65] Concerned again with power relations, he reflects on his misfortune in being born to participate in an age which holds 'that nothing faithful, vulnerable, fragile can be durable or have any true power. Death waits for these things as a cement floor waits for a dropping light bulb'.[66] This last, marvellously evocative image painfully summons up the reality against which the Bellow hero in the later novels refuses to dash himself. The only powers that hold sway in this prevailing condition of man are the practical ones, those that appeal to man 'in a mass. Transformed by science. Under organized power. Subject to tremendous controls. In a condition caused by mechanization'.[67]

Practical energies can still operate in contexts that confound the poor human imagination. Where the twentieth-century carnage has overwhelmed the individual with his useless *agape*:

> You think history is the history of loving hearts? You fool! Look at these millions of dead. Can you pity them, feel for them? You can nothing! There were too many. We burned them to ashes, we buried them with bulldozers. History is the history of cruelty, not love, as soft men think. We have experimented with every human capacity to see which is strong and admirable and have shown that none is. There is only practicality.[68]

Herzog refuses to succumb to this reality but he also, significantly, understands the danger of taking up arms against it. Though he does, for most of the narrative, wear his 'Herzog standards of "heart"' openly, the conclusion shows him to have realised the prudence of concealment. In a comically telling moment, he knows that even the loan sharks at the police station size him up as a bad risk:

> Some fellows always make a nice impression. I never had that ability. Due to my feelings. A passionate heart, a bad credit risk.

Asked to make this practical judgement on myself, I wouldn't make it any differently.[69]

The novel as a whole reveals Herzog's reality largely by means of contrasts such as the above. He knows himself in terms of his distance from the reality commonly assented to by those close to him like his brother, as much as by the reluctance of bondsmen to consider him as a client. The honesty of his self-judgement is in marked contrast to Augie's self-delusion, though it is reminiscent of Joseph's concern to live in the heart of an authentic and immarcescible reality. He is keenly aware of the way others perceive him, 'a loving brute – a subtle, spoiled, loving man. Who can make use of him? He craves use. Where is he needed? . . . Oh, that mysterious creature, that Herzog!'[70] and in the depth of that awareness is his defence.

Some critics have seen the end of *Herzog* as one that presages the hero's return to the world with a new understanding of his place in it. Thus Malcolm Bradbury:

> Herzog finds his 'new angle on the modern condition', recognizes a vividness and worth in the world, finds equilibrium without librium, accepts diurnality and history, finds a hint of the patterned secret. We may doubt the ending in the rural playground of Ludeyville, with its natural transcendence and its pleasure-principle associations, and find it a conventional pastoral set outside the city and society where the anguish is made.[71]

And others, such as Tony Tanner, feel compelled to doubt the credibility of the novel's conclusion, seeing it as a kind of evasion of what would be the true conclusion, the hero's 'renewed encounters with the non-pastoral realities of the city'. For Tanner, the ending has a 'soft focus' and 'there is something a little too easy, and even self-satisfied, in the way in which Herzog achieves the desired disburdenments and reconciliations in the pastoral moment of the last chapter.[72] Indeed this would seem to be the opinion of the majority of commentaries which deal with the conclusion. The climax offers a 'fatty sigh of middle-class intellectual contentment'[73] or is otherwise treated as a weakeningly indeterminate way to end a novel which had gained so much of its drama out of polemicism and confrontation. In fact such criticisms are based upon a failure to understand that Herzog's posture of apparent complacency at the end is wholly consistent with his intelligent and positive response to that reality which has been displayed throughout as implacable and hostile. There *is* a peace for Herzog at the end, but it derives not from a complacent indifference to the world outside Ludeyville, but from his certain knowledge of its operations and of his need to tactfully distance himself from them. At the end of the novel's penultimate chapter, Herzog comes to a decision (overlooked by the above critics) that throws much light upon the meaning of his return to Massachusetts. The scene takes place in the doctor's surgery, and Bellow has carefully arranged it so as to stress Herzog's physical and psychic captivity:

> The white modern lights of the small room were going round, wheeling. Herzog himself felt that he was rotating with them as the doctor wound the medicinal-smelling tapes tightly about his chest. Now, to get rid of all such falsehoods . . .[74]

Coming to the end of Herzog's struggle with the 'falsehoods' of modern life, the above scene with its tropes of constriction and sterility does more than hint at his determination 'to get rid of' the supervisory elements of such life. Bellow uses a hard-edged imagery to suggest how easily self might be sacrificed to the agencies of external management. So Herzog rotates in a trance-like response to 'the white modern lights', consciousness dimmed beneath the artificial glare. To those who would seek to doctor that consciousness, he is more than physically wounded, the tapes set to bind more than cuts and grazes. Maladjusted, Herzog has a 'heart without guile', an innocent abroad in the world, 'in need of protection, a morbid phenomenon, a modern remnant of other-worldliness'.[75] And his brother, one who 'knows-the-world-for-what-it-is', one 'just as glad to be rid of his private or "personal" side',[76] regards Herzog as a very suitable case for treatment. Herzog's refusal to capitulate and become a ratification of that 'type' he has been classified as, 'that mysterious creature, that Herzog! awkwardly taped, helped into his wrinkled shirt by brother Will',[77] is due to his self-knowledge, that allows him to gently preserve his dignity while the ether of 'complete bed rest' is being pressed on him.

Like Augie, Herzog has cause to know the seductive attraction of type. Unlike Augie he refuses the blandishments offered to mass man in exchange for self. The price he has to pay, however, is in the painful knowledge of his divorce, in all the truest ways, even from those nominally closest to him. But to 'accept ineffectuality, banishment to personal life, confusion'[78] as a precondition of being admitted to 'the collective and historical progress of mankind'[79] is to accept too much. Yet Herzog has his moments of joy, too, especially in his sudden discovery of his release from Madeleine:

> He was surprised to feel such contentment ... contentment? Whom was he kidding, this was joy! For perhaps the first time he felt what it was to be free from Madeleine. Joy! His servitude was ended, and his heart released from its grisly heaviness and encrustation.[80]

The sadness behind the joy is that Herzog knows that it must be secretive, concealed from those who would probably misconstrue it as further evidence of his 'insanity'. So even his friend Asphalter must have no wind of his exalted state, of 'all this overflow! It wouldn't make him happier. Keep it to yourself if you feel exalted. Anyway, he may think you've simply gone off your nut'.[81] This, as Bellow will suggest in both *Humboldt's Gift* and *The Dean's December*, is the necessary condition of joy for men like Herzog, Citrine and Corde. Their withdrawal marks no end to the intensely lived life, or to a joyful appreciation of it, but such pleasure will be less open, less public. Nor does secession mean that the Bellow hero becomes more misanthropic. Herzog's humanity is fully shown in several closing reflections which are deep in their care for others ('The light of truth is never far away, and no human being is too negligible or corrupt to come into it').[82] Yet hope more and more becomes a solemn duty in these later characters, something they owe themselves and the world, a debt which is constitutional to their natures. *Herzog* establishes the debts that must be paid, but is more continually concerned to show the concessions that must be refused, the line that cannot be crossed into an unconscionable degeneracy of being.

As Corde will nominate feeling as the mediator between man and transcendence, so Herzog will not relinquish his language of the heart. To his dead mother he says 'I want to send you, and others, the most loving wish I have in my heart. This is the only way I have to reach out – out where it is incomprehensible'.[83] And his knowledge of the compromises his brother has made to 'the actual sphere' is freighted with a loving sorrow:

> Moses could remember a time when Willie, too, had been demonstrative, passionate, explosive, given to bursts of rage, flinging objects on the ground ... But that was long ago. Thirty-five years ago, easily. And where had it gone, the wrath of Willie Herzog? my dear brother? Into a certain poise and quiet humor, part decorousness, part (possibly) slavery. The explosions had become implosions, and where light once was darkness came, bit by bit. It didn't matter. The sight of Will stirred Moses' love for him.[84]

Willie has become dessicated, his intensity of being given up for the normative model of being and doing. Inevitably, what most condemns Herzog in Willie's eyes is his 'intense way of doing everything',[85] and it is as a concession to that normative reality that, at least while his brother is present, Herzog chooses to dissemble, 'taking special pains to give an impression of completest normalcy ... under no circumstances must he utter a single word that might be interpreted as irrational'.[86]

Herzog's final letter, addressed to himself, is an endeavour to make philosophical sense of those emotions which have come to seem the measure of his humanity. Madeleine, Himmelstein, Gersbach, those in the law court, his brother – all have been conspicuous by their emotional emptiness. Herzog comes close to concluding that the emotions are vital not only in their connection with the human factor, but also in their power to reveal spiritual truths to man:

> I look at myself and see chest, thighs, feet – a head. This strange organization, I know it will die. And inside – something, something, happiness ... 'Thou movest me'. That leaves no choice. Something produces intensity, a holy feeling, as oranges produce orange, as grass green, as birds heat. Some hearts put out more love and some less of it, presumably. Does it signify anything? There are those who say this product of hearts is knowledge. *'Je sens mon coeur et je connais les hommes'* ... I couldn't say that, for sure. My face too blind, my mind too limited, my instincts too narrow. But this intensity, doesn't it mean anything? Is it an idiot joy that makes this animal, the most

peculiar animal of all, exclaim something? And he thinks this reaction a sign, a proof, of eternity?[87]

This is an early statement of that mysticism of feeling so much a part of Citrine's and Corde's experience, though Herzog does not have their more assured tone. But in the very last moments of the narrative, with Herzog's decision to desist from letter-writing, this faith in the relationship between the provinces of heart and spirit is given climactic emphasis.

Perhaps it required the sight of *Humboldt's Gift* and *The Dean's December* for *Herzog*'s true meaning to be perceived. As is revealed in my chapter on *Humboldt's Gift*, Bellow had gone through a period of considerable intellectual revision in the decade that intervened between the appearance of *Herzog* and that of *Humboldt*. It is possible that Bellow, in writing his later works, consolidated ideas which had seemed to some a little tentative when they were first broached in *Herzog*. But looking back from *More Die of Heartbreak* we can see the large extent to which *Herzog* was the progenitor of these later novels. The hero of this novel has come to understand a good deal about the pathology of American reality and about the necessity for concealing himself from it. Even in the pastoral sanctuary of Ludeyville he remembers the need for circumspection, the law of survival being 'if you have some happiness, conceal it. And when your heart is full, keep your mouth shut also':

> And, back in the darker garden, he looked for peonies; perhaps some had survived. But then it struck him that he might be making a mistake, and he stopped, listening to Mrs. Tuttle's sweeping, the rhythm of bristles. Picking flowers? He was being thoughtful, being lovable. How would it be interpreted? (He smiled slightly.) Still, he need only know his own mind, and the flowers couldn't be used; no, they couldn't be turned against him. So he did not throw them away.[88]

That smile is formed out of complex ironies, out of his realisation that to be 'thoughtful, lovable' is to be an odd fish in that angry, turbulent sea. Those who display such guileless hearts may have to be 'protected' for their own good. Herzog's silence at the end may, therefore, be seen as a self-defensive strategy on his part, an aspect of his withdrawal from that 'actual sphere' which will always refuse to tolerate his 'type', with its palpitant heart.

The letter-writing Herzog is an exile in his own land, and his mood at the end is as complex in its composition as his wide-ranging thought has been throughout the narrative. Though there is joy in it, there is, too, the sadness of exile. Perhaps Herzog's mood is precisely expressed by the persona of Ezra Pound's poem 'Exile's Letter' who also is led to address someone who may not be listening, who recognises both the futility and the necessity of speaking through the heart:

> What is the use of talking, and there is no
>   end of talking,
> There is no end of things in the heart.
> I call in the boy,
> Have him sit on his knees here
>   To seal this,
> And send it a thousand miles, thinking.[89]

The knowledge that in him such 'things' are inexhaustible is the source of Herzog's joy and also his decision to make the public expression of that joy a cautious and furtive one.

MR SAMMLER'S PLANET

It is not uncommon to find critics who regard *Mr Sammler's Planet* as a watershed in Bellow's fiction. Malcolm Bradbury refers to the novel's 'tone of outrage and detachment' which 'dismayed a number of Bellow's critics who ... felt in it both a waning of imaginative power and an angry conservative withdrawal from liberal humanism'.[90] The reader of this study will not be surprised at such dismay. I have attempted to demonstrate in previous chapters the extent to which Bellow's critics have misunderstood how Bellow's fiction provides the moral rationale for withdrawal from American culture which 'having failed to create a spiritual life of its own, investing everything in material expansion, faced disaster'.[91] This impoverishment of spiritual life, this obsession with the gratification of material and corporeal desire, this 'collaboration of all souls spreading madness and poison' are presented in *Mr Sammler's Planet* as the issue of a recreant age from which Sammler justifiably withdraws. The novel was Bellow's most sustained attack on the conditions that passed for reality in American life, and it suggested that the ugliness of that reality could not be challenged, only confirmed. Surprisingly, there were still some reviews and essays which believed we could still find in the novel 'Bellow's most forceful defense of humanism'.[92] but such judgements slur the vision and cumulative force of Sammler's conclusions. Though he is tired, has had his three score and ten years of experience upon 'this great blue, white, green planet', and feels, with 'secret dismay' that 'others had more strength for life than he', this is no old man's lament for 'the salmon-falls, the mackerel-crowded seas'. Others may possess greater vigour, but 'given the power of the antagonist, no one had strength enough'.[93]

Some critics struggled to find some degree of irony in Bellow's portrayal of his cynical hero.[94] Perhaps Bellow himself might not be fully implicated in Sammler's lack of faith in the human community? Surely, such critics, asked, 'It would be ingenuous to assume that Bellow had lost the complexity displayed in his portrait of Herzog'?[95] Unfortunately, there are few grounds for arguing that Sammler is intended to be an ironic portrait. Given that the novel is narrated by a third-person voice, it is remarkable that Bellow refused the opportunity to exploit the potential subtleties of point-of-view afforded by third-person narration. The narrator, on most occasions, is hardly to be differentiated from Sammler in his outbursts at modern life in general and the novel's cast of other characters. We know, for instance, that Sammler is exasperated by his daughter, Shula, and her eccentric, obsessed personality. But it is Bellow's narrator, not Sammler, who provides us with the first extended satire of Shula's character:

> She wasn't old, not bad looking, not even too badly dressed, item by item. The full effect would have been no worse than vulgar if she had not been obviously a nut.[96]

The narrator seems so hand-in-glove with Sammler that the reader is taken aback on those few occasions (I could only recall two) when he places Sammler in a reproving manner or context. At one point the narrator compares Sammler to 'the majority' of mankind who 'walked about as if under a spell, sleepwalkers, circumscribed by, in the grip of, minor neurotic trifling aims', describing Sammler as 'only one stage forward' from this majority, 'awakened not to purpose but to aesthetic consumption of the environment'.[97] This is an unsteady handling of viewpoint on Bellow's part; we are disturbed by such a general disparagement of Sammler, as it seems to undermine his seriousness, to call the authority of his opinions into question. Fortunately, however, such lapses are rare in the novel, and for the most part the reader experiences a satisfying sense of being buoyed up by the liveliness of Sammler's intelligence and observation. And though on another occasion the narrator appears to invite us to question the worth of that intelligence – 'Old Sammler with his screwy visions!'[98] – our final impression is that of having been in contact with a mind of sane and acute complexion.

In a *Life* interview given just after publication, Bellow described the novel as his 'first thoroughly nonapologetic venture into ideas',[99] perhaps in an effort to forestall criticism of the many lengthy passages of social, historical and cultural analysis within its pages. The 30-page scene in which Sammler and Dr Lal discuss man's estate on the eve of the Apollo moonshot has received particular criticism.[100] Bellow was aware of the likely response to this scene; he retained it at such length despite the contrary advice of one of his respected advisers[101] and must have believed it to be an essential part of the novel's intellectual drama. I agree with John Gross, who, in a review of the novel, thought the Sammler-Lal dialogue 'a daring and wholly successful scene'. It cannot be condemned on the grounds of implausibility, for Bellow had already established Sammler's interest in the kinds of apocalyptic thought ('Like many people who had seen the world collapse once, Mr. Sammler entertained the possibility it might collapse twice . . . You could see the suicidal impulses of civilization pushing strongly')[102] which also concern Dr Lal ('the species is eating itself up. And now Kingdom Come is directly over us and waiting to receive the fragments of a final explosion')[103] and which explain Lal's conviction that the colonisation of the moon is a human necessity. Neither should critics condemn the scene for its length; most of the previous narrative has been to do with Sammler's estrangement from his surroundings and from most of the people he is surrounded by, and, like Albert Corde he has found it difficult to meet with sympathetic minds – 'the right people to talk to – that's the hardest part of all'.[104] It seems natural that, having discovered in Lal a fellow *bien pensant*, a biophysicist who is also interested in metaphysical matters, Sammler should speak at length about his own intellectual dispositions. I cannot agree with those who hold that 'the excitement of the novel resides almost entirely in Mr. Sammler's ruminations. His ideas have the makings of good essays but not of good fiction'.[105] Bellow's strengths have never (with the exception of *The Victim* and some of the short stories) been to do with 'good fiction' as a thing of well-made plot and action. If one is going to criticise *Mr Sammler's Planet* on account of its lack of dramatic activity, the rest of Bellow's fiction will seem an easy target. Just as the reader does not, in Hemingway's fiction, expect his characters to spend a great deal of their time discussing Wittgenstein, so he does not often receive the particular gratifications associated with a fast-moving plot in Bellow's novels.

Other criticisms of *Mr Sammler's Planet* have more to do with the opinions expressed in it than with the way those opinions are expressed. David Galloway, in particular, launched a sharp attack upon the 'Sammleresque' tone of Bellow's voice, its 'avuncular superiority over unwashed radicalism'.[106] 'There are distinctions and discriminations to be made in judging what Sammler calls "the sovereign youth style", but they are not made in the novel.'[107] Galloway does have a point here; it is odd, for instance, that a novel which is, in part, a survey of American youth culture in the 1960s should fail to mention the war in Vietnam.[108] Bellow rather bypasses immediate historical influences in favour of the long view. Rather than attend to the civil repercussions of the Vietnam experience, such as the draft resistance movement and other public expressions of countercultural revolt and display deriving from what was, in effect, America's ideological civil war, Bellow finds it is 'the dreams of nineteenth-century poets' which 'polluted the psychic atmosphere of the great boroughs and suburbs of New York'.[109]

In avoiding mention of Vietnam, Bellow may appear tendentious in his portrayal of what Sammler derisively terms 'the Pepsi Generation', and Sammler himself may seem one who is truly *'out of it, hors d'usage*, not a man of the times'.[110]

Sammler ought, however, to be seen as one who is, in the phrase of a student friend, 'wise, but not hip'.[111] His view of American reality as a species of barbarism has provoked extreme reactions in those who have always seen Bellow as a writer working towards affirmation in the humanist tradition, but Sammler, self-styled 'registrar of madness',[112] has, paradoxically, found reality to be most evident amidst barbarism, in the teeth of pogrom and terror –

'When had things seemed real, true? In Poland when blinded, in Zamosht when freezing, in the tomb when hungry'.[113] In these minimal conditions, life blesses the forms of humanity, the bread brought to him in the Mezvinski tomb by the cemetery caretaker, Cieslakiewicz:

> Some days were missed, but not many, and anyway Sammler saved up a small bread reserve and did not starve. Old Cieslakiewicz was dependable. He brought bread in his hat. It smelled of scalp, of head . . . Cieslakiewicz had risked his life for him. The basis of this fact was a great oddity. They didn't like each other. What had there been to like in Sammler? – half-naked, famished, caked hair and beard, crawling out of the forest . . . After the war Sammler had sent money, parcels to Cieslakiewicz. There was correspondence with the family. Then, after some years, the letters began to contain anti-Semitic sentiments. Nothing very vicious. Only a touch of the old stuff. This was no great surprise, or only a brief one. Cieslakiewicz had had his time of honor and charity.[114]

The old man had the forms for expressing his humanity. Riding along Broadway in Gruner's Rolls Royce 30 years later, Sammler looks out on 'a state of singular dirty misery', a 'poverty of soul . . . you could see in faces on the street'. The Broadway crowds seem to him an articulation of 'the implicit local orthodoxy' which was that 'reality is a terrible thing'.[115] Material excess and devotion to the fat materialist gods has deprived man of spiritual strength, 'given all power to material processes, translated and exhausted religious feeling in so doing'.[116] Sammler had touched reality in the bareness of the tomb, freezing, starving and close to death. In his old age, and in a world unknown to the likes of old Cieslakiewicz, he finds solace in Meister Eckhart's austere injunction, in a metaphysic of isolation and withdrawal from community:

> Blessed are the poor in spirit. Poor is he who has nothing. He who is poor in spirit is receptive of all spirit. Now God is the Spirit of spirits. The fruit of the spirit is love, joy, and peace. See to it that you are stripped of all creatures, of all consolation from creatures. For certainly as long as creatures comfort and are able to comfort you, you will never find true comfort. But if nothing can comfort you save God, truly God will console you.[117]

*　　　*　　　*

Mr Sammler's Planet moves on from Bellow's portrait of the neurosis surrounding Herzog in such characters as Madeleine, to suggest that madness is a generic condition infecting 'the mental masses' of America.[118] The novel shows many examples of the disease, from Eisen's lunging assault on the black pickpocket, to Angela's capitulation to the sex-standards of the Age. Madness is a dispensation, a means of escaping the confrontation with reality, a way of running from the failures of the century's secular faiths:

> Then: a crazy species? Yes, perhaps. Though madness is also a masquerade, the project of a deeper reason, a result of the despair we feel before infinites and eternities. Madness is a diagnosis or verdict of .... man-disappointed minds. Oh, man stunned by the rebound of man's powers.[119]

Madness is a form of insensibility, a perverse state of 'grace'[120] clutched at by those who have been deprived of the numinous pathways. Though 'a few may comprehend that it is the strength to do one's duty daily and promptly that makes saints and heroes' – an early reference to those contractual obligations which Sammler believes Elya Gruner to have met throughout his life – 'most have fantasies of vaulting into higher states, feeling just mad enough to qualify'.[121]

Where Joseph of *Dangling Man* was closing the first chapter of his quest for the authentic, intensely lived life, for a reality which allowed him to be aware of 'the ephemeral agreements by which we live and pace ourselves',[122] Artur Sammler, approaching the final years of his life, has come to similar conclusions about the nature of reality. Mankind, in all its madness and 'degraded clowning'[123] will do anything to escape the reality of selfhood, the bondage of the ordinary and the finite – as Sammler tells Dr Lal, 'there is a peculiar longing for nonbeing'.[124] Like Joseph, Sammler too understands the ersatz and expedient nature of the 'ephemeral agreements' which govern public reality. Reality, he sees, sacrifices truth to the mass need for holistic systems of belief, for models of reality which can satisfy the public desire for the known and the intelligible:

> Arguments! Explanations! thought Sammler. All will explain everything to all, until the next, the new common version is ready. This version, a residue of what people for a century or so

say to one another, will be, like the old, a fiction. More elements of reality perhaps will be incorporated in the new version. But the most important consideration was that life should recover its plenitude, its normal contented turgidity.[125]

This is analogous to Joseph's conclusive insight at the end of *Dangling Man*, though clearly the difference lies in the cynicism with which his elderly successor so easily expresses the key issue of reality as a collaborative fiction.

But Sammler is wiser than Joseph in his realisation that he is himself ensnared in the rage for explanation, for the discovery of design. Such design is, however, a casualty of the plurality of competing cultural interpretations, of the mongrelisation of historical circumstance. Bellow, in a comic retrospect, returns Sammler in memory to the occasion of his first visit to Israel. He encounters there 'a Spanish-speaking Israeli cowpuncher from the pampas' who was 'Bessarabian-Syrian-South American', a bizarre personification of cultural disorder and randomness. 'In Argentinian bloomers tucked into boots, with a Douglas Fairbanks mustache',[126] this gaucho in Galilee mocks Sammler's search to recover the Hebrew homeland and the security and traditions associated with the idea of *patria*. Similarly, on his second visit to Israel, a decade later during the Six-Day War, Sammler's attention is drawn away from the remote tank battle taking place two miles beyond him, to another instance of the culturally disjunct:

Then two more cars came tearing up, joined the group, and cameramen leaped out. They were Italians, *paparazzi*, someone explained, and had brought with them three girls in mod dress. The girls might have come from Carnaby Street or from King's Road in their buskins, miniskirts, false eyelashes. They were indeed British, for Mr. Sammler heard them talking ... The young ladies had no idea where they were, what this was about, had been quarreling with their lovers, who were now lying in the road on their bellies. Photographing battle, the shirts fluttering on their backs. The girls were angry. Carried off from the Via Veneto, probably, without knowing clearly where the jet was going.[127]

This kind of weird coalescence is offered as a satire on Sammler's desire to find relief from the confusions and petty squabbles of domestic life. He had wished to touch bottom again, to recover, in times of war, those conditions when 'things seemed real, true'.[128] But the century has severed Sammler from those times. Ironically he is himself a living example of the kind of acculturation symbolised by the gaucho. With his cosmopolitan credentials, an Anglo-American Polish Jew, he has neglected to notice that diaspora is a stain spreading outwards to affect all peoples and styles of life. Zion and Albion collide in his heritage:

> Mr. Sammler's hired car took him to Capernaum where Jesus had preached in the synagogue. From afar, he saw the Mount of Beatitudes ... Mr. Sammler's heart was very much torn by feelings as he stood under the short, leaf-streaming banana trees.
> And did those feet in ancient time
> Walk upon ...
> But those were England's mountains green. The mountains opposite, in serpentine nakedness, were not at all green ... The many impressions and experiences of life seemed no longer to occur each in its own proper space, in sequence, each with its own recognizable religious or aesthetic importance, but human beings suffered the humiliations of inconsequence, of confused styles, of a long life containing several separate lives. In fact the whole experience of mankind was now covering each separate life in its flood. Making all the ages of history simultaneous. Compelling the frail person to receive, to register, depriving him because of volume, of mass, of the power to impart design.[129]

Such confusion is present in Sammler's eccentric daughter, Shula, 'a nut' whose personality is an embodiment of cultural fragmentation. She surrounds herself with clutter, 'a scavenger' who 'passionately collected things', who is given to 'hunting through Broadway trash baskets',[130] her shopping bags full of 'salvage, loot, coupons, and throwaway literature'.[131] In this respect, she recalls old Miss Lenox, Eugene Henderson's housekeeper, whose mania for collecting 'empty bottles and cartons and similar junk' fills Henderson with despair when, after her death he enters her cottage to find it full of 'shopping bags filled with string and rags'.[132] Such scavenging types bear out Sammler's assertion that 'there is such an absurd craving for actions that connect with other actions, for coherency, for forms'.[133]

And there is also, in this craving, a memory of Herzog's concern for all those who were 'dying for lack of something real to carry home when day is done', their lives blighted by 'their great need, their hunger ... for good sense, clarity, truth'.[134] Shula's fragmented personality would also seem to be connected to that disease of modern consciousness exemplified by Gersbach (himself an early version of Sammler's entrepreneurial student friend, Lionel Feffer) who can, chameleon-like, occupy a range of personality types. Sensing the 'hunger', the market for 'something real' in his audiences, Gersbach sets about simulating the reality with a view to exploiting the need, the mass need of those 'conventional business people and professionals who look after their businesses and specialties well enough, but seem confused about everything else'. This dissociation of being from persona and the consequential distortion of reality, is very much Sammler's concern as he helplessly observes the 'many open elements in his daughter':

> Things that ought but failed actually to connect. Wigs for instance suggested orthodoxy; Shula in fact had Jewish connections ... She became well acquainted with the rabbi, the rabbi's wife and family – involved in Dadaist discussions about faith, ritual, Zionism, Masada, the Arabs. But she had Christian periods as well ... Almost always at Easter she was a Catholic. Ash Wednesday was observed, and it was with a smudge between the eyes that she often came into clear focus for the old gentleman. With the little Jewish twists of kinky hair descending from the wig beside the ears and the florid lips dark red, skeptical, accusing, affirming something substantive about her life-claim, her right to be whatever – whatever it all came to.[135]

Bellow often creates fine comedy out of such chaos. And Sammler himself, though often condemned by critics for being cross-grained, without fellow-feeling, as one whose 'refinement seems repressive ... his sagacity detached and cold',[136] is sometimes made the comic butt. He is 'a considerate father' who is still able to mutter 'appreciation of each piece of rubbish' as Shula presented it to him. He plays the role of straight man to the many clowns who surround him. Forced to use 'the bathroom where Shula kept an Easter chick from Kresge's until it turned into a hen that squawked on the edge of the tub' and to endure 'the Christmas decorations which lasted into Spring', can we blame him if 'the hen with yellow legs in his room on his documents and books was too much one day'?:

He was aware that the sun shone brightly, the sky was blue, but the big swell of the apartment house, heavyweight vase like baroque, made him feel that the twelfth-story room was like a china cabinet into which he was locked, and the satanic hen-legs of wrinkled yellow clawing his papers made him scream out.[137]

When Sammler is given one of Eisen's portraits which makes him look 'like a kewpie doll from the catacombs',[138] it is little wonder that he eventually comes to regard himself as justifiably 'separated from the rest of his species, if not in some fashion severed'.[139] Eisen's dehumanised portraits, the product, Sammler thinks, of 'an insane mind and a frightening soul',[140] are very much in the grain of the American moment, in the mainstream, what the age demanded. Eisen may be crazy, but in being so in the New York of the 1960s he has found his niche and his subject, the accelerated grimace, the mad complexion of an unstable culture in which 'so many highbrows have discovered that madness is higher knowledge. If he painted Lyndon Johnson, General Westmoreland, Rusk, Nixon, or Mr. Laird in that style he might become a celebrity of the art world'.[141]

Decadence in America is wholesale, democratically available to all, 'to everyone who had eyes to read the papers or watch the television, to everyone who shared the collective ecstasies of news, crisis, power'.[142] Public events elicit no moral response from 'the mental masses', having reality only inasmuch as they are bathed in what Bellow's narrator in *The Dean's December* calls 'a kind of event-glamour'.[143] The possibility that sensational public events can have an ethical reality, can be more than a sort of journalism made material, is, as Sammler discovers in the streetfight scene, a futile hope. The scene is an exposure of Sammler's naivety, his vestigial belief in community – the ghost of old Cieslakiewicz – receiving a sharp rebuttal:

Again Mr Sammler turned to the crowd, staring hard. Wouldn't anyone help? So even now – now, *still!* – one believed in such things as help. Where people were, help might be. It was an instinct and a reflex. (An unexasperated hope?) So, briefly examining faces, passing from face to face to face among the people along the curb – red, pale, swarthy, lined taut or soft, grim or adream, eyes bald-blue, iodine-reddish, coal-seam black – how strange a quality their inaction had. They were expecting gratification, oh! at last! of teased, cheated, famished needs. Someone was going to get it! Yes. And the black faces? A similar desire ... Then it struck him that what united everybody was a beatitude of presence ... They are here and not here. They are present while absent. So they were waiting in that ecstatic state. What a supreme privilege![144]

Though observing reality, the crowd does not react to the moral imperatives of the scene of violence and conflict unfolding in front of them; instead, zombie-like, they prefigure Bellow's attack in *The Dean's December* upon the public apprehension of events. There Bellow locates 'new strange forms of blindness'[145] and these are specifically related to the pernicious influence of the media, to the proliferation of theories and discourse, 'the false representations of "communication"'.[146] The siren song of the newspapers, television, the communicators, has taken the place of real experience, and corrupted the forms that made true experience possible. Waiting in the Mezvinski tomb, Sammler remembered how 'there were no events. Events had stopped. There was no news. Cieslakiewicz ... had no news or would not give it'.[147] Decades later, man is being overwhelmed in his essential humanity by the unceasing torrent of news, events, all of which creates a bogus and grotesque passivity, a spectatorial indifference infecting the consciousness which could be 'present while absent'. In a curious reversal of Hemingway's famous attack on the vacuity of high-sounding words such as honour, courage, and glory,[148] Bellow complains about the 'terrible dumbness' deriving from the absence of the 'forms and signs' available to humanity:

> It was not the behaviour that was gone. What was gone was the old words. Forms and signs were absent. Not honor but the word honor. Not virtuous impulse, but the terms beaten into flat nonsense. Not compassion; but what was a compassionate utterance? And compassionate utterance was a mortal necessity. Utterance, sounds of hope and desire, exclamations of grief. Such things were suppressed, as if illicit.[149]

The new reality demands a new breed of man, a new Olympian with vast powers of analysis, self-control, and knowledge of all the discourse, the information-systems, the theories of communication. The modern phase could be triumphed over, comprehended, only by the rare intellect, the perhaps as yet uncreated panepiste-mon of Manhattan:

> Because of the high rate of speed, decades, centuries, epochs condensing into months, weeks, days, even sentences. So that to keep up, you had to run, sprint, waft, fly over shimmering waters, you had to be able to see what was dropping out of human life and what was staying in. You could not be an old-fashioned sitting sage. You must train yourself. You had to be strong enough not to be terrified by local effects of meta-morphosis, to live with disintegration, with crazy streets, filthy nightmares, monstrosities come to life, addicts, drunkards, and perverts celebrating their despair openly in midtown. You had to be able to bear the tangles of the soul, the sight of cruel dissolution. You had to be patient with the stupidities of power, with the fraudulence of business. Daily at five or six a.m. Mr. Sammler woke up in Manhattan and tried to get a handle on the situation. He didn't think he could.[150]

The age demanded not only 'an accelerated grimace', but 'it demanded accelerated exaltation, accepted no instant without pregnant meanings as in epic, tragedy, comedy, or films'.[151] Herzog had watched man 'practicing' his 'future condition already', a condition of amoral automatism 'free from human dependency'.[152] Sammler, too, faces up to the same dehumanised projection of the race, the evolving species of the scientific revolu-tion, 'the future person, a colossal figure, a beautiful green color, with a hand that had evolved into a kit of extraordinary instru-ments, tools strong and subtle, thumb and forefinger capable of exerting thousands of pounds of pressure. Each mind belonging to a marvelous analytical collective, thinking out its mathematics, its physics as part of a sublime whole'.[153]

Bellow introduces the black pickpocket as a supreme exponent of the Age; in his cool and sublime *hauteur*, his absolute self-possession, he is a symbol of what 'millions of civilized people wanted' – 'oceanic, boundless, primitive, neckfree nobility . . . a strange release of galloping impulses . . . the peculiar aim of sexual niggerhood for everyone'.[154] Feffer, too, 'in the furious whirling of his spirit'[155] is a paid-up member of the Now Generation, his 'voice resembling an instrument played with higher and higher intensity but musically hopeless'.[156] Both Feffer and the pickpocket are ones who do have 'a handle on the situation' as opposed to Sammler the 'old-fashioned sitting sage'. In his satirical portrayals of such crazies as Eisen, Shula and Wallace, Bellow offers his most pointed critique of the American Dream. James Truslow Adams, one of the first to popularise the concept of the Dream in his history *The Epic of America* (1931), referred to 'that dream of a land in which life should be better and richer and fuller for every man, with opportunity for each according to his ability or achievement'.[157] America in the 1960s is desperately at work trying to realise this ideal and thereby providing the *reductio ad absurdum* – all have been issued with a bill of rights, but too many are attempting to cash it in too often – 'as one were to smoke ten cigarettes simultaneously; while also drinking whisky; while also being sexually engaged with three or four other persons; while hearing bands of music; while receiving scientific notations – thus to capacity *engagé* . . . the boundlessness, the pressure of modern expectations'.[158]

The ending of *Mr Sammler's Planet* does contain an affirmation, but it is not one that can in any sense balance the weight of futility encountered by Sammler's liberal hopes. As Daniel Fuchs has noted, 'humanistic, liberal affirmation seems not to survive the novel's air'.[159] The desperately repeated cry of the novel's final utterance cannot shield the reader from the truth that emerges from Sammler's many more carefully considered expressions of disillusionment. The hope 'that there is the same truth in the heart of every human being, or a splash of God's own spirit'[160] is one that Sammler 'wouldn't count on'. Similarly, the belief that 'there is still such a thing as a man . . . there are still human qualities . . . was a thing he often thought. At the moment it was only a formula. He did not thoroughly feel it'.[161] Again and again throughout the narrative Sammler is forced to revise his old sense of living in a shared universe, to realise his isolation, his foreignness – 'voice, accent, syntax, manner, face, mind, everything, foreign'.[162] When he most needs others, as in the streetfight scene, or, crucially, in his appeal that Angela ask forgiveness of her dying father, 'come to terms' with him 'at the last opportunity', he fully knows that his ideal of community is very much, like himself 'out of it'.[163] In such conditions, the appeal of Meister Eckhart is obvious.

5

Tuning Out of America:
Humboldt's Gift

In Baudelaire I had found the following piece of curious advice:
Whenever you receive a letter from a creditor write fifty lines
upon some extraterrestrial subject and you will be saved. What
this implied was that the *vie quotidienne* drove you from the
globe, but the deeper implication was that real life flowed
between *here* and *there*. Real life was a relationship between *here*
and *there*.[1]

That last sentence has been an accurate description of Bellow's
field of operations. In his fiction we have been shuttled between
the 'here' of an America that resists the cultured and the humane,
and the 'there' of his characters' efforts at transcendence. If *Mr
Sammler's Planet* had offered, at most, a 'very chilly' invitation to
participate in ordinary life,[2] Bellow's next novel would seem to
provide the rationale and the medium for withdrawal from that
life. The transcendental postulates contained in Dr Lal's heavenly
Utopia are here removed from the margins to become, in the dress
of theosophy, Bellow's major subject. Charlie Citrine finds the
spiritual accountancy of Baudelaire to be both prudent and necessary. This is a novel full of debtors and creditors, a story which
illumines the hard countenance of an early 1970s America, a world
chronically afflicted by avarice, a society of makers and takers.
Mired in their 'melancholy of affluence',[3] they express Bellow's
conviction that 'real life' can only be sustained by deploying
strategies of withdrawal from *la vie quotidienne*. Spiritual secession
is articulated through the ultramundane theories of Rudolf Steiner's anthroposophy.[4] This is the 'extraterrestrial subject' of the
novel and its spiritually redemptive properties are there writ large.

The reaction of reviewers and critics to this novel is worth
considering. Only a very few could welcome its clear rejection of
humanism as signalled by its embrace of a highly-foregrounded

mysticism, cognisant of those 'unconscious sources'[5] of human life in a more strident way than ever before in Bellow's fiction. Those critics who had had Bellow typecast as a gritty realist were especially taken aback by the new novel. One critic properly pointed to the presence of mystical ideas in Bellow's previous work, noting that 'both Moses Herzog and Artur Sammler, for instance, though tough-minded rationalists committed to confronting "the phony with the real thing", are readers of such mystics as William Blake, Meister Eckhart, John Tauler, and Jacob Boehme. They, too, attempt to satisfy yearnings towards a higher, intuitive awareness'[6] of the wellsprings of human life. To the majority of reviewers, however, Bellow's visionary desiderata in *Humboldt's Gift* came as an unwelcome surprise and they treated this aspect of the novel as either aberration or weakness. David Lodge tried to dismiss the theosophical discourse as 'a dead end'[7] to which Bellow gives only partial credence. Others read Citrine's transcendental probings as a continuation of the author's comic voice, so clearly missing throughout *Mr Sammler's Planet*. How seriously, they asked, did Bellow expect his readers to take this kind of 'dubious quasi-mysticism'?[8] It was, surely, a joke, and the joke would be on them if they failed to see this. One reviewer wrote that there was nothing in Bellow's previous work, or indeed in *Humboldt's Gift* itself, to persuade her that Bellow's 'skeptical intelligence can be in agreement with Steiner's pompous elaborations of the invisible'.[9] Howard Eiland regards Citrine as 'a predictably halfhearted visionary' whose 'cosy mysticism'[10] cannot mask an underlying lack of seriousness. But Eiland also tried to do more than dismiss this aspect of the novel and went on to offer an intelligent appraisal of it:

Still, though Citrine's mystical speculations are regarded even by him as hortatory poetry, sketchy in essentials, I do not think Bellow means for us to dismiss them. Like Sammler's 'moon visions' and Herzog's 'holy feeling,' they claim to originate in a kind of primitive awe or wonder that both precedes and comes after philosophy, even the most skeptical. If this rambling counsel on omens and hereafters in the text of our most intelligent living novelist seems cranky, at least from a common-sensical point of view, it is hardly more so than the consideration of destiny and divinities in the post-war, post-modern Heidegger, who arrives at the uncanny by first going through classical metaphysics. Both the novelist and the philosopher instance a new-old religiosity that dwells outside of conventional churches and dogmas, and that hence must appear odd to the world.[11]

And in a 1976 interview, Bellow, unsportingly for the critics, wore a po-face to applaud Steiner's 'great vision', and with no obvious irony declared that the latter was furthermore 'a powerful poet as well as philosopher and scientist'.[12]

If, then, it was no joke, the critics were determined to get serious too, and went back to their desks to pen solemn castigations. Their expectations had been damaged by this novel and the deflection from humanism and community they now saw as ideologically ill-advised and artistically enfeebling. Thus, Keith Opdahl discerns an unfortunate decline into the abstract:

> Mr Sammler rejects figurative thinking, leaning away from the flesh to a world of pure thought. And so too does Charles Citrine ... to Citrine too the world is crazy ... a frantic, superficial, sliding world that might belong to pop music, say, or the sleazier movie companies ... He almost drowns in it but consciously develops the ability to turn away from it to his own mind ... Thus Bellow has come full cycle ... Charles Citrine succeeds in doing what Joseph sought: to dismiss the distracting world and to get down to his business, conducted pretty much in his own head. Bellow's latest art has suffered, I think ... because he is abstract, having lost interest in the physical world that supplied his rich detail.[13]

The criticism here is of the same order as that levelled by reviewer John Aldridge who had found Bellow occupying the wrong pigeon-hole – 'we expect a novelist to be a chronicler and not a visionary, an observer and analyst rather than a seer'.[14] If real life was 'a relationship between here and there' then, for a good many critics, Bellow had decided to spend too much time in remote distances. To some it appeared that *Humboldt's Gift* drowned in its abstracted world.

Now that 'Baudelaire desire to get out'[15] has become much more entrenched, and withdrawal in *Humboldt's Gift* is seen not, as in *Sammler* an evasion of 'the pain of duty',[16] but as a duty in itself, a necessary strategy of spiritual survival which demands that Citrine turn his back on 'all this stuff, the accidental, the merely phenomenal, the wastefully and randomly human'.[17] Bellow's fiction has come to typify that 'demand for life as pure spirit' which Lionel Trilling once observed to be a peculiarly American longing:

> From one point of view, no people has ever had so intense an idea of the relationship of spirit to its material circumstances as we in America now have ... Somewhere in our mental constitution is the demand for life as pure spirit. It is this that explains the phenomenon of our growing disenchantment with the whole idea of the political life, the feeling that although we are willing, nay eager, to live in society, for we all piously know that man fulfills himself in society, yet we do not willingly consent to live in a particular society of the present, marked as it is bound to be by disorderly struggles for influence, by mere approximations and downright failures.[18]

Charlie Citrine is one who cannot give his willing consent any longer. In *Humboldt's Gift* Bellow acknowledges that in its 'society of the present' America's 'failures' have become so conspicuous, the reality of American life so distempered that the full range of individual humanity can only be expressed by cultivating faculties of withdrawal from society. It is a bleak diagnosis, but its bleakness is strongly tempered by Citrine's sturdy conviction that '*this* could not be *it*', that beyond death we achieve the apotheosis denied to us in life.

*   *   *

Though born in Appleton, Wisconsin (so that Bellow can introduce the Citrine-Houdini association: both born in Appleton, both practitioners of escape from material bondage), Charlie Citrine is a Chicagoan. And while he was earnest enough on the subject of anthroposophy, Bellow did take reviewers to task for neglecting his novel's comic aspects, complaining that 'they didn't seem to realize that this is a funny book. As they were pursuing high seriousness, they fell into low seriousness'.[19] Much of that comedy derives from the mismatched coupling of Citrine, man of letters, cultural celebrity, earnest intellectual, 'higher-thought clown', and Chicago, forcing-bed and *milieu* of his antagonists, the band of swindlers and blood-suckers who were intent on 'reinterpreting the twentieth century'[20] for him. He is very aware of this comic discrepancy, aware that he is 'a lover of beauty who insisted on living in Chicago'.[21] That city's heart is as hard and indifferent as it had been at the turn of the century in Dreiser's *Sister Carrie*, its people as grasping, its material prizes still as seductive. If Dreiser had characterised it as 'a magnet', Bellow chooses an image which similarly, but with overtones of greater pain, conveys the compelling nature of the life it holds, for it 'had all the voltage. Once you had picked up the high-voltage wire and were *someone*, a known name, you couldn't release yourself from the electrical current. You were transfixed'.[22] The typical tropes of the novel are adversarial and combative; it is inner life against outer, the here as against the there, the world of flesh against that of spirit, public life swallowing private life. There can be no *détente* and no compromise since America, 'an overwhelming phenomenon', will claim 'more and more of your inner self'; it 'infects you with its restlessness. It trains you in distraction, colonizes consciousness as fast as consciousness advances'.[23]

Memory is what one critic has called Citrine's 'only defense against the anonymous mutability of the city and its silent millions. For the Bellow survivor, each shard of life is unique and precious; it it is not remembered, it is the same as never having existed at all'.[24] Only the past, benign in the sepia of memory, brings Citrine some fleeting consolation. The takings were good then 'in the Twenties' when 'kids in Chicago hunted for treasure in the March thaw. Dirty snow hillocks formed along the curbs and when they melted, water ran braided and brilliant in the gutters and you could find marvellous loot – bottle tops, machine gears, Indian-head pennies'.[25] Since then Citrine's pile has grown large, aligned with his rising stock on 'the cultural Dow-Jones'. He was the victim of capitalism which had made his money 'for dark comical reasons of its own'.[26] This loot was no marvellous thing and his guilty possession of it makes those boyhood memories prelapsarian. In those days before the fall into affluence, he willingly fell victim to the great influence of his life, poet Von Humboldt Fleisher. While Citrine's star rose the latter's fell; as Citrine flies in a helicopter above New York with John F. Kennedy, Humboldt moves towards further impoverishment and eventual death in the Bowery. It could almost be Dreiser again, recast Hurstwood and Carrie, except for Citrine's far greater susceptibility to the guilty feelings engendered by Humboldt's decline. The latter's ever-more splenetic charges that Citrine was in his debt ('he did steal something

from me – my personality'[27]) only serve to heighten his growing
fear of being too closely in the grip of that American reality,
spiritually consumptive and emotionally weak, which could tolerate Humboldt's sad demise.

The critic who accuses Bellow of having 'lost interest in the
physical world that supplied his rich detail' in past novels is at best
half right. Bellow is still a lucid chronicler of the reality of
appearances; indeed he reads at times like Dreiser the social
historian. Where Dreiser would think nothing of sacrificing the
flow of his plot to tell us about Chicago's new telephone system,
Bellow too can stop to remark that 'lying at the southern end of the
Great Lakes – twenty percent of the world's supply of fresh water –
Chicago with its gigantesque outer life contained the whole
problem of poetry and the inner life in America'.[28] Much of this
novel's achievement lies in its ability to summon up the baroque
efflorescence of a teeming 'outer life' while at the same time
providing a critique and a repudiation of the human factor in it.
Any novelist who can give his readers such monstrously credible
characters as the hoodlum Cantabile and law court sharks like
Tomchek and Cannibal Pinsker (*and* delight us with the painful
lyricism of such names) can hardly be said to have slid into the
abstract. At the end of the novel Citrine, with a good deal of
self-directed irony, refers to himself as 'a city boy' and it is true that
he is (like his successor, Albert Corde) very much involved with
the public world. His growing interest in the occult, fantastic
postulates of Steinerian theosophy is, therefore, dramatised as a
reaction to his personal experience of 'turmoil and ideological
confusion, the principal phenomenon of the present age'.[29] If he
does find increasing solace by 'tuning out' of that reality to inhabit
'some phantom Atlantic City boardwalk of the mind'[30] it is a
fugitive impulse well-justified by the logic Bellow has built into the
novel:

Maybe America didn't need art and inner miracles. It had so
many outer ones. The USA was a big operation, very big. The
more *it*, the less *we*. So Humboldt behaved like an eccentric and a
comic subject. But occasionally there was a break in his eccen-
tricity when he stopped and thought. He tried to think himself
clear away from this American world (I did that, too).[31]

Bellow's targets remain unchanged. As Citrine says, 'it was my inner civil war versus the open life which is elementary, easy for everyone to read, and characteristic of this place, Chicago, Illinois'.[32] Citrine's belief in the exhaustion of secular epistemologies, in the contemporary uselessness of 'social ideas, political, philosophical theories, literary ideas (poor Humboldt!), sexual ones, and, I suspect, even scientific ones'[33] is never undermined by Bellow. These latter ideas, and their influence in the field of American politics and society at large, become a particular target of attack in this novel, preparing the ground for the continuation and heightening of the attack in *The Dean's December*. Bellow's quarrel is not with the scientific worldview *per se*, but with its predominant, enforcing influence as a cast of mind. Those who insist on the existence of a spiritual life are made to feel like outsiders, unhistorical, immature. In an important sense this has been the case with Humboldt. A language of the spirit becomes difficult to sustain – 'as none of this is Scientific, we are afraid to think it'.[34]

With *Humboldt's Gift* Bellow became a major figure in the van of a large body of American writing which expresses what one critic has called a 'new consciousness', and which is 'hungry for informed cosmology, for holistic views of life, for individual connections to the many and directly to the divine, for metaphysics'.[35]

In his Nobel lecture Bellow made reference to another state of reality, 'the genuine one, that we lose sight of'; devoid of the heightened consciousness which would allow us access to this reality we are left with nothing but what Bellow, quoting Proust, calls 'a terminology for practical ends which we falsely call life'.[36] In the years immediately following *Humboldt's* publication Bellow further explained, in a number of interviews, his desire to use the art of his fiction as a means of penetrating 'what pride, passion, intelligence, and habit erect on all sides – the *seeming* realities of this world'.[37] He castigated the timidity of modern writing which refused to express the 'much-neglected metaphysical unconscious' in human life, content to rest instead in the 'meager measures' afforded by realism. Contemporary writers must be prepared to throw off such constraints and transgress that 'line between what is visible and what is not', to deny the prohibitions of 'our "rational" or "critical" or "scientific" standards'.[38] For too long writers have chosen the safety of the hither side of that line, cowed by the dogmas of rationalism and merely sighing 'in longing for the gorgeous kingdoms beyond'.[39] *Humboldt's Gift* was clearly to be

taken as a part of this new programme, as a novel which de-
molishes the line which suggests that the reality beyond appearances is unknowable. Under the aegis of this new aesthetic, the
task of the writer was to provide man with the images and the
vocabulary of this spiritual rebirth, for 'the greatest things, the
things most necessary for life, have recoiled and retreated. People
are actually dying of this, losing all personal life, and the inner
being of millions, many many millions, is missing ... Under
pressure of public crisis the private sphere is being surrendered'.[40]
Humboldt's Gift is a work which endeavours to replenish the flow of
writing which could help to claw back the territory lost to 'gigantesque outer life'. The recovery of such territory requires the
elevation of language, for this has atrophied in common with the
life of the spirit. Proust's 'terminology for practical ends' is
expressed by Citrine as a sub-human grunting, for 'our daily
monkeyshines are such, our preoccupations are so low, language
has become so debased, the words so blunted and damaged, we've
said such stupid and dull things, that the higher beings hear only
babbling and grunting and TV commercials – the dog-food level of
things'.[41]

Bellow returns in *Humboldt's Gift* to those metaphors of sleep and
wakefulness which he had made good use of in earlier novels in
order to point up man's spiritual lethargy. Thus, on one occasion,
Citrine is at the theatre with his small daughters; the production is –
what else? – *Rip Van Winkle* and that play's fable is exploited as we
would expect. Citrine casts himself as a latter-day Rip, 'asleep in
spirit' for most of his life and only now, provoked by the tragic
waste of Humboldt's life, waking to face up to his responsibilities.
As Rip staggers up from his sleep of years he has Citrine's
sympathy. 'Knowing what he was up against, I groaned. The real
question was whether he could stay awake'.[42] Where Henderson
burst his spirit's sleep by sitting at the feet of King Dahfu and
willingly submitting to a rite of passage, Citrine practices techniques of withdrawal from ordinary life and learns the rubric of
anthroposophy under the tutelage of Dr Scheldt. Steiner's theories
allow Bellow to posit a framework of spiritual expansion: un-
moored from its rational base, the self begins to assert itself against
an outer world which had threatened to overwhelm it:

Soul and spirit are poured out upon the world which normally
we perceive from within ... This external world we no longer

see, for we are *it*. The outer world is now the inner. Clairvoyant, you are in the space you formerly beheld. From this new circumference you look back to the center, and at the center is your own self. That self, your self, is now the external world . . . and with this glory comes also a knowledge of stars which exist in the space where we formerly felt ourselves to stand inert. We are not inert but in motion together with these stars. There is a star world within us . . . In life and in death the signature of the cosmos is within us.[43]

Henderson's 'grun-tu-molani', his ebullient love of life, is succeeded by Charlie Citrine's 'light-in-the-being'. His retiral into this fantastic star world within is in direct reaction against a socially conditioned reality which victimises many. There are, indeed, some passages which read like extreme evangelical tracts, as, with missionary purpose Citrine busies himself with 'business on behalf of the entire human race'. His destiny is to be a saviour for all:

My very fingertips rehearsed how they would work the keys of the trumpet, imagination's trumpet, when I got ready to blow it at last. The peals of that brass would be heard beyond the earth, out in space itself. When that Messiah, that savior faculty the imagination was roused, finally we could look with open eyes upon the whole shining earth.[44]

There is a good deal of similar, hierographical rhetoric throughout *Humboldt's Gift*, though none quite so inflamed as this. Yet at no point in the narrative is Citrine seriously undermined as an authoritative voice, and especially not when he speaks on such subjects as the above. Though his women regard him as a crank they are themselves discredited[45] as materially or sensually-driven creatures with whom Citrine can have no real communication. Bellow stands squarely behind his character on these matters of ideology and makes no effort to disparage them. Indeed he searches for philosophical and intellectual categories with which to further bolster the divide between a collectively ratified reality and that concept of the real as advocated by Citrine. Thus, some literary big guns are brought forward in defence:

Gertrude Stein used to distinguish between a person who is an 'entity' and one who has an 'identity'. A significant man is an entity. Identity is what they give you socially. Your little dog recognizes you and therefore you have an identity. An entity, by contrast, an impersonal power, can be a frightening thing. It's as T. S. Eliot said of William Blake. A man like Tennyson was merged into his environment or encrusted with parasitic opinion, but Blake was naked and saw man naked . . . and this made him terrifying.[46]

This is an example of the hard dualism that the novel sets up. The two states of being are mutually exclusive and those critics who still insist that we are not being asked 'to choose one over the other', that what the book teaches is that we 'must attend, sometimes simultaneously, to the competing needs of both'[47] miss the point entirely. Citrine has an urgency and a conviction that express the inspirational character of his vision, its wholehearted effect upon him:

> I want it to be clear, however, that I speak as a person who had lately received or experienced light. I don't mean 'The light'. I mean a kind of light-in-the-being . . . and this light, however it is to be described, was now a real element in me, like the breath of life itself. I had experienced it briefly, but it had lasted long enough to be convincing and also to cause an altogether unreasonable kind of joy. Furthermore, the hysterical, the grotesque about me, the abusive, the unjust, that madness in which I had often been a willing and active participant, the grieving, now had found a contrast. I say 'now' but I knew long ago what this light was. Only I seemed to have forgotten that in the first decade of life I knew this light and even knew how to breathe it in. But this early talent or gift or inspiration, *given up for* the sake of maturity or realism (practicality, self-preservation, the fight for survival), was now edging back.[48] (my emphasis)

Now that the scales have dropped, Citrine's delayed task is to recover the light, but to do so by withdrawing from 'realism' (here associated with states of distortion, with madness, hysteria, the grotesque). Transported by his theosophical faith Citrine is cast adrift in a fantastic firmament through which he rushes in an almost Whitmanesque ecstasy. 'I often felt unusually light and swift-paced, as if I were on a weightless bicycle and sprinting through the star-world. Occasionally I saw myself with exhilarating objectivity, literally as an object among objects in the physical universe'.[49]

Bellow has revealed that the novel grew out of a period of considerable intellectual revision; he told an interviewer, 'my mind at the moment is a mass of transition. I'm in the midst of multiple revision. Almost everything that I used to consider stable in life I now doubt. And much that I doubted before now seems to me stable'.[50] But if *Humboldt's Gift* was written in order to partially rectify a state of literary affairs that caused Bellow concern, his belief that 'modern literature has not dealt confidently with the intimations of the far side',[51] his own fiction is not short of characters who strike out for that territory, as I have shown in earlier chapters. Humboldt Fleisher had the nerve to doubt that his feet, too, were made of clay; he had made 'raids behind the lines to bring back beauty'[52] only to be worn down by the effort. His outrage, so disturbing to the establishment, was eventually quelled, tamed and domesticated. The kinds of knowledge Humboldt was privy to were intolerable to the reigning orthodoxy, 'the going mental rules of a civilization that proved its right to impose such rules by the many practical miracles it performed',[53] and the 'bastards, the literary funeral directors and politicians ... had no use for old-hat Humboldt'.[54]

Humboldt was bullied by those who trivialised his insights and, in effect, corrupted his genius before consigning him to the anonymity of 'one of those vast, necropolitan developments' in 'Deathsville, New Jersey'.[55] The sustained attack on the values of the public world that takes place in this novel, and its philosophical renegation of the ordinary, is largely justified by the case study offered by Humboldt's experiences. Bellow's growing awareness of a 'human understructure ... much larger than any measure our culture gives us',[56] in the necessity of release from the stranglehold of 'the scientific world view',[57] leads his central character to cast off all such restrictions:

> In the past the self had had garments, the garments of station, of nobility or inferiority, and each self had its carriage, its looks, wore the sheath appropriate to it. Now there were no sheaths and it was naked self with naked self burning intolerably and causing terror. It felt ecstatic.[58]

This is the point of freedom in *Humboldt's Gift*, the advance on Herzog's 'inspired condition'.

The animating metaphysic of the novel is rooted in part in what is essentially a Neoromanticism. Steiner's thinking was heavily influenced by English Romanticism as was the work of Owen Barfield (whom Bellow interviewed while at work on *Humboldt's Gift*), Steiner's most loyal disciple in this century.[59] Though Bellow has often expressed his contempt for the legacy of Romantic thought upon modern consciousness – that extreme solipsism that dissolves everything into itself – finding in it an untenable hubris, he has in this novel taken up a strain of late Romantic thought which found in Thomas Carlyle its major exponent. In fact the above extract, with its clothing metaphors, reads like something from Carlyle's work of 1834, *Sartor Resartus*. In that volume Carlyle fashioned a critique of his age which held that outer reality be seen as a mere set of clothes which covers the world of spirit, for Carlyle the only reality. The scientific advances of the nineteenth century made possible its argument that the universe was governed by natural laws, that miracles were impossible and the supernatural a myth. It was an age when utilitarian standards reigned supreme, an age which saw the birth of that scientific worldview to which Bellow has taken such great exception. Carlyle, too, believed in the need for a new apprehension of reality and in *Sartor* he accomplishes his argument by reiterating the assertion that 'the beginning of all wisdom is to look fixedly on clothes . . . till they become transparent',[60] and, with his amazing vision of a naked House of Lords, he urged his readers to discard everything but the essential reality behind forms and symbols. It might, of course, be argued that Carlyle's thinking had been subsumed by American intellectual history in the guise of Transcendentalism and that Bellow's ideology here is more fruitfully seen as a development of Emersonian ideas. But while Carlyle and Emerson shared a great deal in common, believing in an immanent deity which suffuses the visible universe, they differed on one crucial point of dogma – the deification of man. In *The Reign of Wonder* Tony Tanner notes the important criticism of Emerson by Carlyle and quotes the latter's address to the American – 'we find you a Speaker indeed, but as it were a Soliloquizer on the eternal mountaintops only, in vast solitudes where men and their affairs all lie hushed in a very dim remoteness; and only *the man* and the stars and the earth are visible'.[61] As Tanner remarks, Carlyle criticised Emerson's stress on the entire independence of man so that he was without history, location, or society. The type of Romantic-related thought I have pointed to in *Humboldt's Gift* is, in these crucial respects, non-

American. Indeed, as early as *Dangling Man* Bellow was discriminating between self-valuation and self-congratulation ('it is a different thing to value oneself and to prize oneself crazily')[62] and so his repudiation of solipsism, his continuing 'assault on the follies of romantic subjectivism'[63] in this novel is not unexpected. All of Citrine's contemplations lead to an *objectification* of self ('I saw myself with exhilarating objectivity, literally as an object among objects in the physical universe').[64] The *naiveté* of Emersonian Transcendentalism could never have attracted Bellow; the remoteness of his heroes is a complex, historically rooted and socially urgent response to a particular crisis of reality. In 1973, between the publication of *Mr Sammler* and, presumably, during the writing of *Humboldt*, he told an audience of his opposition to 'the absurd ideas of originality which belong to the Romantic tradition' and especially to the idea of Romantic hubris, of our 'being self-created individuals of genius, etc., as if we don't *derive* from anything'.[65] In his final letter to Citrine, Humboldt speaks from the grave to wag a final, admonitory finger at him and to hand down in his last sentence what is, we presume, a hard-won wisdom – 'last of all – remember: we are not natural beings but supernatural beings'.[66]

And in the climactic chapter of *Sartor*, titled 'Natural Supernaturalism', Carlyle asserts the spiritual dictum both writers share, that the reality which is based upon the world of appearances is a fool's reality, that the visible world only masks the more fabulous realms of the spirit which lie beyond.

Keith Opdahl, in his otherwise unfriendly account of *Humboldt's Gift*, points to its strengths as 'one of the few novels in which private religious experience is incorporated fully into the novel', and to its 'spiritual mysticism that shuts out the social world of man and makes matter mere appearance'.[67] It is against the depredations of the basely real, against those systems of material and amoral power which bear down on him so remorselessly, the Chicago in which, to survive, one became a 'connoisseur of the near-nothing'[68] and developed 'a deep no-affect belt, a critical mass of indifference',[69] that Citrine moves towards the epiphanies provided by 'the gorgeous kingdoms beyond'. In the grip of what he calls 'a Chicago state' he tells us:

I infinitely lack something, my heart swells, I feel a tearing eagerness. The sentient part of the soul wants to express itself . . .

at the same time I have a sense of being the instrument of external powers. They are using me either as an example of human error or as the mere shadow of desirable things to come.[70]

Citrine yields himself, as no previous Bellow hero has before, to that which Trilling described as peculiarly American, the demand for life as pure spirit. He consorts with a supernal universe in a last-ditch effort to rid himself of the 'many cantankerous erroneous silly and delusive objects actions and phenomena'[71] which encumber him. In the following passage Citrine explains his *modus operandi*. Pursued by Tomchek and Srole, who 'had the assistance of Denise, Pinsker, Urbanovich, and a cast of thousands'[72] he shuts the door on them all:

I visualized an old black iron Chicago lamppost from forty years back ... I was a young boy and I watched from my bedroom window. It was a winter gale, the wind and snow banged the iron lamp, and the roses rotated under the light. Steiner recommended the contemplation of a cross wreathed with roses but for reasons of perhaps Jewish origin I preferred a lamppost. The object didn't matter as long as you went out of the sensible world. When you got out of the sensible world, you might feel parts of the soul awakening that never had been awake before.[73]

No doubt it is passages such as this which have led critics to accuse Bellow of giving us a parboiled mysticism in this novel, and to question his seriousness or his artistic sense. There is a difference between the art which is fiction and the 'lay sermons',[74] the metaphysical *longeurs* which, they believe, are too indulged in this novel's prose. Their irritation is, to an extent, understandable. Bellow does employ a species of chop-logic in his dealings with theosophical axioms, accepting those which are commensurate with his own thinking and rejecting those which are not. However, by refusing the whole package he perhaps undermines the reader's faith in the remainder. Bellow is happy to borrow a context and a profundity from Steiner; Citrine's other-worldly excursions are ratified, to an extent, by that context. Yet Bellow is clearly anxious not to be too closely identified with the entire holistic system of anthroposophy. In his conversations with his anthroposophy tutor, Dr Scheldt, Citrine reveals a scepticism not only about

Scheldt himself ('I'm speaking to his interested and plain face, calm as a bull's face and trying to determine how dependable his intelligence is – i.e., whether we are real here or crazy here'),[75] but about the substance of what is said. It was Wilhelm in *Seize the Day* who, aware of Tamkin's con-talk, nevertheless admits 'I guess I am a sucker for people who talk about the deeper things of life, even the way he does',[76] and Citrine too needs the pabulum offered by Dr Scheldt – 'the strange things he said were at least deep things. In this day and age people had ceased to say such things'.[77] In some sense, then, the respect is granted to the sincerity and profundity of Scheldt's views rather than their validity. But, Bellow seems to suggest, humankind can only bear so much crankiness; there are degrees of crankiness, and Citrine lays down the bottom line:

> I was fairly sceptical still, I couldn't make my peace with things like the Moon Evolution, the fire spirits, the Sons of Life, with Atlantis, with the lotus – flower organs of spiritual perception or the strange mingling of Abraham with Zarathustra, or the coming together of Jesus and the Buddha. It was all too much for me. Still, whenever the doctrine dealt with what I suspected or hoped or knew of the self, or of sleep, or of death, it always rang true.[78]

And so Bellow uses an edited version of anthroposophy, Steiner without the knobs on. It gave him a context, a language of the spirit, and must have seemed to him an important expression of his developed interest in the phenomenology of the self. Forced beyond the 'failed ideas' of his age, Citrine crosses the border into exile. But until he learns again how to revive those faculties of reception which have fallen into desuetude ('this early talent ... given up for the sake of maturity or realism'), to learn through the tuition of Dr Scheldt the liberating possibilities of that exile, he has, in effect, no reality:

> I was aware that I used to think I knew where I stood (taking the universe as a frame of reference). But I was mistaken ... it was now apparent to me that I was neither of Chicago nor sufficiently beyond it, and that Chicago's material and daily interests and phenomena were neither actual and vivid enough nor symbolically clear enough to me. So that I had neither vivid actuality nor symbolic clarity and for the time being I was utterly nowhere.[79]

Citrine's experiences illustrate the divide between what Bellow has called 'the seeming realities of this world' and 'another reality, the genuine one, that we lose sight of'.[80] In possession of this knowledge, Citrine knows the pain of exclusion from his habitat, finding that 'suddenly Chicago was not my town at all. It was totally unrecognizable. I merely imagined that I had grown up here, that I knew the place, that I was known by it. In Chicago my personal aims were bunk, my outlook a foreign ideology'.

Nowhere is this schism more sadly apparent than in the scenes between Citrine and his brother. The latter, a wealthy financier, is about to undergo open-heart surgery. His genius is to compose 'capitalistic fugues',[81] to draw up balance sheets which have the compelling power of 'Chapman's *Homer*, illuminated pages, realms of gold'.[82]

There is real brotherly love between the Citrines, but Julius wears the livery of a different court. As Citrine tries to find the words which could console his brother and offer him hope for what may be his last days, he realises that the eschatology he subscribes to is untransmissible:

> He'd say, 'What do you mean, Spirit! Immortality? You mean that?' . . . and now the fatal coastline was in view before him and I wanted to say, as he sat looking sick behind the wheel, that this brilliant, this dazing shattering delicious painful thing (I was referring to life) when it concluded, concluded only what we knew. It did not conclude the unknown, and I suspected that something further would ensue. But I couldn't prove a thing to this hardheaded brother of mine.[83]

Any intimations he could offer were 'certainly not acceptable to one of the biggest builders of southeast Texas',[84] prohibited as they were by that scientific worldview which could stitch the heart together but which regarded death as final.

It is therefore apt that towards the end of the narrative we find Citrine exiled in literal terms, communing Herzog-like with the dead and happily free from having to deal with 'the mental respectability of good members of educated society',[85] an establishment he wholly despises.

The concluding scene of the novel has caused critics some confusion (almost inevitably, given the critical reaction to previous Bellow endings) and Bellow has been charged with not giving enough clarification to its symbols.[86] The crucial moment appears to be one of shocking epiphany wherein Bellow stresses the finality of death:

> I observed, however, another innovation in burials. Within the grave was an open concrete case. The coffins went down and then the yellow machine moved forward and the little crane, making a throaty whir, picked up a concrete slab and laid it atop the concrete case. So the coffin was enclosed and the soil did not come directly upon it. But then, how did one get out? One didn't, didn't, didn't! You stayed, you stayed! ... Thus, the condensation of collective intelligences, and combined ingenuities, its cables silently spinning, dealt with the individual poet.[87]

The scene is capable of causing confusion in a number of ways. Citrine's exclamation seems to suggest a sudden understanding that death can have no spiritual aftermath, and the funeral thus becomes a very dramatic *memento mori* for him. However, I do not believe that this scene ought to be taken as an unequivocal refutation of the novel's transcendental logic. Certainly the symbolism of the funeral mechanism is powerful and conveys Citrine's grief at Humboldt's wasted life, but beyond this it is not a symbolism which countermands his reiterated faith in the existence of 'the gorgeous kingdoms beyond'. Earlier in the same scene Citrine had made his continuing loyalty to this faith clear enough when, touching Humboldt's coffin, he reflects that the bodily remains were 'very possibly the signature of spiritual powers, the projection of the cosmos'.[88] And his exclamation in the quoted passage above may be seen to derive from the fear sustained throughout the narrative – that the individual dissent of those, like Humboldt, imbued with a vigorous spiritual sensibility, will be overwhelmed by the mass orthodoxies, the 'collective intelligences and combined ingenuities' which are sinisterly represented by the 'yellow machine' which lays the slab on top of Humboldt's coffin. That this is the dominant meaning of the novel's final scene and its symbolism becomes clear in an earlier passage:

> In the long years since I had last attended a burial, many mechanical improvements had been made. There stood a low yellow compact machine which apparently did the digging and bull-dozed back the earth. It was also equipped as a crane.

Seeing this, I started off on the sort of reflection Humboldt himself had trained me in. The machine in every square inch of metal was a result of collaboration of engineers and other artificers. A system built upon the discoveries of many great minds was always of more strength than what is produced by the mere workings of any one mind, which of itself can do little.[89]

This fear of the futility of individual dissent from overpowering systems is very much a part of Citrine's experience. However, it only serves to further justify the novel's major argument that there is no alternative to 'tuning out', to withdrawal from the intimidating mechanisms of such systems. They cannot be publicly challenged, but they may be privately avoided. This, too, will be Albert Corde's discovery.

6

Everything Merely Human: *The Dean's December*, The Short Fiction, *More Die of Heartbreak*

THE DEAN'S DECEMBER

After the mystical departures of *Humboldt's Gift*, *The Dean's December* may at first sight seem a novel in which Bellow returns to more familiar territory. Certainly it was with something like relief that many reviewers remarked this apparent reconciliation. Salman Rushdie confidently asserted that 'like his dean, Bellow looks up to the stars with awe; but he knows the stars are not his job; his place, and his subject, is the earth'.[1] And in the figure of Albert Corde, embroiled as he is with a very ugly Chicagoan reality, Bellow seemed to have turned away from that astral metaphysic which had been so much a part of *Humboldt's Gift*, of Citrine's conviction that 'in life and death the signature of the cosmos is within us', towards his new hero's awareness that 'the cosmos was beyond him'.[2] There were few first readers to suggest the continuities between the novel and its predecessor, with its overtones of withdrawal which had distressed so many. Robert Towers, reviewing the novel for the *New York Times Book Review*, guarded his allusion to *Humboldt's Gift* within the walls of a parenthesis, remarking that Corde's vision 'partly existentialist, partly mystical (in a way adumbrated by the anthroposophic passages of *Humboldt's Gift*) ... entails the recovery of "the world that is buried under the debris of false description or non-experience"'.[3] The majority of Bellow's admirers did not regard *Humboldt* as an advance and so their unwillingness to point out the extent to which the new novel connected with it is hardly surprising. John J. Clayton, in a new edition of his *Saul Bellow: In Defense of Man*, had admonished the novelist for the life-evading tendencies which had issued forth in *Humboldt's Gift*, and in a severely-toned final paragraph urged Bellow to reject a fiction which 'cuts itself off from life'.[4] With *The Dean's December* Bellow seemed to have accepted this kind of critical rebuke and started to make amends. But just as I have argued in previous chapters for a reappraisal of Bellow's vision of reality, so here I find that the general critical response is based upon a misreading of a work which is, if anything, even more explicit in its portrayal of those forces of modern consciousness which debase the spirit and cannot be dislodged. And though the novel is a record of Corde's endeavour to persevere within this context, acknowledging his duty to others, working for change, finally, his effort to point the finger of reproach in his *Harper's* essays leads to his professional disgrace, his resignation from his post as dean, and his own recognition of failure.

Corde's moment of freedom, of searing insight, is given to him, and, with real dramatic power, to the reader, at the very last when he is visiting the Mount Palomar observatory with his astronomer wife, Minna. The truth he is there given to understand is one that urges a revision of existential reality, that undermines the 'merely human'[5] as fully as had Citrine's overtures to the Oversoul of anthroposophy. Once again under the mystical influence of the stars a Bellow character is drawn to reflect upon the nature of reality as it revealed itself to man – as through the dark glass of the senses, and, more profoundly, through the agency of feeling:

> And what he saw with his eyes was not even the real heavens. No, only white marks, bright vibration, clouds of sky roe, tokens of the real thing, only as much as could be taken in through the distortions of the atmosphere. Through these distortions you saw objects, forms, partial realities. The rest was to be felt. And it wasn't only that you felt, but that you were drawn to feel and penetrate further, as if you were being informed that what was spread over you had to do with your existence, down to the very blood and the crystal forms inside your bones. Rocks, trees, animals, men and women, these also drew you to penetrate further, under the distortions (comparable to the atmospheric ones, shadows within shadows), to find their real being with your own.[6]

The allusion here to a mysticism of feeling as the means towards disclosing existential truth is closer to Charlie Citrine's programme for spiritual regeneration than other commentators have allowed. Both men are acted upon by a sense of immanence which endows them with spiritual strength and compels them towards a quest for the essentially human in themselves and others. But whereas for Citrine this effort to rise above the empoisoned 'dog-food level' of things entails an almost total withdrawal from the distractions of everyday life, an ever-more frequent 'tuning-out', Corde is characteristically a more humanly tolerant being, willing to expose himself to the public world in an effort to clarify, and thereby begin to remedy, its worst failings. In the end, however, his efforts to do this are repelled and at the close of the narrative he is, like Sammler and Citrine before him, poised between 'here' and 'there', between that duty to the human bond, a duty and a bond which have been almost completely traduced by this novel's Grand Inquisitor, Dewey Spangler, and the antithetical drive towards the purging chill of cosmic space. To be absorbed by that inhuman immensity, by the welcoming 'cold *out there*' with 'its power to cancel everything merely human',[7] by 'the living heavens' which 'looked as if they would take you in',[8] comes to seem a most serene kind of oblivion to Corde. *The Dean's December* as a whole is an explanation and, I believe, a justification of this willingness on Corde's part to entertain the cancellation of 'everything merely human'.

*   *   *

All of Bellow's fiction is, as I have argued, an effort to grasp a more authentic reality, to suggest the means by which we may be released from the increasingly entrenched view of reality which encourages us to surrender our claim to a spiritual life. In his Nobel speech the writer described the art of the novel as a celebration of the plurality of life, an art which at its best 'tells us that for every human being there is a diversity of existences, that the single existence is itself an illusion in part, that these many existences signify something, tend to something, fulfil something'.[9] And in a 1982 post-publication interview Bellow defined 'the real task of a writer' as an attempt to 'penetrate, to find the essentially human under all the disguises, the appearances'.[10] Like Citrine, Albert Corde is made to find that 'the first act of morality was to disinter the reality, retrieve reality, dig it out from the trash, represent it anew as art would represent it'.[11] Together with that climactic passage quoted above, all of these extracts suggest the tendency at work in the novel as a whole – one of existential penetration, a process of continual ingression, a working towards those elements of individual and collective humanity which remain unsullied by the 'trash' of cultural degradation. This is the significant difference between Corde and Citrine. Rather than devote himself to finding the vestigially human in others, Citrine takes Humboldt's experience as a definitive example of how the world treats the man of feeling and he turns away towards the cultivation of a mystical and visionary sensibility. As a result, Bellow opens himself to the critical charge of being an ideologue more than an artist. 'The central problem in Bellow's novels,' complains one such critic, is that 'the imaginative structure fails to provide adequate support for the intellectual structure, so that at crucial moments the author's ideas fail to be embodied in character, action, or image.'[12] Citrine's secession may be justified but is not sufficiently rendered as such. In comparison, Corde, and the novel in which he appears, do not suffer from this potentially damaging dissociation; his rejection of the public world, and that world's reciprocal rejection of him, is an integral part of the novel's drama.

Always fully entitled to his eminence as a novelist of ideas, Bellow has now written a work which illustrates his conviction that 'nothing is legitimate in literature or any work of art which does not have the support of some kind of emotional conviction. The ideological conviction means almost nothing. The emotional conviction means everything'.[13] On one level this is one of the most peculiar of all the author's many statements on fictional aesthetics. The dissociation of intellect from feeling has been one of the risk areas which Bellow has had to encounter in his sustained effort to dramatise ideas in literature. He has not always been fully successful in this, but that he has accomplished a great deal in this most difficult vein makes him a literary artist of the first rank. His detractors have nevertheless found this risk area an Achilles' heel to be attacked. Frank Tuohy, reviewing *The Dean's December*, homes in on the target when he complains that it is a work which 'comes through as the product of a hyperactive intelligence, rather than as a celebration of a creative gift'.[14] The aesthete's constitutional distrust of a fiction of ideas is clear enough in that castigating 'hyperactive'. The intellectual and the artist are, to such critics, impossible bedfellows. That Bellow has, much more often than not, united his fertile ('hyperactive') intellect with his artistic sensibility, creating such memorable *savant*-heroes as Herzog, Sammler and Joseph, is a convincing demonstration of his rare ability. As if to prove the point further, *The Dean's December* places great stress upon 'the emotional conviction' by elevating it into *the* means of insight for Albert Corde the intellectual, providing through it a basis of communication and understanding which goes beyond, beneath 'the disguises, the appearances'. These latter supply the large structure of a novel which exploits the dissimulation of reality common to both East and Western European and American culture.

Though ostensibly one of contrast, this structure is deftly used by Bellow to point up the ironical similarities between the 'free' world and the penitentiary society of Romania. Though no apologist for the latter, Bellow sees that it presents surprising compensations to those who suffer within it, compensations which are the direct result of having to exist under totalitarian control and repression. Under the latter one was forced to lead 'a crypto-emotional life in the shadow of Party and State. You had no personal rights, but on the other hand, the claims of feeling were more fully acknowledged'.[15] Such claims are given little or no credence by the American creed which, as the novel makes clear, regards the indulgence of feeling as a symptom of weakness. And though Corde spends most of the novel's time-present in Romania, it is this American ethos which becomes Bellow's main critical target. We get few sustained exposures of totalitarianism at large, though the reader is very much aware of the austerity, political and social, beyond Corde's immediate environment in Bucharest. The creation of this environment is one of Bellow's achievements here. It was important to Bellow's structural and philosophical design that he succeed in this matter, for it is this sympathetic society which underpins the claims of feeling for which the novel argues so strongly and which stand against the world represented by the Romanian secret police Colonel and the American newsmonger, Dewey Spangler. The Bucharest of old Europe, a lingering *ancien régime* of men, and particularly women,[16] whose waning lives are full of eccentric defiances and refusals to surrender the residual gentility of their youth – Bellow evokes this secret culture (Bucharest's underclass, only one of this novel's many points of comparison, to be set alongside that Chicagoan underclass so harrowingly portrayed later in the book) with convincing precision.

The externals of this world, the cracked stucco walls of the Haussmann-style blocks, the Raresh parlor with its reliquary feel, the plum brandy Corde sips mainly for thermal purposes, all of the material privations felt so keenly by one fresh from West to East, are together sturdy enough as a backcloth to allow Bellow's narrator to set off, as he frequently does, upon his excursions into his recent past in Chicago. The Romanian Colonel, a secret police potentate whose unyielding protocol prevents the Cordes having free access to the dying matriarch, Valeria, still lags far behind those American monsters who disturb us later in the narrative. Their malevolence is 'the true voice of Chicago', an expression of the brutal *Zeitgeist*, 'the spirit of the age speaking from its lowest register'.[17] It might indeed be argued that the repressions of the Communist State are too weakly suggested in this novel, and that the venality of Romanian officialdom, easily bribed with a packet of Kents, hardly does justice to the unconscionable reality of life in the Communist bloc. Bellow tends to trade on his readers' preconceptions in this area, using them in place of detailed description. However, it is not so much this life he seeks to undermine as certain spurious aspects of East-West 'polarisation'. The Communist system is used here as an element of comparison, a low point against which is measured the American use and abuse of a liberal political constitution. Thus, the bugging system in the Raresh flat is, Corde thinks, probably of American origin, and, whatever the inhumane logic used by the Colonel ('you use the most extreme case to reduce all the rest'),[18] it was fully matched by the so-called rectitude of ethical values in the West. Throughout the novel, Bellow's structure of comparison and contrast is one that continuously suggests not the disparities, but the affinities that exist between East and West and their complicity in the dehumanisation of human life.

Like Citrine, Corde plays the part of a fifth column. Firmly centred in American public life, he progressively finds himself at odds with the language of that life and the reality it purports to express. 'Assembling a dean who was less and less a dean within'[19] becomes increasingly difficult for him, and standing outside of his natural habitat in Bucharest he can be an assessor ('I administered my own Rorschach test to the U.S.')[20] of its mainstream realities, and, more germane to Bellow's purpose here, its exclusions. As in *Humboldt's Gift*, the powers of darkness are seen to derive from the scientific worldview with its monopolistic hold over the public mind, its rigid allegiance to, and elevation of, the empirical and the pragmatic categories of knowledge, and its concomitant contempt for the province of the heart and the spirit:

> So, then, the problem: Deeper realizations were accorded only to the sciences, and there within strict limits. The same methods, the same energies, could not be applied to the deeper questions of existence. It was conceivable, even, that science had drawn all the capacity for deeper realizations out of the rest of mankind and monopolized it. This left everyone else in a condition of great weakness. In this weakness people did poetry, painting, humanism, fiddle-faddle – idiocy.[21]

The attack on scientific atheism carried through with growing vigour in *Humboldt* and *The Dean's December* is one which had one of its first, and perhaps its finest, fictional expressions a century ago in *The Brothers Karamazov*. There, Dostoyevsky, a writer with whom Bellow has sometimes been compared and whom Bellow himself admires,[22] saw the dangers inherent in scientific rationalism with its antagonism towards matters of the spirit. 'They have science.', wrote Dostoyevsky, 'but in science there is nothing but what is subject to the senses. The spiritual world, however, the higher half of man's being, is utterly rejected, dismissed with a sort of triumph, even with hatred.'[23] A century later the desacralisation of life feared by Dostoyevsky has, in Bellow's view, reached chronic proportions. His is the most high-pitched of contemporary voices to be raised against the continuing triumph of the scientific temper, the latest in a line of Americans including, most notably, Henry Adams and William Carlos Williams, to be so disturbed. With Bellow, both men attributed the flaws in the American temper to a confounding weight of pragmatism and a positivistic distrust for any display of feeling except under the most confined conditions. In his essay 'Jacataqua' included in *In the American Grain*, Williams directs his asperity against this rigorous exclusion, noting how his countrymen live a life which 'drives us apart and forces us upon science and invention – away from touch' and the physical expression of feeling:

> Our breed knows no better than the coarse fibre of football, the despair we have for touching ... drives us to scream in beaten frenzy at the great spectacle of violence – or to applaud coldness

and skill. Who is open to injuries? Not Americans. Get hurt;
you're a fool. The only hero is he who is not hurt. We have no
feeling for the tragic. Let the sucker who fails get his. What's
tragic in that? That's funny! To hell with him. He didn't make
good, that's all.[24]

And in an observation of brilliant acuity Williams states the
culturally centred impediment to the fully lived American life
when he states that 'the impact of the bare soul upon the very twist
of fact which is our world about us, is un-American'.[25] To recoil
from this impact, to prevent it by the cultivation of that mind,
made up in Henry Adam's phrase of 'a mere cutting instrument,
practical, economical, sharp, and direct',[26] is the way to participate
in the mainstream culture of hardboiled-dom. Bellow had ex-
claimed against this insensate reality in the first paragraph of his
first novel, and the La Salle Street characters of *The Dean's
December*, though they be 'the spirit of the age speaking from its
lowest register', were still regarded as impressive because 'they
had the backing of the pragmatic culture of the city, the state, the
region, the country'.[27]

In contrast, Corde still recognises that 'this beatitude language'
he associates with Valeria would be condemned as 'unreal ...
foreign, bookish – it was Dostoevsky stuff'[28] if spoken in public by
him, 'an American who had been around'.[29]

The Dean's own sense of reality is intensely encountered and
viscerally felt, a convergence that illustrates that 'impact of the bare
soul upon the very twist of fact'. He is assailed by an overwhelming consciousness of dissolution both in terms of the deaths of
those close to him like Valeria, or that of the student, Rick Lester,
and, more widely, through his sensitivity to the distempered
Zeitgeist:

> No, it wasn't only two, three, five chosen deaths being painted
> thickly, terribly, convulsively inside him, all over his guts, liver,
> heart, over all his organs, but a large picture of cities, crowds,
> peoples, an apocalypse, with images and details supplied by his
> own disposition, observation, by ideas, dreams, fantasies, his
> peculiar experience of life.[30]

More vulnerable to the sources of this premonitory anguish than
Charlie Citrine, more willing to challenge their dominance than

Artur Sammler, Corde has used his *Harper's* essays to exclaim against the erosion of humane principles, specifically in Chicago prisons, though more extensively throughout American and Western society. With the possible exception of Joseph of *Dangling Man*, Corde is the most physically aware of all Bellow characters, the most open to life's press of images. This is a facility he shares with the third-person narrator and Bellow's style here, with its effective bursts of detailed description, is strongly allied to his philosophical design. Both *Humboldt's Gift* and *The Dean's December* are novels that reveal the exhaustion of orthodox modes of communication, the resultant impoverishment of our deeper impulses and the stress this places upon those, like Corde, like Citrine, unable to accept such a reduced reality.

Citrine's disenchantment compelled him towards the language of anthroposophy. And in his new novel the search for a possible grammar of the soul is still very much a part of Bellow's form and subject. The fastidiously described physical world is given to us as if under microscopic scrutiny, as if by such scrutiny that further penetration might be achieved, going under the distortions to retrieve the 'real being' of a dissembled world. So Corde pursues what glimpses he can find, the telling nuance that gathers, for example, in 'that strangely communicative tip'[31] of his sister Elfrida's upper lip. There, Corde thinks, is concentrated her essence, there can be seen a reading of those human qualities which resist the passing of time, so that 'through all the transformations of middle age, the point of her upper lip ... told you (told her brother, at least) what sort of woman she was – patient in disappointment, skeptical, practical, good access to her heart, if you knew where to look. It was all in the rising point of the lip'.[32] And just as Corde doesn't listen to Elfrida's chatter ('as he drank his martini, he tuned out, now and again. But if he paid little attention to her words, he listened closely to the sound of her voice, watched her face')[33] so the developing argument of the novel suggests that Corde may be forced, finally, beyond language, beyond conventional, heavily contaminated modes of communication, beyond the intellect alone, toward profound emotional commitment in his effort to sustain real correspondence with others. His intellectual resources and rhetorical persuasion have been unavailing as exemplified by the *Harper's* débâcle. It is in the face of this impasse that Corde gives himself up to a recognition of the mystical power invested in deep feeling. The head can only take him some of the way: 'the rest was to be felt', the rest lay in what Joseph Conrad once referred to as 'the surrender to one's impulses, the fidelity to passing emotion which is perhaps a nearer approach to truth than any other philosophy of life'.[34]

It is this division which is exploited as one of the novel's East-West contrasts. Ironically, Corde is able to find a greater opportunity for such meaningful expression in the Raresh household of Bucharest than in his indigenous Chicago. In Bucharest he discovers that Tanti Gigi's preposterous Beatrix Potter English is no impediment to real understanding between them, whereas sitting behind his dean's desk in Chicago he conducts a pained 'dialogue' with his nephew Mason as with one speaking an utterly foreign idiom, a language whose characters have ceased to bear meaning. Mason speaks the tongue of a lumpen-class, the argot of a debased culture. In contrast Gigi is a senior member of that matriarchy headed by the dying Valeria which had as a group the task of being 'defenders of feeling', of being 'custodians of the emotional life'[35] so atrophied in the West. Under the cosh of totalitarian rule, this 'extended feminine hierarchy'[36] will not relinquish its right to emotional intercourse. Back in Chicago, Corde, facing another form of coercion, finds himself more and more unprotected from its enforcers:

he deserved to be penalized for meddling, for interfering with reality as the great majority of Americans experienced it – to which that majority actually sacrificed itself. As if everybody were saying, 'This is life, this is what I give myself to. There is no other deal. No holding back, go with the rest'. Then a man like Corde came haunting around ... Corde remembered how in the office he had wanted to open his heart to Mason, to tell him that under the present manner of interpretation people were shadows to one another, and shadows within shadows, to suggest that these appalling shadows *condemned* our habitual manner of interpretation. Grant this premise and ... But the kid would never have listened to this. In his opinion (his portion of the prevailing chaos, but let's call it opinion), Uncle Albert was flirting with a delusive philosophy and trying to have an affair with nonexistent virtues. Mason's statement would have been, 'Uncle, you're unreal, you're out of it'.[37]

In Mason's voice of condemnation is the note of triumphant

dismissal as heard at the beginning of the reign of rationalism by Dostoyevsky, the impatience of those bereft of feeling for those 'suckers' stupid enough to have a 'bare soul' to be hurt. A similar scenario had occurred in *Humboldt's Gift* with Citrine's inability to find an acceptable language with which to convey his feelings to his brother. Denied this opportunity to 'open his heart', Citrine resigns himself to 'tuning-out' of the consensus in order to pursue a path which is beset by solipsistic dangers. In a sense *The Dean's December* documents Corde's route towards a similar secession; the difference is in his greater reliance upon the principle of emotional interaction, his greater tolerance of, and care for his fellow man. Citrine's compassion, his aspiration towards a higher means of communication, has always a rather theoretic, provisional dimension to it, largely because it is mediated through the mystic theory of Steinerism. In contrast, Corde will strive always to find what the narrator felicitously calls 'the depth-level' in those around him. Even the odious Mason has some humanity left in him, and though it was 'as hard to see as the thin line of mercury in some thermometers' it was there for those, like Corde, who cared to persevere, whose insight was good enough to find 'the lucky angle'[38] which would disclose the tiny trace. Corde quarries all he encounters until this seam is struck. Whereas Citrine immerses himself in an abstract world of dead souls, Corde's movement, characteristically, is an inner one, a desire to forego distraction and to find reality by penetrating its modern simulacra:

[He] asked himself where the depth level was. Not in the ladies'-magazine pedagogy or the Lake Forest psychiatry, but in the natural warmth of his sister. In him it was represented if you liked by his feeling for Elfrida – for the length and smoothness of her head, the Vidal Sassoon dye job, the damaged skin, the slender nose with its dark nostrils ... All these particulars, the apperceptive mass of a lifetime ... The depth level he was looking for was in the heat that came from her patchy face, from the art with which she was painted about the eyes ... from an aching sort of personal history ... He thought this to be a reading of true feelings and no mere projection. These times we live in give us foolish thoughts to think, dead categories of intellect and words that get us nowhere. It was just these words and categories that made the setting of a real depth level so important.[39]

Such a passage as the above exemplifies the stresses Bellow places upon style as a conveyor of meaning in this novel. Since one of Corde's difficulties is the correct identification of authentic expression in himself and those around him, Bellow has to dramatise not only the matter obstructing such identification ('shadows within shadows') but, more importantly, the moment of breakthrough. In some ways he fails to achieve this drama. The use of language in the above excerpt is rather trite when it needed to be precise and evocative. The three particulars which Corde sees as containing Elfrida's 'depth level' are, if anything, clichés of the feminine 'mystique', something like sexual chemistry, the body's heat, its 'paint', its smell, and then, smuggled in at the end of this somewhat 'dead category', an allusion to her 'aching sort of personal history', about which we have been told very little indeed. Corde's search is for a language beyond shibboleth, beyond the 'dead categories of intellect and words'. The language of the novel is, at times, ironically deficient. The above passage might possibly be effective in conveying the perceived depth level if it is taken as an 'apperceptive mass', a catalogue, rather than an array of discrete particulars, each one open to analysis. Bellow, one senses, was hoping to convey depth of meaning by a species of stylistic *legerdemain*: by giving a list of Elfrida's surface features (damaged skin, hair style and so on) we were supposed to glimpse the profundities in recess below.

But Bellow is more successful with more fully drawn characters. It is no surprise that Dewey Spangler, the Walter Cronkite-clone of the book, is one of Bellow's successes. Spangler's being is fully expressed on the level of the idea he exemplifies; he is an idea-monger who, unlike Elfrida, has no emotional life, at least no deep emotional life, no 'aching history' to be confessed. His personality is one of this novel's most sinister creations; he is the arch-purveyor of those 'dead categories', a journalist whose moral sense has been completely sacrificed to the impossible task of attempting to salve the mass *anomie* of his cultural audience. His emotional destitution is played off against Valeria's moral concern and emotional rectitude. As the novel later makes clear, Spangler's unscrupulous quest to find news-fodder has led him, vulture-like, to feed off Corde's bereavement. Against the hard-won dignity and quiet observation of the funeral rites, Spangler waits in the background like a vulture, biding his time, waiting for the opportunity to get his information on Corde which he can use to finish him off as a public figure.

Once again, as in *Humboldt's Gift*, Bellow delineates two competing versions of reality: that which has a tolerance of what Spangler
scathingly terms 'that glorious stuff', the high ideas expressed in
the fields of philosophy and literature, and founded upon the
heritage of *belles-lettres*, and that which occupies the cultural centre
of American public life, a reality based upon 'hardness, patience,
circumspection, craft',[40] attributes possessed in large measure by
the likes of Dewey Spangler.[41] The culture that values and rewards
the possession and cultivation of such an outlook is simultaneously one that looks blankly on the atrophy of feeling. Spangler is the
babble-king of this demi-life, his brief only 'to keep talking', to
convey to 'the great public'[42] the fraudulent sense that it was, like
him, in the van of sensational public news, bathed in 'a kind of
event-glamour'[43] like the journalist-elect. He both defines and is
defined by this vulgus which craves significant experience but
which lacks the 'forms that made true experience'.[44] Again this
lack on the part of American culture is thrown into relief by
comparison with the private life of Corde's Bucharest in-laws. The
'extraordinary respect' he finds it possible to pay Valeria is partly
due to the knowledge that 'her personal humanity came from the
old sources'.[45] A harsh history has identified those 'forms that
made true experience', such as that rite of passage, a kind of
vetting process, to which Corde is subjected by Valeria before
gaining her *imprimatur* to marry Minna. Lacking these forms,
people become wedded to a 'bogus and grotesque' world of 'false
consciousness'.[46] In his concern with this radical maladjustment of
reality, Bellow again echoes Carlos Williams' fear that the lack of
such forms would provoke 'the pure products of America' to 'go
crazy'. Minds which have 'no peasant traditions to give them
character' will be erratic and dissociated from true experience. The
result, as expressed in a poem like 'To Elsie', will be fragmentation
and partial development of a culture so that 'it is only in isolate
flecks that/something/is given off/No one/to witness/ and adjust,
no one to drive the car'.[47]

Dewey merely succumbed to what the age demanded; his
'newspaper language'[48] is that of his mass audience who have
become addicted to living amidst the meretricious climate created
by that language. This climate is one in which all experience,
whether true or otherwise, must be souped-up and doctored so
that it, like Elsie's Saturday nights, is tricked out with the gauds of
a false excitement. From Bucharest, Corde worries over the hidden

reality not of life behind the Iron Curtain but behind the curtain of
'false consciousness' in the United States:

> In the American moral crisis, the first requirement was to
> experience what was happening and to see what must be seen.
> The facts were covered from our perception. More than they had
> been in the past? Yes, because the changes, especially the
> increase in consciousness – and also in false consciousness – was
> accompanied by a peculiar kind of confusion. The increase of
> theories and discourse, itself a cause of new strange forms of
> blindness, the false representations of 'communication', led to
> horrible distortions of public consciousness. Therefore the first
> act of morality was to disinter the reality, retrieve reality, dig it
> out from the trash, represent it anew as art would represent it. So
> when Dewey talked about the 'poetry', pouring scorn on it, he
> was right insofar as Corde only made 'poetic' gestures or passes,
> but not insofar as Corde was genuinely inspired. Insofar as he
> was inspired he had genuine political significance.[49]

One of Corde's failings, for Spangler who knew him as a youth,
was not to have relinquished what for Spangler was just a boyish
phase. 'The old Chicago was far away . . . the thrills of Shakespeare
and Plato, the recitations from "The Garden of Proserpine" and
"Lapis Lazuli" . . . all of that, old pal, was boyhood, and one must
detach oneself'.[50] Such interests, according to Spangler's kind,
were pre-pubertal, and ought to have succumbed to the march of
maturity along with acne and short pants. To mature meant to learn
the language and rules of mainstream American reality, to graduate
into a culture that was virile and therefore indifferent to the finer
feelings generated by 'Socrates in the Phaedrus' or 'Rilke in Paris'.
'Do you have an emotional life? It is nobody's business but your
own'[51] – so spoke Joseph of *Dangling Man* in accurate summary of
the ruling code. In a 1975 interview, Bellow talked of the rage for
significance in American life, of the individual's need for *gravitas*,
however faked:

> Life . . . has become very current-eventish. People think they are
> political when they are immersed in these events – vicariously
> . . . society is monopolizing their brains, and taking their souls
> away from them by this interest, by the news, by spurious
> politics.[52]

This remoteness from experience, from real experience, is responsible for some of this novel's most acute ironies. Corde is so aware of his un-American inclinations, of his withdrawal from this culturally ratified view of things, that he, like Citrine and Herzog, realises the necessity of keeping quiet, laying low. 'He was, more or less in secret, serious about matters he couldn't even begin to discuss with Dewey. There was, for instance, the reunion of spirit and nature (divorced by science). Dewey . . . was rough on writers who talked about "spirit", intellectuals in flight from the material realities of the present age.'[53] To bring up the subject of one's spiritual or emotional life is to be dismissed as a bleeding heart, as a wet, or finally, if one insists on going public with this complaint as had Corde in his *Harper's* essays ('the trained urbanologists had found the articles too emotional'),[54] as a subversive in need of muzzling. In Bucharest Corde finds a society upon which to model his challenge to such a destructively partial and sterile orthodoxy, finding in 'the woman connection'[55] a timely corrective to it.

In *Humboldt's Gift*, Bellow's attack upon this scientifically oriented, emotionally drained reality had been confined to revealing its hegemony and its power to lock out and eventually destroy a man like Humboldt, a 'genuinely inspired' poet. And, of course, Citrine spends most of his time knocking against it, attempting to find in Steiner's wisdom a structured alternative. Now, in the figure of the geophysicist, Beech, with his theory of lead insult, Bellow has furthered his attack upon that life which 'drives us apart and forces us upon science and invention – away from touch'. Beech's investigations reveal that science, the god of progress, has brought not universal improvement but global contamination. The scientific worldview can now be palpably indicted, its toxic influence responsible in large part for 'wars and revolutions' and for the 'mental disturbances' which result in a general state of 'cultural degradation'.[56] In the plot of *The Dean's December*, the lead insult idea is a shrewd stratagem on Bellow's part; Citrine had seen the scientific worldview as a polluter of the spiritual life and its healthy development, but in Beech Corde discovers a 'burning moral visionary' who had 'incorporated the planet itself into his deepest feelings',[57] a type capable of bringing a humane ethic to bear upon the excesses of the scientific worldview ('I'm asking whether certain impulses and feelings which play no part in the scientific work of a man like Professor Beech and lie ignored or undeveloped in his nature may not suddenly have

come to life').[58] The man of science and the man of feeling, the
marriage of these two types – this is the felicitous conjunction that
Bellow considers, and promotes, in this novel. It is no accident that
this marriage is already present, literally, in Corde and Minna – 'he
was justified to Minna the scientist as Albert the human
husband'.[59] But whereas Minna is irretrievably the victim of
Valeria's maternal solicitude, her innocence in a sense guaranteed
by the nature of her career ('What an innocent person! She did
stars; human matters were her husband's field . . . Science would
save her from evil'),[60] Beech, by virtue of his new susceptibility to
those 'certain impulses and feelings', unites the dualism within
himself. Yet Beech and Corde still need each other. The former
with his revised mass of scientific knowledge – 'he was only
investigating lead levels and this led him into horror chambers'[61] –
the latter with his ability as a communicator and his gift for seeing
the large picture, together constitute an ideal positive in the novel.
In the end Corde agrees to help Beech compose his article on lead
insult, while at the same time reserving judgement about its
absolute validity – 'those lead conclusions are his, not mine.
Something deadly is happening. I'm with him to that extent. So I'll
advise him about language only. Then I won't have to agree
ignorantly'.[62]

Corde's own articles in *Harper's* are, ostensibly, an attempt to
account for the existence of the alienatees in Chicagoan life, the
criminals, the underclasses, black and white, a lower depth which
is tolerated, to an extent engendered by the 'reduced consciousness' of the age. His interview with lawyer Sam Varennes illustrates the extent of this 'tolerance'. Both Varennes and Spofford
Mitchell his client, who is standing trial for murder and rape, are
infected and damaged by this consciousness. Indeed Corde's
articles provoke the retribution they do because they are indict-
ments not of those directly touched by prison conditions, not of the
prisoners or the wardens, but of people like Sam Varennes and
even Corde's boss Provost Alec Witt, unwitting perpetrators of a
climate of violence and deprivation:

the advanced modern consciousness was a reduced consciousness inasmuch as it contained only the minimum of furniture
that civilization was able to install (practical judgments, bare
outlines of morality, sketches, cartoons instead of human
beings); and this consciousness, because its equipment was

humanly so meager, so abstract, was basically murderous. It was for this reason that murder was so easy to 'understand'.[63]

The *Harper's* pieces are in reality an examination of this parvanimity and its effects. They disturb the likes of Witt and Spangler not because they are sociological analyses of a depraved few, but because they see the city and its human flotsam ('many, many square miles of civil Passchendaele or Somme')[64] as manifestations of an endemic condition, a debased inner being. Life, individual and collective, is being traduced and denied; thus, 'it was not so much the inner city slum that threatened us as the slum of innermost being, of which the inner city was perhaps a material representation'.[65]

Devoid of a significant human factor, this 'murderous' modern consciousness resembles that of the Romanian Colonel with his 'simple' sliding-scale of retribution. Corde inveighs against the cause and the effect of this decline into inhumanity and in so doing sets himself well apart from his predecessor in Bellow's fiction, Charlie Citrine. Where the latter took the route of an abstract salvation through anthroposophy, Corde regards the tendency towards abstraction as one damaging effect of the widespread flight from a reality properly based on experience:

> We prefer to have such things served up to us as concepts. We'd rather have them abstract, stillborn, dead. But as long as they don't come to us with some kind of reality, as facts of experience, then all we can have instead of good and evil is ... well, concepts. Then we'll never learn how the soul is worked on. Then for intellectuals there will be discourse or jargon, while for the public there will be ever more jazzed-up fantasy. In fact, the two are blending now. The big public is picking up the jargon to add to its fantasies.[66]

For Bellow, a writer renowned for the intellectual eminence of his work, the above seems an extraordinary indictment of intellectual process. The attack, however, is more properly seen as one levelled at what passes for a moral use of such process. Instead of an intellectual response based upon 'facts of experience', minds such as Spangler's, trained to entertain rather than edify, can only add to the rift between reality, moral reality and its public travesty. The development of a moral sense depends upon this judicious correspondence between intellect and experience, and without it there can only be the most depressed kind of intelligentsia.

Corde's search for the 'depth-level' in those around him, the authentic, often deeply-buried quiddity beneath 'the debris of false description or nonexperience',[67] is given to the reader as a kind of antidote to this flight from experience. This, Bellow seems to say, is one way forward, one way to begin to recover our decayed sense of 'what a human being really was':

> Then for some reason, with no feeling of abruptness, he became curiously absorbed in Dewey: blue eyes, puffy lids, tortoise-shell beard, arms crossed over his fat chest, fingers tucked into armpits, his skin scraped and mottled where the beard was trimmed, the warm air of his breathing, his personal odors, a sort of doughnut fragrance, slightly stale – the whole human Spangler was delivered to Corde in the glass-warmed winter light with clairvoyant effect ... Maybe on this death day Corde was receiving secret guidance in seeing life. Perhaps at this very moment the flames were finishing Valeria, and therefore it was especially important to think what a human being really was.[68]

Experience here becomes a kind of meditation, a purposeful endeavour to see not 'cartoons' but 'human beings'. Such an immersion in the other is one way to prevent what is presented in this novel as the overwhelming imbalance of the age: its evasion of the real, its passive acceptance of a second or third-hand report of experience, the jargonising of moral realities, the trivialisation of the spirit in man. John J. Clayton, in a passage already referred to, saw *Humboldt's Gift* as a book that at times offered a 'merely speculative' allegiance to life, but 'to the extent that it is at points in deep contact with life, it succeeds'.[69] Though I cannot agree with Clayton's criticism of *Humboldt's Gift*, there is no doubt that in *The Dean's December* Bellow fastidiously reveals his concern for keeping 'deep contact with life'. Even where the human subject, like Spangler, is hardly promising, Corde perseveres, keenly aware that what might be a mere carcase for others had, for him, urgent existential overtones:

> What, for example, did he know about Dewey Spangler? Well, he knew his eyes, his teeth, his arms, the form of his body, its doughnut odor; the beard was new but that was knowledge at

first sight. That vividness of beard, nostrils, breath, tone, was real knowledge. Knowledge? It was even captivity.[70]

To overlook nothing, to underestimate nothing, to see humanity not for that which it 'represented' but for the life it was – these are the stark imperatives of Corde's developing philosophy.

Against Charlie Citrine's 'deep no-affect belt', his 'critical mass of indifference' in the face of his Chicago, Bellow has placed Corde with his urgent need to commit himself to an extreme literalism, his reverence for the knowledge deriving in the first instance from the senses. Against Citrine's fugitive aspirations, his need 'to think himself clear away from this American world', Corde soaks himself in its presence, devoted to the empirical as a first base:

This organic, constitutional, sensory oddity, in which Albert Corde's soul had a lifelong freehold, must be grasped as knowledge. He wondered what reality was if it wasn't this, or what you were 'losing' by death, if not this . . . What you didn't pass through your soul didn't even exist, that was what made the literal literal. Thus he had taken it upon himself to pass Chicago through his own soul. A mass of data, terrible, murderous. It was no easy matter to put such things through. But there was no other way for reality to happen. Reality didn't exist 'out there'. It began to be real only when the soul found its underlying truth. In generalities there was no coherence – none. The generality-mind, the habit of mind that governed the world, had no force of coherence, it was dissociative.[71]

By this stage in the novel, Corde's intense awareness of particularities (at first described as 'an instinct with Corde – maybe it was a weakness – always to fix attention on certain particulars, in every situation to grasp the details')[72] has gathered more profound significance, has become, indeed, an operative metaphysic. The self as a display of closely registered surfaces ('Himself, too, he knew with a variant of the same oddity – as, for instance, the eyes and other holes and openings of his head, the countersunk entrance of his ears and the avidity expressed by the dilation of his Huguenot-Irish nostrils')[73] becomes the gateway to spirit, a means of access to a reality unsullied by abstraction, unmediated by distortion. While this was also Citrine's terminus (cf. his Blakean vision of 'naked self with naked self burning intolerably and causing terror'),[74] his path towards it was radically different. Corde has a sense of being rigorously bound by his habitat, of being made existentially whole by his implication in its life. Unlike Citrine, he opens himself to Chicago and its 'mass of data'. It is, for the most part, an almost indigestible potage, a gruel which is nearly too much even for Corde's spiritual intestines. The data, after all, include such costive elements as Maxie Detillion whom it was not easy to digest, whose 'vividness was unwanted, repugnant, but nothing could be done'.[75] If *Humboldt's Gift* was, to one critic, 'the most renunciatory of Bellow's novels'[76] in its revolt from a public corporate vision and its espousal of a world of abstract promise, *The Dean's December* is surely the most willing to accept the confrontation.

The various strands of the novel's thematic structure come together in this conclusion with real dramatic force, propelled by Spangler's hatchet-job on Corde. This final *coup de main* discloses the impotence Corde comes to feel. It is an impotence of language, of communication, enforced by a society equipped to understand only Spangler-speak, 'the passwords, the code words',[77] and which rejects as unAmerican, as treasonable, seditious, Corde's *Harper's* essays. With considerable effect, Bellow's East-West structure is again used to make a trenchant criticism of American values here, for Spangler represents the voice of an American totalitarianism, becomes, indeed, the agent of that totalitarian machinery which silences Corde as effectively as any KGB crackdown. The muzzle will stay on Corde until he is willing to learn the language of American realism – as insidious and implacable in its influence on American life as socialist realism has been on Soviet dissidents:

> What a smart little monster Dewey was, and what a keen schemer, and how rivalrous. He disposed of the Dean by describing him as an unwitting alien. How cleverly he got rid of him ... In touch with the Sadats and the Kissingers, the Brezhnevs and the Nixons, interpreting them to the world, Dewey was a master of the public forms of discourse. If you were going to be a communicator, you had to know the passwords, the code words, you had to signify your acceptance of the prevailing standards. You could say nothing publicly, not if you expected to be taken seriously, without the right clearance. The Dean's problem had been one of language. Nobody will buy what you're selling – not in those words. They don't even know what your product *is*.[78]

The realisation of this state of affairs brings Corde's political enlightenment to a head. The novel's conclusion is played out against this background of defeat and Bellow offers Corde no way out of the impasse. 'To be able to say what you mean, mean what you say'[79] is Corde's difficulty throughout as he searches for both a language of truth and a constituency of those sufficiently well-equipped to hear and understand. His earlier work as a journalist had taught him that 'nothing true – really true – could be said in the papers'[80] and just as Citrine finds only the somewhat crazy Dr Scheldt as an available correspondent, so Corde has spent the greater part of his life seeking out 'the right people to talk to – that's the hardest part of all'.[81] And later, attempting to explain to Minna how he had been gullible enough to drop his guard in front of Spangler, Corde reiterates – 'there's the whole thing – having people to talk to'.[82] Years before he had retired into a self-imposed silence 'to cure himself of bad habits, bad usage'[83] of language. Now, letting himself be heard in the *Harper's* pieces, he wonders if he has not been intemperate, whether the years of frustrated feeling have not resulted in an outburst of spleen alone. However, since it is the snake-like Spangler who is most critical of Corde's essays ('I'm frankly surprised that the *Harper's* people let you go on as you did. The language you used from time to time . . .'),[84] it seems that the reader is being urged to accept them as valid, authorially ratified expressions of outrage.

With such a great distrust of the accepted channels and modes of communication, a distrust fully justified in the light of Spangler's betrayal, it is little wonder that Corde is seen to reject these for new ways of reaching the 'depth level' which lies so far beneath the operating consciousness of those around him. My suggestion that these new ways are best described as a mysticism of the feelings, of deep emotion experienced as truth, is one that is upheld by Bellow's creation of a central character in whom 'exclusively mental acts seldom occurred'[85] and a novel in which the significant moments are often ones experienced privately, initiated by a heightened sensual receptivity, moments during which the concept of reality is extended, deepened and made to enclose the impalpable as a signal of transcendent possibilities:

Here in the Midwest there sometimes occurred the blues of Italian landscapes and he passed through them, very close to the borders of sense, as if he could do perfectly well without the help of his eyes, seeing what you didn't need human organs to see but experiencing as freedom and also as joy what the mortal person, seated there in his coat and gloves, otherwise recorded as colors, spaces, weights. This was different. It was like being poured out to the horizon, like a great expansion. What if death should be like this, the soul finding an exit. The porch rail was his figure for the hither side. The rest, beyond it, drew you constantly as the completion of your reality.[86]

Or else the significances in the novel are concentrated in carefully understated, unembellished moments in which emotional passages between characters are given only the briefest verbal statement, as when Minna confirms that Valeria had 'trusted' Corde and fully accepted his love for her. This posthumous bond stands out against the duplicitous 'friendship' attested to in Spangler's article. If Corde has no language with which to successfully address 'the big public', Spangler, and, this novel implies, the masses he addresses, have no language of the heart. 'In two sentences he did the friendship'[87] is a statement which fully expresses not Spangler's malevolence (I accept here Bellow's comment that the undermining of Corde is not malice on Spangler's part, but rather a species of amorality)[88] but, more insidiously, his complete absorption by those forces he submits to and is the agent of, forces which falsify and discredit authentic experience. Spangler's article shows him to have been a single-minded plotter, assembling his copy while participating in Corde's Bucharest bereavement, turning up at Valeria's funeral to make sure he secures his afternoon 'appointment' with Corde. His mind is precisely 'a mere cutting instrument, practical and economical, sharp and direct', a mind that impatiently dispensed with the formalities of 'friendship' in a few lines of what Corde, quoting Mencken, elsewhere calls 'the usual hypocrisies'. Spangler meets reality, if he can be said to confront it at all, heavily armoured with that mind Bellow describes as 'dissociative'.

Despite the reassurance that *The Dean's December* will offer to those critics who saw *Humboldt* as a turning away from humanism, its conclusion will cause them renewed anxiety. The exquisitely modulated coda at Mount Palomar sees Corde on his wife's territory; once again he is unable to make sense of a language, in this case the vernacular pass-words, the 'right ascension, mirrors, refractions, spectrum analysis'[89] of astronomy. Once again, however, 'that he understood so little of the ... lingo made no difference'[90] to him for, as in his dialogue with Valeria, communication and knowledge here takes place beyond language in a preternatural region of mystical correspondence. Corde is strongly drawn to the icy remoteness of the heavens, attracted by their 'power to cancel everything merely human'.[91] Their reality is, for the human eye, only an approximate condition, a reality the true nature of which can only be approached by means of an empathetic feeling towards the essence. To cancel out the human is for Corde, after all he has discovered about its purblind nature and its deep-seated morbidity of mind, a manumission and enlightenment:

> Once, in the Mediterranean, coming topside from a C-class cabin, the uric smells and the breath of the bilges, every hellish little up-to-date convenience there below to mock your insomnia – then seeing the morning sun on the tilted sea. Free! The grip of every sickness within you disengaged by this pouring out. You couldn't tell which was out of plumb, the ship, or yourself, or the sea aslant – but free! It didn't matter, since you were free! It was like that also when you approached the stars as steadily as this.[92]

Once again freedom is expressed in terms which suggest a release from self, from consciousness as a state of sickness, a 'pouring out' of self figured as a kinetic, exhilarating surge. The freedom is vertiginous, unexamined, an escape from trammelling forces. Even if the experience of liberation at Palomar is, for Corde, only a temporary remission from what Sammler called a 'collaboration of all souls spreading madness and poison', it is powerful enough to cast considerable doubt upon the validity of a conclusion like that of Salman Rushdie, quoted on the first page of this chapter. Descending from the top of the Palomar telescope towards the earth, Corde's final utterance implies not an acceptance, but a rejection of that inevitable destination. If approaching the stars had provoked a desiderative mood in Corde, the return trip ('I almost think I mind coming down more') is freighted with antipathetic overtones. This novel has spent most of its time amidst scenes of enclosure and constraint, whether behind a geopolitical and ideological Iron Curtain or behind the nominally libertarian world of America. Corde's reluctance to return to 'the breath of the bilges', to rejoin that bogus free world, is the stressed element of the novel's climax.

THE SHORT FICTION

Bellow's latest books have been a collection of short fiction, *Him With His Foot in His Mouth and Other Stories* (1984), a novel *More Die of Heartbreak* (1987) and the novella *A Theft* (1989). Although my concern throughout this study has been with the novels, Bellow is an accomplished writer of short fiction as, indeed, both *Dangling Man* and *Seize the Day* testify. From his 1969 book of short stories, *Mosby's Memoirs*, one remembers particularly 'The Old System' and 'Looking for Mr. Green' for their powerful epiphanic conclusions and for the technical craft that makes their emotional force so credible and complete. There is a sense, too, in which the discipline needed to compose short fiction restrains that 'metaphysical garrulity'[93] which some critics have seen as an occasional weakness in Bellow's novels. In a study such as this, one can also turn to the short stories as indicators of the direction his themes and interests are likely to take in the novels.

The ending of 'The Old System', for instance, is surely an adumbration of that of *The Dean's December*. Like Albert Corde, Dr Braun is driven by doubt and futility, by the apparent inconsequentiality of anguish and the shapelessness of suffering ('And these tears! When you wept them from the heart, you felt you justified something, understood something. But what did you understand? Again, *nothing*! It was only an intimation of understanding'),[94] towards the kind of mystic fundamentalism generated by a contemplation of the heavens:

> And again, why these particular forms – these Isaacs and these Tinas? When Dr Braun closed his eyes, he saw, red on black, something like molecular processes – the only true heraldry of being. As later, in the close black darkness when the short day ended, he went to the dark kitchen window to have a look at stars. These things cast outward by a great begetting spasm billions of years ago.[95]

Of course, Corde's moment of insight is more fully drawn and glossed by Bellow's narrator in the novel; but there is in Dr Braun's reaching towards this cosmic source of origin the same 'cold eye',[96] the same yearning for a human principle, a human reality, that, being fundamental to all life, could not be undermined or questioned. For Dr Braun, 'something like molecular processes', for

Corde 'the very blood and crystal forms inside your bones'. There is in both men a susceptibility to the power of the firmament 'to cancel everything merely human', that 'crude circus of feelings'[97] which can only distract man from the necessity of comprehending 'why life, why death'.[98] Henry Adams once averred that 'true ignorance approaches the infinite more nearly than any amount of knowledge can do'.[99] Both Braun and Corde show a willingness to open themselves up in this way.

Bellow's latest short story collection does not signify any considerable shift in that vision I have described throughout this study. The critique of American values is carried through with a similar implacability, and the chief targets remain the political and business ethos, 'this life to which all have consented'.[100] Degeneration is seen as radical and ubiquitous, written into the constitution of national life so that 'the foundations of political stability, of democracy, according even to its eminent philosophers, are swindle and fraud'.[101] As Frank Kermode wrote in his review of the collection, Bellow's tone throughout is a distinctive one 'of exasperated regret, delight in (mostly lost) abundance'.[102] The finest stories are without doubt those, like 'A Silver Dish', 'Cousins' and 'Zetland: By a Character Witness', which display the author at his lyrical best, those rooted in the recall of Chicago's Jewish-American past, full of healing nostalgia but tempered by a concomitant indictment of what Chicago has become, 'a model of modern America, where crime and business merge'.[103] The intensity of this cultural recollection is extraordinary, both in terms of the wealth of material detail, and of what one may term the evocation of historical character. This lyrical vein is, I think, too rarely present in Bellow's novels, though one remembers instances of it, notably the first chapters of *Augie March*.

As well as delighting us with this descriptive prose, Bellow expertly uses these narratives of memory to provide a backdrop against which the venality of contemporary life can be exposed, in much the same way as the Romanian family circle was used to generate the critical dynamic of *The Dean's December*. The opening of 'A Silver Dish' shows this technique, and hints at the ironic possibilities it affords:

What do you do about death – in this case, the death of an old father? If you're a modern person, sixty years of age, and a man who's been around, like Woody Selbst, what do you do? Take this matter of mourning, and take it against a contemporary background. How, against a contemporary background, do you mourn an octogenarian father, nearly blind, his heart enlarged, his lungs filling with fluid, who creeps, stumbles, gives off the odors, the moldiness or gassiness, of old men. I *mean*! As Woody put it, be realistic. Think what times these are. The papers daily give it to you – the Lufthansa pilot in Aden is described by the hostages on his knees, begging the Palestinian terrorists not to execute him, but they shoot him through the head. Later they themselves are killed. And still others shoot others, or shoot themselves. That's what you read in the press, see on the tube, mention at dinner.[104]

Once again, as in *The Dean's December* and elsewhere in Bellow's later novels, the media agencies are guilty of perpetuating, even of creating, that 'contemporary background' which has such an enervating effect upon private experience. The forms for acknow-ledging the significance of that experience, and the reality of that experience itself, are diminished and trivialised. Like his antece-dents in Bellow's fiction, Woody Selbst finds that his honest needs are not to be accommodated by contemporary 'realistic' norms. He finds a way to mourn his father by withdrawing from them into memory, into a faithful and loving vignette from his childhood, one that concentrates with splendid irony upon his father's dis-honesty in stealing a silver dish from the home of a wealthy philanthropist. The story hinges upon Woody's struggle with the moral tenor of this act, his struggle to see it as his father did, as an act of defiance, of necessary irreverence. He comes to understand that honesty has little to do with what the narrator of 'Cousins' calls 'the low language of high morals',[105] but is more an elemental quality held in the nature of those, like his father, who refused to succumb to the orthodoxies of his 'contemporary background'. As Woody remembers, 'in regard to Pop, you thought of neither sincerity nor insincerity. Pop was like the man in the song: he wanted what he wanted when he wanted it ... Pop was elemental'.[106]

Grieving for his dead father on a Sunday morning, Woody finds his honest memory in the 'straight' ringing of Chicago's Sunday bells which 'broke loose ... wagged and rocked, and the vibrations and the banging did something for him – cleansed his insides, purified his blood. A bell was a one-way throat, had only one thing to tell you and simply told it. He listened'.[107] 'A Silver Dish' is another of Bellow's definitions of the reality beyond appearances. And in a culture in which 'all the words were up for grabs',[108] in which '"We Care" is stenciled on the walls of supermarkets and loan corporations',[109] and in which the Chicago mobsters are on good terms with 'aldermen, city officials, journalists, big builders, fundraisers for charitable institutions',[110] Bellow's endeavour to penetrate beneath the seeming realities of this world is vital.

What the new short stories continue to demonstrate is their author's conviction that the reality of American life in the second half of this century is, in all the truest, most human matters, beginning 'to roll towards oblivion'.[111] Twenty-five years ago Tony Tanner concluded the first book-length study of Bellow's fiction with the reservation that though that fiction stressed the need for 'some new positive values', it had not been able to 'produce an authentic image of the desiderated new way of life'.[112] That image was one of the individual finding fulfillment and affirmation in and through the American community. Yet even when Bellow began writing, this component of the American promise was dying. There is, as the narrator of 'Cousins' puts it, an iniquitous '*new* democracy' in existence in America, the product of '*new* abstractions'.[113] America, once the grail's end for the rootless, a continent where one could be 'found', is now a community of the lost. Accepting this, Bellow (*pace* Tanner) has indeed produced authentic images of a new way of life in that new democracy. Such images are, however, based upon assumptions of loss, lost ideals of community and moral integrity:

> Being an American always had been something of an abstract project. You came as an immigrant. You were offered a most reasonable proposition and you said yes to it. You were *found*. With the new abstractions you were *lost*. They demanded a shocking abandonment of personal judgement.[114]

Bellow's heroes learn to accept this loss as an irremediable condition. They find their freedoms in their various strategies of withdrawal from the fallen community around them. Real being is in retreat, on the run from that 'contemporary background' of dissolution. Yet Bellow's greatness lies in his refusal to merely record the new disorder; his heroes have the phoenix touch, the will to survive, to modify their outlook so as to find reality in times of crisis:

The seams open, the bonds dissolve, and the untenability of existence releases you back again to the original self. Then you are free to look for real being under the debris of modern ideas, and in a magical trance, if you like, or with a lucidity altogether different from the lucidity of *approved* types of knowledge ... Disorder, if it doesn't murder you, brings certain opportunities. You wouldn't guess that when I sit in my Holy Sepulchre apartment at night ... I am concentrating on strategies for pouncing passionately on the freedom made possible by dissolution.[115]

MORE DIE OF HEARTBREAK

Bellow's *More Die of Heartbreak* came out in 1987 to mixed reviews. In the *New York Times Book Review* there was acclamation from William Gaddis who was able to welcome back 'the calamitous wit of "The Adventures of Augie March" and "Herzog"'.[116] The British reviews were, however, much less enthusiastic. For David Holloway there was too much pessimism in Bellow's vision and not enough effort to do more than report the worst news from 'a sad, sad world'.[117] Holloway's response ends in exasperation – 'you want to grab hold of the author and say: "OK. Admittedly everything may be as bad as you say it is, but what are you going to do about it?"'.[118] But this is, of course, Bellow's point here, as it has consistently been since *Herzog*; there is nothing that *can* be done except acknowledge the pre-eminence of anti-humanistic forces leading to the 'march of declining humankind'.[119] Professor Benn Crader, Bellow's hero in *More Die of Heartbreak*, finds the icy wastes of the Arctic tundra more hospitable than an America in which 'more people die of heartbreak than of radiation'.[120] The novel provides a definitive confirmation of those arguments I have presented in previous chapters, making it abundantly clear that for Benn Crader as for Albert Corde life amidst American conditions is untenable.

Those conditions make their presence known in a fictional setting which is Chicago in all but name, a mid-West Rustbelt metropolis, it offers 'a mixture of barbarism and worn-out humanist culture' though 'the latter had never had much of a chance to flower in these parts'.[121] At the centre of the novel is Benn Crader, an internationally respected botanist whose life has come to have an exemplary interest for his nephew, the novel's narrator Kenneth Trachtenberg. A specialist in Russian philosophy, Kenneth has decided to return to America in order to essay his 'Project Turning Point', a kind of humanist's charter which holds that 'conscious existence might be justified only if it was devoted to the quest for a revelation, a massive reversal, an inspired universal change, a new direction, a desperately needed human turning point'.[122] But the resumption of life in America will also bring him closer to his uncle whom he regards as 'a plant visionary', 'a communicant in a green universal church'.[123] At 35, Kenneth is looking for metaphysical aid and Benn is the unlikely eminence chosen to supply the grace.

Bellow's interest in men of science and feeling has a lengthy pedigree, stretching back to Dr Lal in *Mr Sammler's Planet* and more recently Professor Beech and Minna Corde in *The Dean's December*. Like Beech, Benn Crader is a visionary, though the gift he has for deep communication with plants lets him down when it comes to dealing with men and women. There he is a 'middle-aged botanist in the kindergarten',[124] a soft target for the no-mercy types who reign supreme in this barbarous portion of America. For them Benn is the 'dodo botanist' easily victimised by the crafty exponents of 'middle-class diabolism'.[125] So Kenneth appoints himself his uncle's spiritual minder while at the same time hoping that he can learn to do 'for human subjects what Uncle Benn did for the ... lichens'.[126] To preserve Benn 'in his valuable oddity' is a task Kenneth fails to accomplish as his uncle succumbs to the increasingly dubious charms of Matilda Layamon, whose 'sharp teeth' and shoulders 'heavier than solid bronze'[127] chase him out of the narrative at the end, as he escapes further entanglements by fleeing to 'an incomprehensible location in reindeer country, far out on the tundra'.[128]

More than anything else Benn's 'valuable oddity' derives from Kenneth's sense that his uncle is a humanist in an age of fabricated feeling, a vestigial part of that 'worn-out humanist culture' almost extinct now. Benn is a test-case, perhaps able 'to keep track in this day and age of the original feelings, the feelings referred to by some Chinese sage as "the first heart"'.[129] For though Benn is a scientist he remains uncontaminated by that Bellow *bête noire*, 'the scientific worldview', so much a target for attack in *The Dean's December* and *Humboldt's Gift*. Benn 'never spoke of "the scientific worldview"' and 'not even the "laws" of physics or biology were permitted to inhibit him'.[130] He is the scientist as seer and taking plants 'as his arcana' is a potent *entrée* into the spiritual realm enabling him 'to make discoveries, to prepare for the communication of a spiritual mystery'.[131] All of this we are told by Kenneth, and this is just one part of the problem of this novel. *More Die of Heartbreak* is the author's weakest novel since *Henderson the Rain King* and nowhere are its weaknesses more acutely exposed than in this area of narrative stance.

Reviewing the book for the *Times Literary Supplement* Galen Strawson correctly notes that while 'Benn is perfect in blueprint . . . he doesn't quite come off in speech and action. It would help to hear more about him from the inside; but this is ruled out by Kenneth's plashy custody of the narrative voice'.[132] Nothing that Benn says or does convinces us that he deserves to be saddled with the portentous credentials assigned him by his disciple Kenneth. He is, we are told, almost a card-carrying 'Citizen of Eternity' worthy of being ranked with the Great Dead:

> To name at random a number of such Citizens will reveal what the word 'Eternity' signifies: Moses, Achilles, Odysseus, the Prophets, Socrates, Edgar in *King Lear*, Prospero, Pascal, Mozart, Pushkin, William Blake. These we think about and, if possible, make our souls by . . . If Benn was not yet a Citizen, if Eternity was not ready to give him his second papers, he was as close to it as I had ever been able to come.[133]

Billed to star amongst such giants of the human stage, we may begin to feel a little sorry for Benn, and to ask some serious questions about his promoter.

All of this may of course be taken as a slice of that 'calamitous wit' cheered by William Gaddis in his review of the novel. However, we face here the other major difficulty in the telling of this story, for the slapstick generated when Benno 'the blockhead botanist'[134] is routed by the Layamon lions is curiously misplaced. Certainly the confrontation between Benno and his new in-laws (exquisitely portrayed representatives of 'this selfish, low-down age')[135] is intended to be farcical; the farce is conveyed not only in specific narrative incidents but also through Kenneth's narrative style which is ponderous, self-involved, and at times insufferably pompous. This latter source of humour is, however, at times a trial to the reader's patience. As Paul Taylor put it in his review of the novel, its 'anguished, manic comedy . . . stems from the fact that its serious pained issues are all mediated through the mind of this fundamentally humourless, interfering jerk'.[136] However, I would question Taylor's judgement that Bellow has accomplished 'an artful variation of the "unreliable narrator" convention' by making that unreliability depend upon Kenneth's 'inability to judge the appropriate weight to grant to any of the events in his own or in his uncle's life'.[137] This, it seems to me, is precisely the artistic lapse that damages *More Die of Heartbreak*. For if Bellow intended us to both laugh and lament, grow weary in the company of a narrator who is by turns a tedious self-promoter and endearing buffoon, what *are* we to make of this novel's serious issues? For assuredly Bellow's subject matter so tragically and bleakly rendered in *The Dean's December* makes its return throughout this new novel. The thematic ground is almost identical, with a few new stresses, yet the narrative treatment is one that continually undermines a seriousness of response. It seems that in this novel Bellow set out to retrieve some of his reputation as a comic writer; but to use as comic fodder so many of the same preoccupations which justifiably provoked Albert Corde's rage and anguish – this seems at best a disturbing lapse in judgement.

Perhaps in an effort to put some distance between himself and his narrators (a point some critics felt had damaged point-of-view in *The Dean's December*)[138] Bellow created a sensibility younger and less experientially wise than that possessed by Corde or Citrine. But this sensibility is only partially realised, and where it does succeed there are unfortunate side-effects. As Galen Strawson remarks, 'Kenneth's good thoughts are weakened just by being his'.[139] Finally there is a glaring credibility-gap to contend with as Bellow muscles in on the narrative action so that 'when Kenneth suddenly releases a full-scale Bellow description of Doctor Layamon, Benn's new father-in-law, it isn't believable'.[140] It is, however, all too easy to believe in the Kenneth who strikes us as a callow idea-monger. The problem is, why should we show any interest in such a person? Aren't his ideas discredited as Strawson says, 'just by being his'? He is, he admits, irresponsible even to the claim of ideas upon sense, elated by the rush and glide of thought for its own sake:

> I was unusually – that is, emotionally – open to associations. It was esthetically intoxicating to entertain them all. Furthermore, it was characteristic – it was me: me as it excited me to be, fully

experiencing the fantastic, the bizarre facts of contemporary reality, making no particular effort to impose my cognitions on them. I didn't especially wish to make sense; I wanted only to follow the intoxicating flow of those facts.[141]

So when he points us to 'the sufferings of freedom'[142] or the 'mortally dangerous choices which would determine the future of civilization'[143] we hear the Bellow note, we know the gravity with which such concerns have been explored in his fiction and essays, but in *More Die of Heartbreak* that note is all too often refracted by Kenneth's giddy mentality. It's not that his ideas are indeed cranky, though in some cases they are made to seem facile by virtue of being contextually forced; the point is rather that when, for instance, he lectures his mother on the politics of suffering ('the ordeal of desire' in the West versus 'the ordeal of privation' in the East) it takes him a mere two pages where it took Bellow a whole novel to do justice to the same theme in *The Dean's December*. That novel takes the theme and thoroughly involves us in its human effects. One cannot help but sympathise with Kenneth's mother who, he tells us, 'was scandalized by my theorizing'. But Kenneth sees himself as 'an express train' rushing past at 100 mph, with his mother dismissed patronisingly as 'this frail person in her sixties, waiting at a whistle-stop to flip a ride'.[144] Placed alongside Corde's strictures on the same East-West theme, Kenneth's whistle-stop tour strikes us as an exercise in self-gratifying rhetoric. Apparently the Trachtenbergs are famous for thrilling themselves with their own talk, for as he tells us 'in this regard he was like his pa, in whose list of pleasures lecturing came right after sex'.[145]

The America on view in this novel is as corrupt and as inhospitable to the making of souls as Bellow revealed it to be in his previous work. It is a place where one goes to get 'spiritual headaches'[146] and the costs of its dynamism are measured in the coinage of lovelessness and empty hearts. Surrounded on all sides by a profusion of 'events' and by the inescapable inanities of the media who peddle crisis chatter, 'a disguise for kitsch entertainment . . . often passing for "information"',[147] America is in the grip of 'the ordeal of desire'. Materialism and carnality have taken the place of 'enduring human bonds'[148] as the masses lunge in pursuit of neurotic yearnings and erotic pleasures. In such a world love and affection go unacknowledged and, perhaps, 'more people die of heartbreak than of radiation'.[149] Kenneth returns to the USA 'because that's where the action is now – the real modern action';[150] with his ethic of engagement, his 'Project Turning Point', he goes in search of community and commitment:

> Inner communion with the great human reality was my true occupation, after all. It was a field without much competition, so few took it up. I did it out of a conviction that it was the only worthwhile enterprise around ... unless you made your life a turning point, there was no reason for existing. Only you didn't *make*, you *found* the turning point that was the crying need ... of humankind.[151]

With his own relationship (to the all-too-plausibly named Treckie) on the rocks and with Uncle Benn's final flight into polar oblivion at the close of the narrative, Bellow has given us in Kenneth the tale of yet another humanist *manqué*. His efforts to find inner communion with others, what Albert Corde would have called 'the depth level' in his fellow man, are comically inept. From Treckie (although Kenneth still believes he and Treckie were 'ideally suited for a lifetime of intimacy'[152] she deserts him for Ronald, a macho ski instructor who wins her heart by kicking her in the shins) to Dita (who has to have the acne on her face sandblasted by 'one of those old-time clap doctors'[153] before Kenneth realises she is making 'a love offering'), he blunders his way through human relationships. Far from being a discovery of a humanist turning-point, Kenneth's story is a ludicrous catalogue of social ineptitude. At the end of the novel we are left to wonder whether poor Benn is on the run not just from the Layamons but from his greatest admirer.

The power sources against which Bellow ranges his protagonists derive from the 'post-human' universe of capitalist energy – 'the main enterprise was America itself, and the increase of its powers'.[154] Such powers as belong to the technocrats, the media barons, the entertainment and commercial culture; against their *force majeure* Uncle Benn is a prehistoric curiosity:

> Did he understand what Paul Volcker was saying about interest rates? Or anything to do with jet propulsion? Or electrical engineering? ... If Uncle had done something or other in television, in mutual funds, in advertising, in commercial music, in hydraulics, in protein chemistry, how different the attitude of the Layamons would have been![155]

Expecting Benn to get up and go in this world would be like giving
'a Melanesian aborigine a new Yamaha motorcycle and [turning]
him loose on the expressway. He couldn't even start, much less
stop'.[156] This is a world that chews up the humanistic 'project'
Kenneth sees as so necessary to the survival of civilisation. The
sole countervailing power is concentrated for him in the example
of his uncle – 'to bring to the human world what Uncle brought to
plant life'.[157] But the odds against this are stacked as high as the
Ecliptic Circle Tower, built upon old world real estate where
Benn's family used to live before they were swindled out of it by
his own Uncle Villitzer (aka 'the Big Heat'), a pol and ward boss 'as
crooked as they came'.[158] Certainly Kenneth knows what's at
stake, knows the inestimable cost of late twentieth-century indulgence and puts against this his own defiant survival declaration:

> if you think that historical forces are sending everybody straight
> to hell you can either go resignedly with the procession or hold
> out, and hold out not from pride or other personal motives but
> from admiration and love for human abilities and powers to
> which, without exaggeration, the words 'miracle' and 'sublimity'
> can be applied.[159]

More Die of Heartbreak is, though, less acute in its identification of
those forces which have hastened 'the declining march of humankind'. Though there is Bellow's now familiar attack upon the
rampant philistinism of American rationalistic and scientific culture in all its excessive material forms, this is attributed to 'a huge
force that advances, propels ... it demands the abolition of such
things as love and art'[160]; and though the 'historical forces'[161] have
their say in this decline, Kenneth, with his background in the
Russian mystics, can't resist describing this huge force in terms of a
demonological *coup*. Apparently angels and demons have been
struggling for American souls while they sleep, but angelic love
has lost out to devilish lust:

> Denied access to the soul, the angels work directly on the
> sleeping body. In the physical body this angelic love is corrupted
> into human carnality. Such is the source of all the disturbed
> sexuality of the present age ... planetary demons of electricity
> were entering us from beneath, coming from the interior of the
> earth. They filled the spinal fluid with their currents of lust. As
> the millenium approached its end, this was the true picture of
> human sexuality.[162]

Into this Sodom Benn ('a plant artist who was not qualified to be a love artist'[163]) is thrown. The resulting marriage to the formidable Matilda Layamon (surely one of the most implausible nuptials in all American fiction) has more to do with the contrivances of a whimsical plot than the maledictions of 'planetary demons'.

Finally *More Die of Heartbreak* is a novel that reminds us of the implacability of the American push for worldly preeminence and of the increasing gulf between the embattled heart and 'the deformities and diseases'[164] of civilisation. This is the Bellow bailiwick, his title to it as vigorously expressed in these statements (from a pre-publication interview) as in all of his fiction since *Herzog*:

> You are struck by the effectiveness of lawyers, surgeons, engineers, and the shabbiness, nullity of their personal lives because they have no inner cultivation. They've shut off access to their own souls . . . where there is no correspondence between inner life and outer, you're a barbarian. You may look civilised, but you're not.[165]

At the end of this novel those readers who still look to Bellow for spiritual uplift will find none. In Daniel Fuch's fine phrase Bellow is once again playing 'a humanist's version of end-game',[166] a version that has Benn Crader packing up to head for tundra country, though 'even that was not remote enough'.[167] Kenneth for his part has witnessed the collapse of his Project Turning Point (at least insofar as it took Benn as its role model) and seen that 'worn-out humanist culture' move one step closer to extinction. In what reads curiously like a gloss on his own reputation amongst critics as a humanist writer, Bellow-Kenneth reviews the battleground in which 'literature tries to hold its old positions'[168]:

> Philip Larkin, a poet much admired, writes, 'In everyone there sleeps a sense of life according to love.' But the sense *is* sleeping . . . Where's the space for love to perform in? And it's not too heartening to set these Larkin statements against the opposite propositions, upheld by a prodigious number of people who renounce love and go it alone – strong, healthy, rational, rationally wicked or at least 'unsentimental' people who are generally more wide awake than others.[169]

In *More Die of Heartbreak* Bellow reveals the futility of trying to hold to a humanist ideology in contemporary times. Perhaps this is the sense in which his creation of Kenneth can be viewed – for if he in all his feeble personality and tedious speechifying is humanism's defendant, then that hope will remain unregenerate. We leave Bellow's novel with the clear sense that there is no known cure for the spiritual and emotional haemorrhage of our time, and that deaths from heartbreak will go on increasing.

7

Afterword: *A Theft*

Bellow's most recent work is the novella *A Theft* (1989), the first of his books to be published as a paperback original.[1] It marks what is perhaps the beginning of a new phase in Bellow's career, with a commitment to the novella as a form particularly suited to the modern mind, a mind already in the author's view afflicted with information overload. Talking about *A Theft* in a recent interview, Bellow described himself as being in 'a different phase', one which had seen him putting aside his 'standing gravity and seriousness' in an effort to reach his audience more immediately.[2] He spoke of a new dedication to plot, to story, to easing reader access:

> Sometimes I've gone too far in the other direction, I admit it; I think I've let myself go in trying to be instructive and edifying. I think it's a bad mistake and it's one of the things that I try to correct in this new novella of mine.[3]

The paperback format, the novella brevity, the fabled plot – all clearly signal Bellow's determination to forge a more direct relationship with his readers. Since finishing *A Theft* he has completed another novella (provisionally titled *The Bellarosa Connection*), to be published in 1990.

The reasons for this new minimalism are not, perhaps, far to seek. He needed to find a way out of the *cul-de-sac* which, since *Herzog*, had increasingly become the perennial terminus of his disenchanted heroes. Herzog, Citrine, Corde and Crader were all men who sought retreat from an America of rank materialism and darkening hopes, exhausted by their efforts to do more than the many, their fellow-citizens mired in a state of moral abjection. In this cultural *impasse*, the humanist thinker-hero becomes a pathetically marginalised clown – Corde, the 'dud dean', or Crader the 'blockhead botanist'. Crader, particularly, seemed too much of an Aunt Sally, too obviously the enfeebled victim of a squalid society. 'You want to understand humanist intellectuals? Think of the

Ruling Reptiles of the Mesozoic . . .'.[4] *More Die of Heartbreak* may well be the last permutation of this ironic type, as well as the last of the big, baggy monster fictions through which they wandered. With *A Theft* Bellow seems to have acknowledged his complicity in creating what he calls 'the congestion of modern consciousness'. The idea-savvy of a Herzog or Corde only scored their defeat more deeply, and caught up in 'the moronic inferno'[5] of life in post-humanist America, their futility is not without consequence:

> So what you have is a grotesquely elaborated consciousness from which people function, which takes less and less note of the external world simply because it is hopeless to look at . . . this life that we lead becomes increasingly a life of mental operations and this is one of the threats to our vitality and indeed to our survival as human beings.[6]

The anti-intellectual reformation of *A Theft* is seen most obviously in its central character, Clara Velde. One of the rare female primary voices in Bellow's fiction,[7] she is a creature of feelings more than ideas. In Bellow's view, 'what distinguishes a woman like Clara is that she's some sort of natural theologian or natural metaphysician'.[8] A successful businesswoman, a company director with all of the life-style tokens – Park Avenue apartment, children in private schools, a czarina of *couture* – she is served up as 'a strange case – a woman who hasn't been corrupted'[9] by life in downtown Gogmagogsville, as Bellow's narrator contemptuously dubs New York City. The elderly sages of Bellow's previous novels owed their humanity to immigrant wellsprings, to a small-town fundamentalism, churchgoing, morally toned and materially frugal. This heritage is firmly present too in Clara, born of the sticks and 'sweet old Bible Hoosiers'.[10] She can still be 'the openmouthed rube'[11] upon whom big-city ways have been grafted. Now an arbiter of fashion, familiar not with pioneer skirts but those of Armani and Gianni Versace, she still knows the magnitude of her debt to 'life in that Indiana town' of her childhood, as remote from contemporary New York now as ancient Egypt. Her humanist credentials are impeccable, obvious in her 'preoccupation with questions which have gone out of style – faith, love, confidence, loyalty, duty . . . which sophistication has put aside in the modern age as having no weight'.[12]

The novella's main plot concerns the theft and return of Clara's emerald ring, a gift to her from Ithiel Regler, her lover, soulmate, and thought-guru. Stolen by the black Haitian boyfriend of Gina, Clara's *au pair*, its significance is that for Clara 'it represented the permanent form of the passion she had had'[13] for Regler. That Gina understands its importance for Clara, and that Clara's daughter Lucy also acts with discretion and maturity in assisting Gina in returning the ring, are for Clara unwonted revelations of integrity and love. Busy 'stockpiling ideas for survival in Gogmagogsville',[14] and hardened by now to the conviction that 'without a slum background' Gina would be easily corrupted by 'those East Harlem types',[15] Clara too readily underestimates the girl's quiet resolve.

The reviews of *A Theft* lamented the absence in it of Bellow's pungent portraits of American city life. New York is hardly present except as a city of interiors, and this presents us with a problem in accepting the novella as 'an ebullient celebration of human survival'[16] as one reviewer saw it. Even Clara's husband, Wilder Velde, is happily housebound. Shamelessly indigent, he sits 'in the middle of his female household like a Sioux Indian in his wickiup'[17] reading pop biographies or 'pedaling his Exercycle while the TV ran at full volume'.[18] The fact that neither Gina (a Viennese *bourgeois*) nor Lucy (who barely exists as a character and who is backgrounded in the narrative's affluent interior) are generic New Yorkers renders their 'survival' a somewhat attenuated achievement. Bellow fails to do more than sketch in New York's big bad wolves which lie in wait for the likes of Gina and Lucy. Lucy, Clara's eldest daughter, is afflicted with nothing more than premature adolescence it seems ('awkward before the awkward age'), and when her mother asks with a kind of weary resignation, 'how did you coach a kid like this, what could you do for her in New York City?',[19] her concern seems just a little excessive.

I think, too, the reviews were right to doubt whether the return of the stolen ring (the theft itself, we are to suppose, is just one example of what 'New York' will do if the locked interiors are ever opened to its perfidy) provides an objective correlative of sufficient weight to justify Clara's tearful epiphany. One reviewer saw this conclusion as 'overblown' and 'out of scale with the slightness of the story',[20] while another sees the resolution as 'perfunctory and without much consequence for either of the leading characters'.[21] The conclusion seems a rather unearned one, inadequately dramatised and too obviously reached for.

However, as so often in Bellow's fiction, this ending cannot, I think, be so easily dismissed. Though the human community is, for Clara, enlarged at the end (in her discovery that though 'there may not be more than one in a xillion' who are in touch with their essential humanity, Gina and Lucy are two such 'complete persons'),[22] yet that ending is also full of images of estrangement, isolation, and alienation from community. Indeed, Clara's passionate release of tears as she hurries alone down a crowded Madison Avenue 'not like a person who belonged there but like one of the homeless',[23] explicitly recalls the conclusion of that earlier novella, *Seize the Day*, where Tommy Wilhelm's breakdown also affirms his human loneliness amidst the urban crowd. Much of the force behind the conclusion of *A Theft* derives from Clara's sense of surprised discovery: to unexpectedly find not only a stolen ring, but a human being is, in Gogmagogsville, an event to write a novella about. I think the reviewers perhaps missed Bellow's irony here. *A Theft* was intended to be a sort of humanist's fairytale of Manhattan. Written in what Bellow called 'a sort of holiday mood',[24] there is in it a real sense of happy endings for Clara, whose 'one and only subject' is, according to Ithiel Regler, 'love and happiness'.[25]

Like most fairy tales though, and particularly those in the American romance tradition, *A Theft* cannot quite sustain the rainbow colours. Clara's tears are ones of both joy and sadness. Bellow, together with his new heroine, in their search for what Albert Corde would have called 'the depth level' in those around them, have been reduced to celebrating it in its most minimal traces. To be in touch with human qualities in late twentieth-century New York means becoming 'a connoisseur of the near-nothing'.[26] Where not 'more than one in a xillion' is so in touch, it is perhaps understandable that Clara feels she has won the jackpot in Gina and Lucy. There is therefore an ironically ambiguous dimension to Clara's unlikely access of joy. Rather like Benn Crader's lifelong search for the rare but brilliant patches of lichens in Arctic tundra, Clara too is entitled to express her joy at finding such unexpected human signs. 'There are curators in the zoo who give more thought to the needs of a fruit bat than any of us give our fellowman'[27] says one of Clara's friends, and this is the kind of prevailing view against which the conclusion of *A Theft* needs to be put. To be a humanist in Gogmagogsville is, like Arctic lichen-hunting, a lonely calling and too often the inventory is an empty one; the pursuit requires endurance, acute vision, and perhaps a life-long wait for the payoff.

All of this suggests that in *A Theft*'s conclusion, Bellow was indulging a bleak irony. Apart from the unstable uplift of the conclusion, there is little about the story that asks us to modify that view of Bellow's fiction I have been exploring throughout this study. Ithiel Regler, the *éminence grise* of Clara's life, and 'a dark horse in the history of the American mind'[28] was, for the reviewers of *A Theft*, too much of a disembodied voice. Yet he remains the authoritative presence in Clara's outlook, the one who 'knows what the big picture is – the big, *big* picture'.[29] His oracular culture-readings sound the deep Bellow note, and for Clara he often speaks with an *ex cathedra* force. The big picture he draws is that of the declining march of humankind still, with heartbreak remaining endemic in the national life, in the body politic, as 'the heart of this whole country aches for itself. There may be occult political causes for this as well. Foreshadowings of the fate of this huge superpower'.[30] However, this gloomy picture is never really substantiated in the narrative itself. Readers familiar with the Bellow of *Humboldt's Gift* or *The Dean's December* will certainly know the cultural coordinates of Regler's wasteland, but in *A Theft* Bellow neglects to remind new readers of them. 'Here, as never before in Bellow', Robert Boyers notes in his review, 'one can say that none of the references amounts to anything'.[31] Regler's view of the culture in which 'all the rules [were] crumbling' is just not realised in this fiction. For Clara he may be 'the Gibbon or the Tacitus of the American Empire',[32] but we need more convincing proof of imperial decay before we can judge Regler's view of it.

Finally, then, *A Theft* lacks the concentrated authenticity of Bellow's early short fiction. It is perhaps unfortunate that he should so recently have remarked that 'minimalism is OK as long as there's a certain amount of pressure behind the words. The trouble with most minimalists is that they're simply minimal in every respect'.[33] And although this latter comment cannot be applied to *A Theft*, one does come away from it with the sense of a story abraded in being told too often. Where, in *A Theft*, is there a voice to match that of Kirby Allbee contemplating, for the first time in Bellow's fiction, New York's tawdry decline?

It's really as if the children of Caliban were running everything. You go down in the subway and Caliban gives you two nickels

for your dime. You go home and he has a candy store in the
street where you were born. The old breeds are out. The streets
are named after them. But what are they themselves? Just
remnants.[34]

Forty years on, *A Theft* still contains Bellow's darling themes, but
the pressure, the outrage, the determination to have us respond to
the reality of such human depletions as Allbee refers us to, are now
transmuted into the resignation of irony. The decline of human
standards remains Bellow's concern, but anxiety has turned into a
wry acceptance, and indignation to the acknowledgement of
unstoppable decay:

Unless heaven itself were to decree that Gogmagogsville had
gone far enough, and checked the decline – time to lower the
boom, send in the Atlantic to wash it away. Not a possibility you
could count on.[35]

Notes

1 INTRODUCTION

1. Matthew C. Roudané, 'An Interview with Saul Bellow', *Contemporary Literature*, 25 (1974), p. 270.
2. Roudané, p. 280.
3. 'Letter to Elaine Feinstein', May 1959, in *The Human Universe and Other Essays*, edited by Donald Allen (New York: 1967), p. 96.
4. 'The Writer and the Audience', *Perspectives*, 9 (Autumn 1954), p. 12.
5. For a concise and lucid exposition of the postmodern aesthetic and its distinctive fictional expression, see David Lodge, *The Modes of Modern Writing: Metaphor, Metonymy, and the Typology of Modern Literature* (London: 1977), pp. 220–45.
6. *A Passage to India* (Harmondsworth: 1961), p. 177.
7. Rockwell Gray, Harry White and Gerald Nemanic, 'Interview with Saul Bellow', *TriQuarterly*, 60 (Spring/Summer 1984), p. 14.
8. *To Jerusalem and Back: A Personal Account* (London: 1976), p. 21.
9. Rosette C. Lamont, 'Bellow Observed: A Serial Portrait', *Mosaic*, 8 (1974), p. 252.
10. *TriQuarterly* interview, p. 34.
11. Examples of such criticism are too numerous to mention here and will be cited at appropriate points throughout this study. Malcolm Bradbury in his *Saul Bellow* (London: 1982), p. 22, accepts the dominance of this tradition.
12. *Saul Bellow: Vision and Revision* (Durham, North Carolina: 1984), p. 9.
13. Fuchs, p. 23.
14. Fuchs, p. 27.
15. *A Sort of Columbus: The American Voyages of Saul Bellow's Fiction* (Athens, Georgia: 1984), p. 2.
16. Braham, p. 2.
17. Fuchs, p. 308.
18. Eugene Hollahan, 'Editor's Comment', *Studies in the Literary Imagination*, 27 (Fall 1984), p. 4.
19. *Saul Bellow* (London: 1982), pp. 27–8.
20. Edmond Schraepen and Pierre Michel, *Notes to Henderson the Rain King* (Place Riad Solh, Beirut: Immeuble Esseily, 1981), pp. 7–8.
21. *On Bellow's Planet: Readings from the Dark Side* (Cranbury, New Jersey: 1985), p. 18.
22. Wilson, p. 19.
23. Wilson, p. 23.
24. Wilson, p. 22.
25. Wilson, p. 19.
26. Wilson, p. 38.
27. Peter Faulkner, *Humanism and the English Novel* (London: 1976), p. 1.

28. *True Humanism* (London: 1938), translated by M. R. Adamson, p. 19.
29. See Judie Newman, *Saul Bellow and History* (London: 1984), pp. 1–4 for relevant sources.
30. Maritain, p. xii.
31. Umberto Cerroni, 'Socialist Humanism and Science', in *Socialist Humanism: An International Symposium* (London: 1967), edited by Erich Fromm, p. 119: a survey of the varieties of humanism is provided by *The Humanist Alternative: Some Definitions of Humanism*, ed. Paul Kurtz (London and Buffalo, New York: 1973). Also helpful are the essays collected in *The Humanist Outlook*, ed. A. J. Ayer (London: 1968).
32. *Religion in American Public Life* (Washington, DC: 1985), p. 344.
33. Reichley, p. 52.
34. Reichley, p. 344.
35. Melvin J. Friedman, 'Dislocations of Setting and Word: Notes on American Fiction Since 1950', *Studies in American Fiction*, 5 (Spring 1977), p. 81.
36. 'The Two Environments', *Encounter*, 25 (July 1965), p. 12.
37. See Alan Wald, *The New York Intellectuals: The Rise and Decline of the Anti-Stalinist Left From the 1930s to the 1980s* (Chapel Hill, North Carolina: 1987), pp. 246–7.
38. Philip Rahv, 'Trials of the Mind', *Partisan Review*, 4 (April 1938), p. 3.
39. *Lionel Trilling and the Fate of Cultural Criticism* (Evanston, Illinois: 1986), pp. 188–9.
40. *Making It* (New York: 1967), p. 165.
41. Podhoretz, p. 165.
42. Podhoretz, p. 162.
43. Roudané interview, p. 279.
44. *Mr Sammler's Planet* (London: 1970), p. 135.
45. *To Jerusalem and Back*, p. 29.
46. *Dangling Man* (Harmondsworth: 1971), p. 56.
47. Bradbury, p. 28.
48. Susan Crosland, 'Bellow's Real Gift', *Sunday Times*, 18 October 1987, p. 57.
49. Crosland, p. 57.
50. *Humboldt's Gift* (London: 1975), p. 250.

2 THE COSTS OF SURRENDER: *DANGLING MAN* AND *THE VICTIM*

1. *Dangling Man* (London: 1946), p. 9.
2. *Dangling Man*, p. 9.
3. *Dangling Man*, p. 32.
4. *Dangling Man*, p. 33.
5. See, for example, Leslie Field and John Z. Guzlowski, 'Criticism of Saul Bellow: A Selected Checklist', *Modern Fiction Studies*, 25 (1979), pp. 149–71.
6. 'Saul Bellow's Ineffectual Angels', in *On the Novel*, edited by B. K. Benedikz (London: 1971), p. 224.
7. Waterman, p. 224.

8. Waterman, p. 224.
9. *Dangling Man*, p. 9.
10. The specific phrase was first used by Maxwell Geismar as a chapter heading in his book *American Moderns: From Rebellion to Conformity* (New York: 1958).
11. *Dangling Man*, p. 12.
12. Waterman, p. 238.
13. *Dangling Man*, p. 38.
14. *Dangling Man*, p. 92.
15. *Dangling Man*, p. 68.
16. *Dangling Man*, p. 123.
17. *Dangling Man*, pp. 135–6.
18. *Dangling Man*, p. 190.
19. 'Alain Robbe-Grillet: The Aesthetics of Sado-Masochism', *Massachusetts Review*, 18 (Spring 1977), p. 119.
20. *Dangling Man*, p. 190.
21. *Dangling Man*, p. 191.
22. *Dangling Man*, p. 190.
23. *Dangling Man*, p. 190.
24. *Dangling Man*, pp. 167–8.
25. *Dangling Man*, p. 26.
26. *Dangling Man*, p. 30.
27. *Dangling Man*, p. 13.
28. *City of Words: American Fiction 1950–1970* (London: 1971), pp. 395–6.
29. *Dangling Man*, p. 164.
30. 'Where Do We Go From Here: The Future Of Fiction', *Michigan Quarterly Review*, 1 (1962), p. 32.
31. *Dangling Man*, p. 96.
32. *The Victim* (London: 1948), p. 9.
33. *Dangling Man*, p. 92.
34. *Dangling Man*, p. 119.
35. *Dangling Man*, p. 119.
36. *Dangling Man*, pp. 190–1.
37. *Dangling Man*, p. 27.
38. *Dangling Man*, p. 68.
39. *Dangling Man*, p. 190.
40. 'The Fictional Criticism of the Future', *TriQuarterly*, 34 (1975), p. 237.
41. *Dangling Man*, p. 183.
42. See, for example, Maggie Simmons, 'Free to Feel: A Conversation with Saul Bellow on One Writer's Search for Authenticity in his Life and Work', *Quest* (February/March 1979, p. 31); and Roudané interview, p. 279.
43. *The Victim*, p. 217.
44. *The Victim*, p. 15.
45. Rockwell Gray, Harry White and Gerald Nemanic, 'Interview with Saul Bellow', *TriQuarterly* (Spring/Summer 1984), p. 60.
46. Roudané interview, p. 279.

47. See, for example, M. Gilbert Porter, *Whence the Power? The Artistry and Humanity of Saul Bellow* (Columbia, Missouri: 1974), p. 49; Tony Tanner, *Saul Bellow* (Edinburgh: 1965), p. 27; Ihab Hassan, *Radical Innocence: Studies in the Contemporary American Novel* (Princeton: 1961), p. 299; and John Jacob Clayton, *Saul Bellow: In Defense of Man* (Bloomington, Indiana: 1968), p. 140.
48. *The Victim*, pp. 130–1.
49. *The Victim*, p. 131.
50. *The Victim*, p. 133.
51. *The Victim*, p. 104.
52. *The Victim*, p. 115.
53. *The Victim*, p. 116.
54. *The Victim*, p. 117.
55. *The Victim*, p. 217.
56. *The Victim*, pp. 228–9.
57. 'Saul Bellow: Novelist of the Intellectuals', in *Saul Bellow and the Critics*, edited by Irving Malin (New York: 1967), p. 16.
58. *After the Tradition: Essays on Modern Jewish Writing* (New York: 1969), p. 102.
59. *The Lessons of Modernism* (London: 1977), p. 69.
60. Tanner, p. 36.
61. *A Dangerous Crossing: French Literary Existentialism and the Modern American Novel* (Carbondale, Illinois: 1973), p. 113.
62. James Gindin, *Harvest of a Quiet Eye: The Novel of Compassion* (Bloomington, Indiana: 1971), p. 313.
63. Clayton, p. 161.
64. *Doings and Undoings* (New York: 1964), p. 214.
65. Clayton, p. 162.
66. Clayton, p. 165.
67. Waterman, p. 225.
68. 'Who Killed Herzog? Or, Three American Novelists', *University of Denver Quarterly*, 1 (1966), p. 66.
69. Tanner, p. 33.
70. 'A Discipline of Nobility: Saul Bellow's Fiction', in *Saul Bellow: A Collection of Critical Essays*, edited by Earl Rovit (Englewood Cliffs, New Jersey: 1975), p. 142.
71. *Herzog* (London: 1965), p. 328.
72. *The Victim*, p. 15.
73. Roudané, p. 270.
74. *The Victim*, pp. 122–3.
75. Porter, p. 59.
76. *The Victim*, p. 15.
77. *The Victim*, p. 22.
78. *The Victim*, p. 26.
79. I am particularly struck by scenes where we find Leventhal representing Allbee and his relations with Allbee to outsiders such as Stan and Phoebe Williston. Such a scene occurs in Chapter 18 of the novel.
80. *The Victim*, p. 169.

81. See, for instance, Bellow's comments in the Gray, White and Nemanic interview.
82. *The Victim*, p. 126.
83. Bradbury, p. 40.
84. *The Victim*, p. 15.
85. Tanner, p. 27.
86. Hassan, pp. 299–300.
87. *The Victim*, p. 31.
88. *The Victim*, p. 105.
89. *The Victim*, p. 179.
90. 'The American Individualist Tradition', in *The Creative Present: Notes on Contemporary American Fiction*, edited by Nona Balakian and Charles Simmons (New York: 1963), p. 116.
91. *The Victim*, p. 27.
92. *The Victim*, p. 30.
93. *The Victim*, p. 31.
94. *The Victim*, p. 32.
95. *The Victim*, p. 214.
96. *The Victim*, p. 33.
97. *The Victim*, p. 27.
98. *The Victim*, pp. 29–30.
99. *The Victim*, p. 32.
100. *The Victim*, p. 37.
101. *The Victim*, p. 26.
102. *The Victim*, p. 174.
103. *The Victim*, p. 51.
104. *The Victim*, pp. 49–50.
105. *The Dean's December* (New York: 1982), p. 193.
106. Roudané interview, p. 270.
107. *The Victim*, pp. 52–3.
108. *The Victim*, p. 52.
109. *The Victim*, p. 27.
110. *The Victim*, p. 54.
111. *The Victim*, p. 54.
112. *The Victim*, p. 132.
113. *The Victim*, p. 57.
114. *The Victim*, p. 55.
115. *The Victim*, p. 135.
116. *The Victim*, p. 64.
117. *The Victim*, p. 64.
118. Hassan, p. 303.
119. *The Victim*, p. 72.
120. *The Victim*, p. 86.
121. *The Victim*, p. 89.
122. *Herzog*, p. 340.
123. *The Victim*, p. 94.
124. Porter, p. 57.
125. *The Victim*, pp. 96–7.
126. *The Victim*, p. 97.

127. *The Dean's December*, pp. 265–6.
128. *The Dean's December*, p. 265.
129. *The Victim*, p. 112.
130. *Herzog*, p. 215.
131. *The Victim*, p. 120.
132. *The Victim*, p. 139.
133. *The Victim*, pp. 141–2.
134. *The Victim*, p. 186.
135. Roudané, p. 273.
136. Roudané, p. 270.
137. *The Victim*, p. 205.
138. *The Victim*, p. 243.
139. *The Victim*, p. 206.
140. *The Victim*, p. 206.
141. *The Victim*, pp. 209–10.
142. *The Victim*, p. 199.
143. *The Victim*, pp. 199–200.
144. *The Victim*, p. 225.
145. *The Victim*, p. 233.
146. *The Victim*, p. 249.
147. *The Victim*, p. 250.
148. *The Victim*, p. 253.
149. *The Victim*, p. 197.
150. *The Victim*, p. 198.
151. *The Victim*, p. 174.
152. *The Victim*, p. 182.
153. *The Victim*, p. 246.
154. *The Adventures of Augie March* (London: 1954), p. 403.

3 A FUGITIVE STYLE: *THE ADVENTURES OF AUGIE MARCH, SEIZE THE DAY, HENDERSON THE RAIN KING*

1. David R. Jones, 'The Disappointments of Maturity: Bellow's *The Adventures of Augie March*', in *The Fifties: Fiction, Poetry, Drama*, edited by Warren French (DeLand, Florida: 1970), p. 84.
2. 'Saul Bellow: Novelist of the Intellectuals', in *Saul Bellow and the Critics*, edited by Irving Malin (New York: 1967), p. 18.
3. 'Saul Bellow', in *Saul Bellow and the Critics*, p. 7.
4. *The Adventures of Augie March* (London: 1954), p. 52.
5. Maggie Simmons, 'Free to Feel: A Conversation with Saul Bellow', *Quest* (February/March 1979), p. 31.
6. *Advertisements for Myself* (London: 1965), pp. 402–3.
7. 'The Adventures of Saul Bellow', *Commentary*, 27 (April 1959), pp 324–5.
8. 'Adventure in America', *Partisan Review*, 21 (January-February 1954), p. 112.
9. Quoted by M. Gilbert Porter in his *Whence the Power? The Artistry and Humanity of Saul Bellow* (Columbia, Missouri: 1974), p. 65.

10. 'Saul Bellow and the Activists: On *The Adventures of Augie March*', *The Southern Review*, 3 (1967), p. 584.
11. Guerard, p. 592.
12. Chirantan Kulshrestha, 'A Conversation with Saul Bellow', *Chicago Review*, 23–24 (1972), p. 13.
13. 'The New Nihilism and the Novel', *Partisan Review*, 25 (1958), p. 579.
14. *Saul Bellow: In Defense of Man* (Bloomington, Indiana: 1968), pp. 74–6.
15. *Augie March*, p. 125.
16. *Augie March*, p. 125.
17. *Augie March*, p. 125.
18. *Augie March*, p. 147.
19. *Augie March*, p. 85.
20. Ralph Freedman, 'Saul Bellow: The Illusion of Environment', in *Saul Bellow and the Critics*, p. 60.
21. *Augie March*, p. 83.
22. *Augie March*, p. 536.
23. *Augie March*, p. 194.
24. *Augie March*, p. 170.
25. *Augie March*, p. 206.
26. *Augie March*, p. 175.
27. *Augie March*, p. 175.
28. *Augie March*, p. 214.
29. *Augie March*, pp. 228–9.
30. Quoted on the dust-wrapper of the first British edition of *Augie March*.
31. *The Dean's December* (New York: 1982), p. 205.
32. *The Dean's December*, p. 205.
33. *Augie March*, p. 297.
34. 'The World of Saul Bellow' in his *Contemporaries* (Boston: 1962), p. 220.
35. John Aldridge, *In Search of Heresy: American Literature in an Age of Conformity* (New York: 1956), p. 135.
36. *Augie March*, p. 330.
37. *Augie March*, p. 330.
38. Kazin, p. 219.
39. *In Search of Heresy*, p. 139.
40. *Augie March*, p. 402.
41. 'Who Killed Herzog? Or, Three American Novelists', *University of Denver Quarterly*, 1 (1966), p. 73.
42. *Augie March*, pp. 402–3.
43. *The Novels of Saul Bellow: An Introduction* (London: 1967), p. 71.
44. Guerard, p. 585.
45. *Augie March*, p. 424.
46. *Augie March*, p. 436.
47. *Augie March*, pp. 447–8.
48. *Augie March*, p. 453.
49. *Augie March*, pp. 454–5.

50. *Augie March*, p. 437.
51. Henry Popkin, 'American Comedy', *Kenyon Review*, 16 (1954), p. 331.
52. *Augie March*, p. 456.
53. *Augie March*, pp. 457–8.
54. *Augie March*, p. 519.
55. *Augie March*, p. 515.
56. *Augie March*, p. 516.
57. Schwartz, p. 115.
58. *Augie March*, p. 536.
59. *Dangling Man* (London: 1946), p. 191.
60. Mudrick, p. 78.
61. *Advertisements for Myself*, p. 402.
62. Saul Bellow, *Seize the Day* (Harmondsworth: 1966), p. 8.
63. See, for example, M. Gilbert Porter, 'The Scene as Image: A Reading of *Seize the Day*' in *Saul Bellow: A Collection of Critical Essays*, edited by Earl Rovit (Englewood Cliffs, New Jersey: 1975), Malcolm Bradbury, *Saul Bellow* (London: 1982), pp. 55–6, and Clinton W. Trowbridge, 'Water Imagery in *Seize the Day*', *Critique*, 9, No. 3 (1967), pp. 62–73.
64. See, for example, Mudrick p. 82, and Ruth Raider, 'Saul Bellow', *Cambridge Quarterly*, 2 (1966–67), pp. 175–6.
65. Andrew Waterman, 'Saul Bellow's Ineffectual Angels', in *On the Novel*, edited by B. S. Benedikz (London: 1971), pp. 228–9.
66. Waterman, p. 228.
67. Bradbury, pp. 55–6.
68. *Seize the Day*, p. 7.
69. *Seize the Day*, p. 7.
70. *Seize the Day*, p. 15.
71. *Seize the Day*, p. 43.
72. Gerald Nelson, 'Tommy Wilhelm', in his *Ten Versions of America* (New York: 1972), p. 135.
73. *Dangling Man*, p. 9.
74. Simmons interview, p. 32.
75. Porter, p. 70.
76. Andrew Jefchak, 'Family Struggles in *Seize the Day*', *Studies in Short Fiction*, 11 (1974), p. 301.
77. Ray B. West, 'Six Authors in Search of a Hero', *Sewanee Review*, 65 (1957), p. 505.
78. *Seize the Day*, p. 125.
79. *Seize the Day*, p. 125.
80. Mudrick, p. 82.
81. *Seize the Day*, p. 14.
82. *Seize the Day*, p. 52.
83. *Seize the Day*, p. 26.
84. *Seize the Day*, p. 26.
85. *Seize the Day*, p. 26.
86. *Seize the Day*, p. 33.
87. *Seize the Day*, p. 60.

88.   *Seize the Day*, p. 62.
89.   Bellow acknowledged (Simmons, p. 31) that 'it isn't Tommy Wilhelm ... that interests me but that crook and phony, Dr. Tamkin'.
90.   Mudrick, p. 79.
91.   *Seize the Day*, p. 67.
92.   *Seize the Day*, p. 99.
93.   *Seize the Day*, p. 10.
94.   *Seize the Day*, p. 88.
95.   *Seize the Day*, p. 14.
96.   *Seize the Day*, p. 89.
97.   William Handy, 'Bellow's *Seize the Day*', in his *Modern Fiction: A Formalist Approach* (Carbondale, Illinois: 1971), pp. 124–5.
98.   *Herzog* (London: 1965), p. 28.
99.   *Herzog*, p. 215.
100. *Seize the Day*, p. 78.
101. *Herzog*, p. 28.
102. *Seize the Day*, p. 74.
103. *Seize the Day*, p. 75.
104. *Herzog*, p. 193.
105. *Seize the Day*, p. 71.
106. *Seize the Day*, p. 73.
107. *Seize the Day*, pp. 89–90.
108. *Seize the Day*, pp. 67–8.
109. *Herzog*, p. 217.
110. *Herzog*, p. 215.
111. *Seize the Day*, p. 69.
112. *Seize the Day*, p. 77.
113. *Herzog*, p. 258.
114. *Seize the Day*, p. 41.
115. *Seize the Day*, pp. 103–4.
116. *Seize the Day*, p. 43.
117. Kulshrestha interview, p. 12.
118. Matthew C. Roudané, 'An Interview with Saul Bellow', *Contemporary Literature*, 25 (1984), p. 279.
119. Richard G. Stern, 'Henderson's Bellow', *Kenyon Review*, 21 (1959), p. 658.
120. Simmons interview, p. 31.
121. *Saul Bellow* (Edinburgh: 1965), pp. 85–6.
122. Mudrick, pp. 77–8.
123. Gordon Lloyd Harper, 'Saul Bellow', in *Saul Bellow: A Collection of Critical Essays*, p. 10.
124. Harper, p. 13.
125. 'Nature and Social Reality in Bellow's *Sammler*', *Critical Quarterly*, 15 (1973), p. 257.
126. *Radical Innocence: Studies in the Contemporary American Novel* (Princeton: 1971), p. 321.
127. Boyers, p. 257.
128. *The Novels of Saul Bellow: An Introduction*, p. 119.

129. 'The Solitariness of Saul Bellow', *Spectator*, 22 May 1959.
130. Quoted in Tanner, p. 80.
131. John J. Clayton, *Saul Bellow: In Defense of Man* (Bloomington, Indiana: 1968), p. 167.
132. Duane Edwards, 'The Quest for Reality in *Henderson the Rain King*', *Dalhousie Review*, 53 (1965), p. 247.
133. *Henderson the Rain King* (London: 1959), p. 22.
134. *Henderson*, p. 21.
135. Eusebio Rodrigues, 'Saul Bellow's Henderson as America', *Centennial Review*, 20 (1976), p. 191.
136. L. Moffitt Cecil, 'Bellow's Henderson as American Imago of the 1950's, *Research Studies*, 40 (1972), pp. 296–7.
137. Howard Eiland, 'Bellow's Crankiness', *Chicago Review*, 32, No. 4 (Spring 1981), p. 104.
138. Melvin J. Friedman, 'Dislocations of Setting and Word: Notes on American Fiction since 1950', *Studies in American Fiction*, 5 (1977), p. 81.
139. *Henderson*, p. 7.
140. *Henderson*, pp. 23–4.
141. *Henderson*, pp. 39–40.
142. *Henderson*, p. 132.
143. *Henderson*, p. 40.
144. *Henderson*, p. 46.
145. Bradbury, p. 61.
146. *Henderson*, p. 38.
147. See, for instance, Rodrigues and Moffitt Cecil.
148. *Henderson*, p. 167.
149. *Henderson*, p. 285.
150. *Henderson*, p. 285.
151. *Henderson*, p. 286.
152. Melvin Maddocks, 'The Search for Freedom and Salvation', in *Critical Essays on Saul Bellow*, edited by Stanley Trachtenberg (Boston: 1979), p. 26.
153. *Henderson*, p. 307.
154. *Henderson*, p. 232.
155. *Henderson*, pp. 22–3.
156. *Henderson*, p. 67.
157. *Henderson*, p. 314.
158. *Henderson*, p. 318.
159. *Henderson*, p. 328.
160. *Henderson*, p. 318.
161. *Henderson*, p. 339.

4 HEARTS WITHOUT GUILE: *HERZOG* AND *MR SAMMLER'S PLANET*

1. See, for instance, Earl Rovit, 'Bellow in Occupancy', *American Scholar*, 34 (1965), pp. 292–8; James M. Mellard 'Consciousness Fills the Void: Herzog, History, and the Hero in the Modern World',

Modern Fiction Studies, 25 (1979), pp. 75–91; Forrest Read, '*Herzog*: A Review', *Epoch*, 14 (Winter 1964), pp. 81–96; and Malcolm Bradbury, 'Saul Bellow's *Herzog*', *Critical Quarterly*, 7 (1965), pp. 269–78.

2. 'Herzog, or, Bellow in Trouble' in *Saul Bellow: A Collection of Critical Essays*, edited by Earl Rovit (Englewood Cliffs, New Jersey: 1975), p. 86. This essay is a revision of 'Bellows to Herzog' which first appeared in *Partisan Review* (Spring 1965).

3. *The Dean's December* (New York: 1982), p. 310.

4. Poirier, 'Herzog, or, Bellow in Trouble', p. 81.

5. See, for example, Tony Tanner, *Saul Bellow* (Edinburgh: 1965), p. 110; Tony Tanner, *City of Words: American Fiction 1950–1970* (London: 1971), pp. 64–73; and J. J. Clayton, *Saul Bellow: In Defense of Man* (Bloomington, Indiana: 1968), p. 8.

6. Poirier, p. 82.

7. Harold Fisch, 'The Hero as Jew: Reflections on *Herzog*', *Judaism*, 18, No. 1 (Winter 1968), p. 52.

8. *Herzog* (London: 1965), p. 1.

9. See, for instance, Bradbury, pp. 76–7; Tanner, *City of Words*, p. 304; and John W. Aldridge, 'The Complacency of *Herzog*', in *Saul Bellow and the Critics*, edited by Irving Malin (New York: 1967), p. 210.

10. 'A Discipline of Nobility: Saul Bellow's Fiction', in Rovit, p. 160.

11. Klein, p. 153.

12. *Herzog*, p. 307.

13. *Herzog*, p. 307.

14. See, for example, pages 49, 106, 201.

15. Some critics have seen *Mr Sammler's Planet* as a turning-point. See Andrew Waterman, 'Saul Bellow's Ineffectual Angels' in *On The Novel*, edited by B. S. Benedikz (London: 1971), pp. 233–8.

16. *Herzog*, p. 28.

17. *Herzog*, p. 28.

18. *The Dean's December*, p. 193.

19. *The Dean's December*, p. 193.

20. *Herzog*, p. 38.

21. *Herzog*, p. 55.

22. *Herzog*, p. 67.

23. *Herzog*, p. 51.

24. *Herzog*, p. 126.

25. *Herzog*, p. 126.

26. 'Skunk Hour', in Robert Lowell, *Selected Poems* (London: 1965), p. 55.

27. *Herzog*, p. 54.

28. *Herzog*, p. 52.

29. *Herzog*, p. 56.

30. *Herzog*, p. 341.

31. *Herzog*, p. 272.

32. *Herzog*, p. 1.

33. *Herzog*, p. 116.

34. *Herzog*, p. 106.

35. *Herzog*, p. 106.

36.   *Herzog*, p. 215.
37.   *Herzog*, p. 106.
38.   See, for example, *Humboldt's Gift* (London: 1975), pp. 393–4, where Herzog's meditation is modified into Citrine's characteristic concern with the theory of meditation, and *The Dean's December*, pp. 289–90, which also involves the main character in a hypersensitive awareness of the physical world as an analogue for matters of the spirit.
39.   *Herzog*, pp. 91–2.
40.   *Herzog*, p. 93.
41.   *Herzog*, p. 93.
42.   *Herzog*, p. 73.
43.   *Herzog*, p. 255.
44.   *Herzog*, p. 164.
45.   *Herzog*, p. 193.
46.   *The Dean's December*, p. 193.
47.   *Herzog*, p. 163.
48.   *Herzog*, p. 196.
49.   *The Adventures of Augie March* (London: 1954), p. 402.
50.   *Herzog*, p. 215.
51.   *Herzog*, p. 215.
52.   *Herzog*, p. 217.
53.   *Herzog*, p. 218.
54.   *Herzog*, p. 50.
55.   *Herzog*, p. 231.
56.   *Herzog*, p. 237.
57.   *Herzog*, p. 238.
58.   *Herzog*, p. 239.
59.   *Herzog*, p. 240.
60.   *Herzog*, p. 240.
61.   *Herzog*, p. 258.
62.   *Herzog*, p. 263.
63.   *Herzog*, pp. 264–5.
64.   *Mr Sammler's Planet* (London: 1970), p. 43.
65.   *Herzog*, pp. 280–1.
66.   *Herzog*, p. 290.
67.   *Herzog*, p. 201.
68.   *Herzog*, p. 290.
69.   *Herzog*, pp. 294–5.
70.   *Herzog*, p. 308.
71.   Bradbury, *Saul Bellow*, pp. 76–7.
72.   *City of Words*, p. 304.
73.   Aldridge, p. 210.
74.   *Herzog*, pp. 307–8.
75.   *Herzog*, p. 307.
76.   *Herzog*, p. 307.
77.   *Herzog*, p. 308.
78.   *Herzog*, p. 314.
79.   *Herzog*, p. 317.

80. *Herzog*, p. 313.
81. *Herzog*, p. 315.
82. *Herzog*, p. 314.
83. *Herzog*, p. 326.
84. *Herzog*, p. 328.
85. *Herzog*, p. 338.
86. *Herzog*, pp. 330–1.
87. *Herzog*, p. 340.
88. *Herzog*, p. 341.
89. *Selected Poems* (London: 1933), p. 115.
90. *Saul Bellow*, p. 83.
91. Saul Bellow, *Mr Sammler's Planet* (London: 1970), p. 145.
92. Hana Wirth-Nesher and Andrea Cohen Malamut, 'Jewish and Human Survival on Bellow's Planet', *Modern Fiction Studies*, 25 (1979), p. 59.
93. *Mr Sammler's Planet*, p. 56.
94. See D. P. M. Salter, 'Optimism and Reaction in Saul Bellow's Recent Work', *Critical Quarterly*, 14 (1972), p. 61, and Susan Glickman, 'The World as Will and Idea: A Comparative Study of *An American Dream* and *Mr Sammler's Planet*', *Modern Fiction Studies*, 28 (1982–83), pp. 569–70.
95. Salter, p. 61.
96. *Mr Sammler's Planet*, p. 22.
97. *Mr Sammler's Planet*, p. 44.
98. *Mr Sammler's Planet*, p. 32.
99. Jane Howard, 'Mr. Bellow Considers his Planet', *Life*, 3 April 1970, p. 59.
100. See Keith Cushman, 'Mr Bellow's *Sammler*: The Evolution of a Contemporary Text', in *Critical Essays on Saul Bellow*, edited by Stanley Trachtenberg (Boston: 1979), p. 152, and David Galloway, '*Mr Sammler's Planet*: Bellow's Failure of Nerve', *Modern Fiction Studies*, 19 (1973), p. 24.
101. The reference is to Edward Shils, whose amendments to Bellow's manuscript are detailed in Cushman.
102. *Mr Sammler's Planet*, p. 33.
103. *Mr Sammler's Planet*, p. 219.
104. *The Dean's December*, p. 60.
105. Max F. Schultz, 'Mr Bellow's Perigree, or the Lowered Horizon of *Mr Sammler's Planet*', in *Contemporary American-Jewish Literature: Critical Essays*, edited by Irving Malin (Bloomington, Indiana: 1973), pp. 128–9.
106. Galloway, p. 28.
107. Galloway, pp. 22–3.
108. This neglect has also been remarked upon by Salter, p. 64.
109. *Mr Sammler's Planet*, p. 33.
110. *Mr Sammler's Planet*, p. 136.
111. *Mr Sammler's Planet*, pp. 119–20.
112. *Mr Sammler's Planet*, p. 118.
113. *Mr Sammler's Planet*, p. 248.

114. *Mr Sammler's Planet*, pp. 90–1.
115. *Mr Sammler's Planet*, p. 280.
116. *Mr Sammler's Planet*, p. 54.
117. *Mr Sammler's Planet*, p. 253.
118. *Mr Sammler's Planet*, p. 33.
119. *Mr Sammler's Planet*, p. 148.
120. *Mr Sammler's Planet*, p. 93.
121. *Mr Sammler's Planet*, p. 93.
122. *Dangling Man* (London: 1946), p. 190.
123. *Mr Sammler's Planet*, p. 313.
124. *Mr Sammler's Planet*, p. 235.
125. *Mr Sammler's Planet*, p. 19.
126. *Mr Sammler's Planet*, pp. 24–5.
127. *Mr Sammler's Planet*, pp. 164–5.
128. *Mr Sammler's Planet*, p. 248.
129. *Mr Sammler's Planet*, pp. 25–6.
130. *Mr Sammler's Planet*, p. 21.
131. *Mr Sammler's Planet*, p. 23.
132. *Henderson the Rain King* (London: 1959), p. 39.
133. *Mr Sammler's Planet*, p. 120.
134. *Herzog*, p. 28.
135. *Mr Sammler's Planet*, pp. 22–3.
136. Wirth-Nesher and Malamut, p. 64.
137. *Mr Sammler's Planet*, p. 27.
138. *Mr Sammler's Planet*, p. 65.
139. *Mr Sammler's Planet*, p. 43.
140. *Mr Sammler's Planet*, pp. 64–5.
141. *Mr Sammler's Planet*, p. 65.
142. *Mr Sammler's Planet*, p. 73.
143. *The Dean's December*, p. 122.
144. *Mr Sammler's Planet*, pp. 288–9.
145. *The Dean's December*, p. 123.
146. *The Dean's December*, p. 123.
147. *Mr Sammler's Planet*, p. 90.
148. *A Farewell to Arms* (New York: 1929), p. 196.
149. *Mr Sammler's Planet*, p. 261.
150. *Mr Sammler's Planet*, p. 74.
151. *Mr Sammler's Planet*, p. 162.
152. *Herzog*, p. 265.
153. *Mr Sammler's Planet*, p. 191.
154. *Mr Sammler's Planet*, p. 162.
155. *Mr Sammler's Planet*, p. 115.
156. *Mr Sammler's Planet*, p. 110.
157. Quoted in Robert H. Fossum and John K. Roth, *The American Dream*, British Association for American Studies Pamphlets in American Studies, 6 (South Shields, 1981), p. 6.
158. *Mr Sammler's Planet*, p. 202.
159. *Saul Bellow: Vision and Revision* (Durham, North Carolina: 1984), p. 227.

160.   *Mr Sammler's Planet*, p. 189.
161.   *Mr Sammler's Planet*, p. 305.
162.   *Mr Sammler's Planet*, p. 287.
163.   *Mr Sammler's Planet*, p. 307.

5   TUNING OUT OF AMERICA: *HUMBOLDT'S GIFT*

1.   Saul Bellow, *Humboldt's Gift* (London: 1975), p. 460.
2.   Marcus Klein, 'A Discipline of Nobility: Saul Bellow's Fiction', in
      Saul Bellow: A Collection of Critical Essays, edited by Earl Rovit
      (Englewood Cliffs, New Jersey, 1975), p. 160.
3.   *Humboldt's Gift*, p. 3.
4.   For details of Bellow's debt to Steiner see Herbert J. Smith, '*Hum-
      boldt's Gift* and Rudolf Steiner', *Centennial Review*, 22 (1978), pp.
      478–89. References to theosophy in Bellow's fiction appear as early
      as those in *Augie March* (London: 1954), pp. 70 and 370.
5.   Maggie Simmons, 'Free to Feel: A Conversation with Saul Bellow',
      Quest (February/March 1979), p. 34.
6.   Ben Siegel, 'Artists and Opportunists in Saul Bellow's *Humboldt's
      Gift*', *Contemporary Literature*, 19 (1978), p. 160.
7.   'Dead Reckoning', *Times Literary Supplement*, 10 October 1975,
      p. 1173.
8.   Richard Gilman, 'Saul Bellow's New Open, Spacious Novel about
      Art, Society and a Bizarre Poet', *New York Times Book Review*, 17
      August 1975, p. 2.
9.   Pearl Bell, 'Bellow's Best and Worst', *New York Leader*, 1 September
      1975, p. 20.
10.   'Bellow's Crankiness', *Chicago Review*, 32, No. 4, (Spring 1981),
      p. 106.
11.   'Bellow's Crankiness', p. 107.
12.   Joseph Epstein, 'A Talk with Saul Bellow', *New York Times Book
      Review*, 5 September 1976, p. 93.
13.   '"Strange Things, Savage Things": Saul Bellow's Hidden Theme',
      Iowa Review, 10, No. 4 (1979), p. 13.
14.   'Saul Bellow at 60: A Turn to the Mystical', *Saturday Review*, 6
      September 1975, p. 25.
15.   Saul Bellow, *Mr Sammler's Planet* (London: 1970), p. 219.
16.   *Mr Sammler's Planet*, p. 233.
17.   *Humboldt's Gift*, p. 291.
18.   *The Opposing Self: Nine Essays in Criticism* (London: 1955), pp. 90–1.
19.   Paul Carroll, 'Q and A – Saul Bellow Says a Few Words about his
      Critics and Himself', *Chicago Sun Times*, 9 November 1975, p. 8.
20.   *Humboldt's Gift*, p. 231.
21.   *Humboldt's Gift*, p. 284.
22.   *Humboldt's Gift*, p. 312.
23.   *Humboldt's Gift*, p. 299.
24.   Earl Rovit, 'Saul Bellow and the Concept of the Survivor', in *Saul
      Bellow and his Work*, edited by Edmond Schraepen (Brussels: 1978),
      p. 100.

25. *Humboldt's Gift*, p. 4.
26. *Humboldt's Gift*, p. 3.
27. *Humboldt's Gift*, p. 4.
28. *Humboldt's Gift*, p. 9.
29. *Humboldt's Gift*, p. 59.
30. *Humboldt's Gift*, p. 9.
31. *Humboldt's Gift*, p. 6.
32. *Humboldt's Gift*, p. 280.
33. *Humboldt's Gift*, p. 250.
34. *Humboldt's Gift*, p. 10.
35. Raymond Olderman, 'American Fiction 1974–76: The People Who Fell to Earth', *Contemporary Literature*, 19 (1978), pp. 504–5.
36. 'The Nobel Lecture', *American Scholar*, 46 (1977), p. 321.
37. 'The Nobel Lecture', p. 321.
38. Simmons interview, p. 34.
39. Simmons interview, p. 33.
40. *Humboldt's Gift*, p. 250.
41. *Humboldt's Gift*, p. 264.
42. *Humboldt's Gift*, p. 295.
43. *Humboldt's Gift*, pp. 393–4.
44. *Humboldt's Gift*, p. 396.
45. See Kerry McSweeney, 'Saul Bellow and the Life to Come', *Critical Quarterly* 18 (Spring 1976), p. 69.
46. *Humboldt's Gift*, p. 311.
47. See, for example, Michael Yetman, 'Who Would Not Sing for Humboldt?', *English Literary History*, 48 (1981), p. 948.
48. *Humboldt's Gift*, pp. 177–8.
49. *Humboldt's Gift*, p. 221.
50. Simmons interview, p. 36.
51. Simmons interview, p. 36.
52. *Humboldt's Gift*, p. 5.
53. *Humboldt's Gift*, p. 392.
54. *Humboldt's Gift*, p. 5.
55. *Humboldt's Gift*, p. 483.
56. Simmons interview, p. 34.
57. *Humboldt's Gift*, p. 364.
58. *Humboldt's Gift*, p. 221.
59. This information is given in Yetman, p. 943.
60. *Sartor Resartus* (London: 1908), p. 50.
61. *The Reign of Wonder: Naivety and Reality in American Literature* (Cambridge: 1965), p. 9.
62. *Dangling Man* (London: 1946), p. 88.
63. Andrew Waterman, 'Saul Bellow's Ineffectual Angels', in *On the Novel*, edited by B. S. Benedikz (London: 1971), p. 237.
64. *Humboldt's Gift*, p. 221.
65. Sansford Pinsker, 'Saul Bellow in the Classroom', *College English*, 34 (1973), p. 979.
66. *Humboldt's Gift*, p. 347.
67. Opdahl, 'Strange Things, Savage Things', p. 114.

68. *Humboldt's Gift*, p. 24.
69. *Humboldt's Gift*, p. 35.
70. *Humboldt's Gift*, p. 66.
71. *Humboldt's Gift*, p. 177.
72. *Humboldt's Gift*, p. 222.
73. *Humboldt's Gift*, p. 223.
74. Lodge, 'Dead Reckoning', p. 1173.
75. *Humboldt's Gift*, p. 261.
76. *Seize the Day*, (Harmondsworth: 1966), p. 74.
77. *Humboldt's Gift*, p. 261.
78. *Humboldt's Gift*, p. 263.
79. *Humboldt's Gift*, p. 260.
80. 'The Nobel Lecture', p. 321.
81. *Humboldt's Gift*, p. 402.
82. *Humboldt's Gift*, p. 396.
83. *Humboldt's Gift*, p. 391.
84. *Humboldt's Gift*, p. 392.
85. *Humboldt's Gift*, p. 439.
86. See, for example, McSweeney, 'Saul Bellow and the Life to Come'.
87. *Humboldt's Gift*, p. 487.
88. *Humboldt's Gift*, p. 485.
89. *Humboldt's Gift*, pp. 485–6.

6 EVERYTHING MERELY HUMAN: *THE DEAN'S DECEMBER*, THE SHORT FICTION, *MORE DIE OF HEARTBREAK*

1. 'The Big Match', *New Statesman*, 2 April 1982, p. 22.
2. *The Dean's December* (New York: 1982), p. 14.
3. 'A Novel of Politics, Wit and Sorrow', *New York Times Book Review*, 10 January 1982, p. 22.
4. *Saul Bellow: In Defense of Man*, 2nd edn (Bloomington, Indiana: 1979), p. 309.
5. *The Dean's December*, p. 310.
6. *The Dean's December*, p. 311.
7. *The Dean's December*, p. 310.
8. *The Dean's December*, p. 311.
9. 'The Nobel Lecture', *American Scholar*, 46 (1977), p. 325.
10. In conversation with Melvyn Bragg, 'The South Bank Show', Thames Television, 28 March 1982.
11. *The Dean's December*, p. 123.
12. David Galloway, 'Culture-Making: The Recent Works of Saul Bellow', in *Saul Bellow and his Work*, edited by Edmond Schraepen (Brussels: 1978), p. 57.
13. Robert Boyers and others, 'Literature and Culture: An Interview with Saul Bellow', *Salmagundi*, 30 (Summer 1975), p. 14.
14. 'An Irish Intelligence', *Guardian*, 1 April 1982, p. 10.
15. *The Dean's December*, p. 73.
16. The importance in this novel of the matriarch figure as the custodian of humane values is the most explicit and sustained

appearance of a character type which had its earliest incarnation in the *grande dame* of *Augie March*, Grandma Lausch. The latter ruled the March home 'like a great lama', her dominance that of 'an autocrat, hard-shelled and jesuitical, a pouncy old hawk of a Bolshevik'. With such an upbringing it is little wonder that Augie tells us he 'had a lot of regard for the power of women'. *The Dean's December* gives Valeria a more subdued, but no less firm dominance.

17. *The Dean's December*, p. 42.
18. *The Dean's December*, p. 64.
19. *The Dean's December*, p. 51.
20. *The Dean's December*, p. 187.
21. *The Dean's December*, p. 141.
22. In his interviews with Kulshrestha, Harper and Galloway, Bellow tells of his admiration for Dostoyevsky and his contemporary Russian novelists.
23. *The Brothers Karamazov* (Harmondsworth: 1958), pp. 368–9.
24. *In the American Grain* (London: 1966), p. 180.
25. *In the American Grain*, p. 178.
26. *The Education of Henry Adams: An Autobiography* (London: 1919), p. 181.
27. *The Dean's December*, p. 42.
28. *The Dean's December*, p. 130.
29. *The Dean's December*, p. 130.
30. *The Dean's December*, p. 70.
31. *The Dean's December*, p. 83.
32. *The Dean's December*, p. 83.
33. *The Dean's December*, p. 89.
34. *The Collected Letters of Joseph Conrad*, Volume I, 1861–97, edited by Frederick R. Karl and Laurence Davies (Cambridge: 1983), pp. 267–8.
35. Bellow, 'South Bank Show'.
36. *The Dean's December*, p. 72.
37. *The Dean's December*, p. 78.
38. *The Dean's December*, p. 51.
39. *The Dean's December*, pp. 89–90.
40. *The Dean's December*, p. 120.
41. The name Dewey Spangler recalls those of John Dewey and Oswald Spengler, both thinkers who have contributed to the ideological climate Bellow appears to be attacking in this novel. Bellow makes deprecatory reference to Dewey in his interview in *Audit*, 3, No. 1 (Spring 1963), p. 22; and Herzog vituperates in Spengler's direction on several occasions (*Herzog* [London: 1965], pp. 74–5). Spengler believed that Western civilisation was without soul, and that it was better for man to be engineer rather than poet, soldier rather than artist, politician rather than philosopher. His conclusions are thought to have greatly influenced Nazi ideology. In the novel his shade is seen in the way Spangler contributes to Corde's experience of totalitarian conditions and in Spangler's

mockery of Corde's humanism. John Dewey's belief in pragmatism was one that saw truth as partaking of no transcendental or eternal reality but, rather, subject to experience that can be tested. Again, the relevance to Spangler's cynical materialism is obvious. I would like to thank my former tutor, Henry Claridge of the University of Kent, who first suggested to me the dual allusion in Spangler's name.

42. *The Dean's December*, p. 122.
43. *The Dean's December*, p. 122.
44. *The Dean's December*, p. 122.
45. *The Dean's December*, p. 105.
46. *The Dean's December*, p. 122.
47. 'To Elsie', in *The Collected Earlier Poems of William Carlos Williams* (New York: 1951), p. 272.
48. *The Dean's December*, p. 122.
49. *The Dean's December*, p. 123.
50. *The Dean's December*, p. 239.
51. *Dangling Man*, p. 9.
52. Boyers interview, p. 11. And as early as 1963 Bellow was casting doubt upon the resistance even the stoutest minds could put up against such omnipresent distractions; he wrote then that 'public life', vivid and formless turbulence, news, slogans, mysterious crises, and unreal configurations dissolve coherence in all but the most resistant minds, and even to such minds it is not always a confident certainty that resistance can ever have a positive outcome'. 'Recent American Fiction', *Encounter*, 21 (November 1963), p. 23.
53. *The Dean's December*, p. 122.
54. *The Dean's December*, p. 300.
55. *The Dean's December*, p. 129.
56. *The Dean's December*, p. 139.
57. *The Dean's December*, pp. 140–1.
58. *The Dean's December*, p. 226.
59. *The Dean's December*, p. 256.
60. *The Dean's December*, p. 256.
61. *The Dean's December*, p. 228.
62. *The Dean's December*, p. 307.
63. *The Dean's December*, p. 193.
64. *The Dean's December*, p. 205.
65. *The Dean's December*, p. 201.
66. *The Dean's December*, p. 243.
67. *The Dean's December*, p. 243.
68. *The Dean's December*, p. 245.
69. Clayton, *In Defense of Man*, p. 310.
70. *The Dean's December*, p. 265.
71. *The Dean's December*, pp. 265–6.
72. *The Dean's December*, p. 16.
73. *The Dean's December*, p. 265.
74. *Humboldt's Gift* (London: 1975), p. 217.
75. *The Dean's December*, p. 265.

76. Howard Eiland, 'Bellow's Crankiness', *Chicago Review*, 32, No. 4 (Spring 1981), p. 104.
77. *The Dean's December*, p. 301.
78. *The Dean's December*, pp. 300–1.
79. *The Dean's December*, p. 305.
80. *The Dean's December*, p. 54.
81. *The Dean's December*, p. 60.
82. *The Dean's December*, p. 305.
83. *The Dean's December*, p. 61.
84. *The Dean's December*, pp. 237–8.
85. *The Dean's December*, p. 17.
86. *The Dean's December*, p. 290.
87. *The Dean's December*, p. 298.
88. Bellow, 'The South Bank Show'.
89. *The Dean's December*, p. 309.
90. *The Dean's December*, p. 310.
91. *The Dean's December*, p. 310.
92. *The Dean's December*, p. 311.
93. Tony Tanner, *Saul Bellow* (Edinburgh: 1965), p. 111.
94. *Mosby's Memoirs and Other Stories* (London: 1969), p. 82.
95. *Mosby's Memoirs*, p. 83.
96. *Mosby's Memoirs*, p. 82.
97. *Mosby's Memoirs*, p. 82.
98. *Mosby's Memoirs*, p. 83.
99. R. P. Blackmur, *Henry Adams*, edited by Veronica A. Makowsky (New York: 1980), p. 192.
100. Saul Bellow, *Him With His Foot in His Mouth and Other Stories* (London: 1984), p. 243.
101. *Him With His Foot in his Mouth*, pp. 243–4.
102. 'The American Thinker Prince', *Guardian*, 28 June 1984, p. 10.
103. 'The American Thinker Prince', p. 10.
104. *Him With His Foot in His Mouth*, p. 191.
105. *Him With His Foot in His Mouth*, p. 243.
106. *Him With His Foot in His Mouth*, pp. 205–6.
107. *Him With His Foot in His Mouth*, p. 195.
108. *Him With His Foot in His Mouth*, p. 251.
109. *Him With His Foot in His Mouth*, p. 227.
110. *Him With His Foot in His Mouth*, p. 227.
111. *Him With His Foot in His Mouth*, p. 282.
112. Tanner, p. 115.
113. *Him With His Foot in His Mouth*, p. 282.
114. *Him With His Foot in His Mouth*, p. 282.
115. *Him With His Foot in His Mouth*, pp. 268/87.
116. 'An Instinct for the Dangerous Wife', *New York Times Book Review*, 24 May 1987, p. 1.
117. 'It's a Sad, Sad World', *Daily Telegraph*, 24 October 1987, p. 11.
118. 'It's a Sad, Sad World', p. 11.
119. *More Die of Heartbreak* (New York: 1987), p. 98.
120. *More Die of Heartbreak*, p. 87.
121. *More Die of Heartbreak*, p. 187.

122.   *More Die of Heartbreak*, p. 315.
123.   *More Die of Heartbreak*, p. 299.
124.   *More Die of Heartbreak*, p. 55.
125.   *More Die of Heartbreak*, p. 292.
126.   *More Die of Heartbreak*, p. 188.
127.   *More Die of Heartbreak*, p. 243.
128.   *More Die of Heartbreak*, p. 335.
129.   *More Die of Heartbreak*, p. 18.
130.   *More Die of Heartbreak*, p. 15.
131.   *More Die of Heartbreak*, p. 27.
132.   'Professor Crader's Satellite', *Times Literary Supplement*, 23–29 October 1987, p. 1158.
133.   *More Die of Heartbreak*, p. 69.
134.   *More Die of Heartbreak*, p. 284.
135.   *More Die of Heartbreak*, p. 119.
136.   'Pontificating Away in the Spiritual Ice Age', *Literary Review* (October 1987), p. 22.
137.   'Pontificating Away in the Spiritual Ice Age', p. 22.
138.   See, for instance, John Updike, 'Toppling Towers Seen by a Whirling Soul', in his *Hugging the Shore: Essays and Criticism* (New York: 1984), pp. 255–63; and Jonathon Wilson, *On Bellow's Planet: Readings from the Dark Side* (Madison, New Jersey: 1986), pp. 32–8.
139.   'Professor Crader's Satellite', p. 1158.
140.   'Professor Crader's Satellite', p. 1158.
141.   *More Die of Heartbreak*, p. 253.
142.   *More Die of Heartbreak*, p. 100.
143.   *More Die of Heartbreak*, p. 100.
144.   *More Die of Heartbreak*, p. 99.
145.   *More Die of Heartbreak*. p. 101.
146.   *More Die of Heartbreak*, p. 301.
147.   *More Die of Heartbreak*, p. 19.
148.   *More Die of Heartbreak*, p. 43.
149.   *More Die of Heartbreak*, p. 87.
150.   *More Die of Heartbreak*, p. 66.
151.   *More Die of Heartbreak*, p. 188.
152.   *More Die of Heartbreak*, p. 63.
153.   *More Die of Heartbreak*, p. 208.
154.   *More Die of Heartbreak*, p. 194.
155.   *More Die of Heartbreak*, p. 194.
156.   *More Die of Heartbreak*, p. 170.
157.   *More Die of Heartbreak*, p. 33.
158.   *More Die of Heartbreak*, p. 40.
159.   *More Die of Heartbreak*, p. 68.
160.   *More Die of Heartbreak*, p. 301.
161.   *More Die of Heartbreak*, p. 68.
162.   *More Die of Heartbreak*, p. 73.
163.   *More Die of Heartbreak*, p. 301.
164.   *More Die of Heartbreak*, p. 279.
165.   Susan Crosland, 'Bellow's Real Gift', *The Sunday Times*, 18 October 1987, p. 57.

166. *Saul Bellow: Vision and Revision* (Durham, North Carolina: 1984), p. 308.
167. *More Die of Heartbreak*, p. 335.
168. *More Die of Heartbreak*, p. 44.
169. *More Die of Heartbreak*, p. 44.

7 AFTERWORD: *A THEFT*

1. In Britain this paperback first edition was quickly followed in June 1989 by a hardback edition (Secker & Warburg).
2. 'Saul Bellow in Conversation', BBC Radio 4, 5 March 1989.
3. 'Saul Bellow in Conversation'.
4. *The Dean's December* (New York: 1982), p. 136.
5. *Humboldt's Gift* (London: 1975), p. 78.
6. 'Saul Bellow in Conversation'.
7. The other two are Katrina Goliger of *What Kind of Day Did You Have?* and Hattie in 'Leaving the Yellow House'.
8. 'Saul Bellow in Conversation'.
9. *A Theft* (London: 1989), p. 58.
10. *A Theft*, p. 6.
11. *A Theft*, p. 15.
12. 'Saul Bellow in Conversation'.
13. *A Theft*, p. 43.
14. *A Theft*, p. 15.
15. *A Theft*, p. 59.
16. Penny Perrick, 'The Days of Naked Lunches', *Sunday Times*, 2 April 1989, p. 64.
17. *A Theft*, p. 45.
18. *A Theft*, p. 6.
19. *A Theft*, p. 11.
20. Paul Taylor, 'Is He Trying to be Satirical or What?', *Literary Review* (April 1989), p. 21.
21. Robert Towers, 'Mystery Women', *New York Review of Books*, 27 April 1989, p. 51.
22. *A Theft*, p. 108.
23. *A Theft*, p. 109.
24. 'Saul Bellow in Conversation'.
25. *A Theft*, p. 16.
26. *Humboldt's Gift*, p. 27.
27. *A Theft*, p. 28.
28. *A Theft*, p. 103.
29. *A Theft*, p. 109.
30. *A Theft*, p. 15.
31. 'Losing Grip on Specifics', *Times Literary Supplement*, 24–30 March 1989, p. 299.
32. *A Theft*, p. 55.
33. 'Saul Bellow in Conversation'.
34. *The Victim* (London: 1948), p. 129.
35. *A Theft*, p. 65.

Bibliography

WORKS BY SAUL BELLOW

Novels and Short Fiction

In each case the first edition is listed, followed by the edition referred to in this study.

Dangling Man (New York: Vanguard, 1944; London: John Lehmann, 1946).
The Victim (New York: Vanguard, 1947; London: John Lehmann, 1948).
The Adventures of Augie March (New York: Viking Press, 1953; London: Weidenfeld & Nicholson, 1954).
Seize the Day (New York: Viking Press, 1956; Harmondsworth, Middlesex: Penguin, 1966).
Henderson the Rain King (New York: Viking Press, 1959; London: Weidenfeld & Nicholson, 1959).
Herzog, (New York: Viking Press, 1964; London: Weidenfeld & Nicholson, 1965).
Mosby's Memoirs and Other Stories (New York: Viking Press, 1968; London: Weidenfeld & Nicholson, 1969).
Mr Sammler's Planet (New York: Viking Press, 1970; London: Weidenfeld & Nicholson, 1970).
Humboldt's Gift (New York: Viking Press, 1975; London: Secker & Warburg, 1975).
The Dean's December (New York: Harper & Row, 1982).
Him With His Foot in His Mouth and Other Stories (New York: Harper & Row, 1984; London: Secker & Warburg, 1984).
More Die of Heartbreak (New York: William Morrow, 1987).
A Theft (New York and London: Penguin, 1989; London: Secker & Warburg, 1989).

Non-Fiction

'The Writer and the Audience', *Perspectives*, 9 (Autumn 1954), pp. 99–102.
'Deep Readers of the World, Beware', *New York Times Book Review*, 15 February 1959, pp. 1 and 34.
'The Sealed Treasure', *Times Literary Supplement*, 1 July 1960, p. 414.
'Where Do We Go From Here: The Future of Fiction', *Michigan Quarterly Review*, 1 (1962), pp. 27–33.
'Some Notes on Recent American Fiction', *Encounter*, 21 (November 1963), pp. 22–9. Reprinted in M. Bradbury (ed.), *The Novel Today: Writers on Modern Fiction* (Manchester and London: 1977).
To Jerusalem and Back: A Personal Account (London: 1976).

INTERVIEWS AND BIOGRAPHICAL MATERIAL

Bragg, Melvyn, 'An Interview with Saul Bellow', *The South Bank Show*, Thames Television, 28 March 1982.

Brans, Jo, 'Common Needs, Common Preoccupations: An Interview with Saul Bellow', in *Critical Essays on Saul Bellow*, ed. by Stanley Trachtenberg (Boston, 1979), pp. 57–72.

Breit, Harvey, 'Talk with Saul Bellow', *New York Times Book Review*, 20 September 1953, p. 22.

Carroll, Paul, 'Q and A – Saul Bellow Says a Few Words About his Critics and Himself', *Chicago Sun Times*, 9 November 1975, p. 8.

Crosland, Susan, 'Bellow's Real Gift', *The Sunday Times* 18 October 1987, p. 57.

Enck, John, 'Saul Bellow: An Interview', *Wisconsin Studies in Contemporary Literature*, 6 (1965), pp. 156–60.

Epstein, Joseph, 'A Talk with Saul Bellow', *New York Times Book Review*, 5 December 1976, p. 93.

Galloway, David D., 'An Interview with Saul Bellow', *Audit*, 3 (Spring 1963), pp. 19–23.

Gray, Rockwell, and others, 'Interview with Saul Bellow', *TriQuarterly*, 60 (Spring/Summer 1984), pp. 12–34.

Harper, Gordon Lloyd, 'Saul Bellow – The Art of Fiction: An Interview', *Paris Review*, 37 (Winter 1965), pp. 48–73.

Harris, Mark, *Saul Bellow: Drumlin Woodchuck* (Athens, Georgia: 1979).

Harris, Mark, 'Saul Bellow at Purdue', *The Georgia Review*, 32 (1978), pp. 715–54.

Howard, Ann, 'Mr Bellow Considers his Planet', *Life*, 68, 3 (April 1970), pp. 57–60.

Kulshrestha, Chirantan, 'A Conversation with Saul Bellow', *Chicago Review*, 23–24 (1972), pp. 715–20.

Lamont, Rosette C., 'Bellow Observed: A Serial Portrait', *Mosaic*, 8 (1974), pp. 241–57.

Pinsker, Sansford, 'Saul Bellow in the Classroom', *College English*, 34 (1973), pp. 975–82.

Robinson, Robert, 'Saul Bellow at 60 – Talking to Robert Robinson', *Listener*, 13 February 1975, pp. 218–19.

Roudané, Matthew C., 'An Interview with Saul Bellow', *Contemporary Literature*, 25 (1984), pp. 265–80.

Simmons, Maggie, 'Free to Feel: A Conversation with Saul Bellow on One Writer's Search for Authenticity in his Life and Work', *Quest*, (February/March 1979), pp 31–6.

CRITICAL STUDIES OF SAUL BELLOW (1)

Book-length Studies and Essays in Books

Aldridge, John, *In Search of Heresy: American Literature in an Age of Conformity* (New York: 1956).

Aldridge, John, 'The Complacency of *Herzog*', in *Saul Bellow and the Critics*, edited by Irving Malin (New York: 1967), pp. 207–10.

Aldridge, John, *The American Novel and the Way We Live Now* (New York: 1983).

Alter, Robert, 'Saul Bellow: A Dissent from Modernism', in his *After the Tradition: Essays on Modern Jewish Writing* (New York: 1969), pp. 97–115.

Amis, Martin, *The Moronic Inferno and Other Visits to America* (London: 1986).

Baumbach, Jonathan, 'The Double Vision: *The Victim*', in his *The Landscape of Nightmare: Studies in the Contemporary American Novel* (New York: 1965), pp. 35–54.

Bloom Harold (ed.), *Saul Bellow* (New York: 1986).

Bradbury, Malcolm, '''The Nightmare in Which I'm Trying to Get a Good Night's Rest'': Saul Bellow and Changing History', in *Saul Bellow and his Work*, edited by Edmond Schraepen (Brussels: 1978), pp. 11–30.

Bradbury, Malcolm, *Saul Bellow* (London: 1982).

Braham, Jeanne, *A Sort of Columbus: The American Voyages of Saul Bellow's Fiction* (Georgia: 1984).

Bryant, Jerry H., 'The Moral Outlook', in his *The Open Decision: The Contemporary American Novel and its Intellectual Background* (New York: 1970), pp. 283–394.

Ciancio, Ralph, 'The Achievement of Saul Bellow's *Seize the Day*' in *Literature and Theology*, edited by Thomas F. Staley and Lester F. Zimmerman (Norman, Oklahoma: 1969), pp. 49–80.

Clayton, John Jacob, *Saul Bellow: In Defense of Man* (Bloomington, Indiana: 1968), 2nd edn, 1979.

Cohen, Sarah Blacher, *Saul Bellow's Enigmatic Laughter* (Urbana, Illinois: 1974).

Davis, Robert Gorham, 'The American Individualist Tradition', in *The Creative Present: Notes on Contemporary American Fiction*, edited by Nona Balakian and Charles Simmons (New York: 1963), pp. 111–41.

Donoghue, Denis, 'Dangling Man', in *Saul Bellow: A Collection of Critical Essays*, edited by Earl Rovit (Englewood Cliffs, New Jersey: 1975), pp. 19–30.

Dutton, Robert, R., *Saul Bellow* (New York: 1971), 2nd edn, Boston, 1982.

Ellison, Ralph, 'Society, Morality and the Novel', in *The Living Novel*, edited by Granville Hicks (New York: 1957), pp. 59–91.

Fiedler, Leslie, 'Saul Bellow', in *Saul Bellow and the Critics*, edited by Irving Malin (New York: 1967), pp. 1–9.

Finkelstein, Sidney, 'Lost Convictions and Existentialism: Arthur Miller and Saul Bellow', in his *Existentialism and Alienation in American Literature* (New York: 1965), pp. 252–69.

Fuchs, Daniel, *Saul Bellow: Vision and Revision* (Durham, North Carolina: 1984).

Galloway, David, 'Culture-Making: The Recent Works of Saul Bellow', in *Saul Bellow and his Work*, edited by Edmond Schraepen (Brussels: 1978), pp. 49–60.

Geismar, Maxwell, *American Moderns: From Rebellion to Conformity* (New York: 1958).

Geismar, Maxwell, 'Saul Bellow: Novelist of the Intellectuals', in *Saul Bellow and the Critics*, edited by Irving Malin (New York: 1967), pp. 10–24.

Gindin, James, 'Saul Bellow', in his *Harvest of a Quiet Eye: The Novel of Compassion* (Bloomington, Indiana: 1971), pp. 305–36.

Glenday, Michael K., 'Some Versions of Real: The Novellas of Saul Bellow', in *The Modern American Novella*, edited by A. Robert Lee (Plymouth and New York, 1989), pp. 162–77.

Gross, Theodore, 'Saul Bellow: The Victim and the Hero', in his *The Heroic Ideal in American Literature* (New York: 1971), pp. 243–61.

Guttman, Allen, 'Mr. Bellow's America', in his *The Jewish Writer in America: Assimilation and the Crisis of Identity* (New York: 1971), pp. 178–221.

Handy, William, 'Bellow's *Seize the Day*', in his *Modern Fiction: A Formalist Approach* (Carbondale, Illinois: 1971), pp. 119–30.

Harper, Howard M., 'Saul Bellow: The Heart's Ultimate Need', in his *Desperate Faith: A Study of Bellow, Salinger, Mailer, Baldwin, and Updike* (Chapel Hill, North Carolina: 1967), pp. 7–64.

Hassan, Ihab, 'Saul Bellow: The Quest and Affirmation of Reality', in his *Radical Innocence* (Princeton: 1961), pp. 290–324.

Hassan, Ihab, *Contemporary American Literature: An Introduction* (New York: 1973).

Hicks, Granville, 'Saul Bellow', in his *Literary Horizons: A Quarter Century of American Fiction* (New York: 1970), pp. 49–63.

Hoffman, Frederick J., 'The Fool of Experience: Saul Bellow's Fiction', in *Contemporary American Novelists*, edited by Harry T. Moore (Carbondale, Illinois: 1964), pp. 80–94.

Hughes, Daniel, 'Reality and the Hero: *Lolita* and *Henderson the Rain King*', in *Saul Bellow and the Critics*, edited by Irving Malin (New York: 1967), pp. 69–71.

Jones, David R., 'The Disappointments of Maturity: Bellow's *The Adventures of Augie March*', in *The Fifties: Fiction, Poetry, Drama*, edited by Warren French (DeLand, Florida: 1970), pp. 83–92.

Josipovici, Gabriel, 'Saul Bellow', in his *The Lessons of Modernism* (London: 1977), pp. 64–84.

Kazin, Alfred, 'The World of Saul Bellow', in his *Contemporaries* (Boston: 1962), pp. 207–23.

Kegan, Robert, *The Sweeter Welcome: Voices for a Vision of Affirmation – Bellow, Malamud, and Martin Buber* (Needham Heights, Massachusetts: 1976).

Kiernan, Robert F., *Saul Bellow* (New York: 1989).

Klein, Marcus, 'A Discipline of Nobility: Saul Bellow's Fiction', in *Saul Bellow: A Collection of Critical Essays*, edited by Earl Rovit (Englewood Cliffs, New Jersey: 1975), pp 135–60.

Lehan, Richard, 'Into the Ruins: Saul Bellow and Walker Percy', in his *A Dangerous Crossing: French Literary Existentialism and the Modern American Novel* (Carbondale, Illinois: 1973), pp. 107–45.

Levenson, J. C., 'Bellow's Dangling Men', in *Saul Bellow and the Critics*, edited by Irving Malin (New York: 1967), pp. 39–50.

Lewis, R. W. B., 'Recent Fiction: Picaro and Pilgrim', in *A Time of Harvest*:

American Literature 1910–1960, edited by Robert E. Spiller (New York: 1962).

Malin, Irving (ed.), *Saul Bellow and the Critics* (New York: 1967).

Malin, Irving, *Saul Bellow's Fiction* (Carbondale, Illinois, 1969).

Malin, Irving, 'Seven Images', in his *Saul Bellow and the Critics* (New York: 1967), pp. 142–76.

McConnell, Frank D., 'Saul Bellow and the Terms of Our Contract', in his *Four Postwar American Novelists: Bellow, Mailer, Barth, and Pynchon* (Chicago: 1977), pp. 1–57.

Nelson, Gerald B., 'Tommy Wilhelm', in his *Ten Versions of America* (New York: 1972), pp. 129–45.

Newman, Judie, *Saul Bellow and History* (London: 1984).

Opdahl, Keith M., *The Novels of Saul Bellow: An Introduction* (London: 1967).

Opdahl, Keith, 'True Impressions: Saul Bellow's Realistic Style', in *Saul Bellow and his Work*, edited by Edmond Schraepen (Brussels: 1978), pp. 61–71.

Pearce, Richard, 'The Ambiguous Assault of Henderson and Herzog', in *Saul Bellow: A Collection of Critical Essays*, edited by Earl Rovit (Englewood Cliffs, New Jersey: 1975), pp. 72–80.

Pearce, Richard, 'Harlequin: The Character of the Clown in Saul Bellow's *Henderson the Rain King* and John Hawkes's *Second Skin*', in his *Stages of the Clown: Perspectives on Modern Fiction from Dostoyevsky to Beckett* (Carbondale, Illinois: 1976), pp. 102–16.

Podhoretz, Norman, 'The Adventures of Saul Bellow', in his *Doings and Undoings: The Fifties and After in American Writing* (New York: 1964), pp. 205–27.

Poirier, Richard, 'Herzog, or, Bellow in Trouble', in *Saul Bellow: A Collection of Critical Essays*, edited by Earl Rovit (Englewood Cliffs, New Jersey: 1975), pp. 81–9.

Rovit, Earl, *Saul Bellow* (Minneapolis: 1967).

Rovit, Earl (ed.), *Saul Bellow: A Collection of Critical Essays* (Englewood Cliffs, New Jersey: 1975).

Rovit, Earl, 'Saul Bellow and Norman Mailer: The Secret Sharers', in *Saul Bellow: A Collection of Critical Essays* (Englewood Cliffs, New Jersey: 1975).

Rovit, Earl, 'Saul Bellow and the Concept of the Survivor', in *Saul Bellow and his Work*, edited by Edmond Schraepen (Brussels: 1978), pp. 89–101.

Rupp, Richard, 'Saul Bellow: Belonging to the World in General', in his *Celebration in Post-War American Fiction* (Gainsville, Florida: 1970), pp. 189–208.

Scheer-Schazler, Brigitte, *Saul Bellow* (New York: 1972).

Scheer-Schazler, Brigitte, 'Epistemology as Narrative Device in the Work of Saul Bellow', in *Saul Bellow and his Work*, edited by Edmond Schraepen (Brussels: 1978), pp. 103–18.

Schraepen, Edmond, and Pierre Michel, *Saul Bellow: Henderson the Rain King* (Immeuble Esseily, Place Riad Solh, Beirut: 1981).

Schraepen, Edmond (ed.), *Saul Bellow and his Work* (Brussels: 1978).

Schultz, Max F., 'Saul Bellow and the Burden of Selfhood', in his *Radical*

Sophistication: Studies in Contemporary Jewish-American Novelists (Athens, Ohio: 1969), pp. 110–53.

Schultz, Max F., 'Mr. Bellow's Perigree, or, The Lowered Horizon of Mr. Sammler's Planet', in *Contemporary American-Jewish Literature: Critical Essays*, edited by Irving Malin (Bloomington, Indiana: 1973), pp. 118–33.

Scott, Nathan A., Jr., 'Bellow's Vision of the "Axial Lines"', in his *Three American Moralists: Mailer, Bellow, Trilling* (Notre Dame, Indiana: 1973), pp. 101–49.

Scott, Nathan A., Jr., 'Sola Gratia: The Principle of Saul Bellow's Fiction', in his *Adversity and Grace: Studies in Recent American Literature* (Chicago: 1968), pp. 27–57.

Siegel, Ben, 'Saul Bellow and Mr. Sammler: Absurd Seekers of High Qualities', in *Saul Bellow: A Collection of Critical Essays*, edited by Earl Rovit (Englewood Cliffs, New Jersey: 1975), pp. 122–34.

Sullivan, Victoria, 'The Battle of the Sexes in Three Bellow Novels', in *Saul Bellow: A Collection of Critical Essays*, edited by Earl Rovit (Englewood Cliffs, New Jersey: 1975), pp. 101–14.

Tanner, Tony, *Saul Bellow* (Edinburgh: 1965).

Tanner, Tony, *City of Words: American Fiction 1950–1970* (London: 1971).

Tanner, Tony, 'Afterword', in *Saul Bellow and his Work*, edited by Edmond Schraepen (Brussels: 1978), pp. 131–38.

Trachtenberg, Stanley (ed.), *Critical Essays on Saul Bellow* (Boston: 1979).

Waterman, Andrew, 'Saul Bellow's Ineffectual Angels', in *On the Novel: A Present for Walter Allen on his Sixtieth Birthday from his Friends and Colleagues*, edited by B. S. Benedikz (London: 1971), pp. 218–39.

Weinberg, Helen, 'The Heroes of Bellow's Novels', in her *The New Novel in America: The Kafkan Mode in Contemporary Fiction* (New York: 1970), pp. 29–107.

Weiss, Daniel, 'Caliban on Prospero: A Psychoanalytic Study of the Novel *Seize the Day*, by Saul Bellow', in *Saul Bellow and the Critics*, edited by Irving Malin (New York: 1967), pp. 114–41.

Wilson, Jonathon, *On Bellow's Planet: Readings From the Dark Side* (Cranbury, New Jersey: 1985).

Wisse, Ruth R., 'The Schlemiel as Liberal Humanist', in *Saul Bellow: A Collection of Critical Essays*, edited by Earl Rovit (Englewood Cliffs, New Jersey: 1975), pp. 90–100.

Yazaburo, Shibuya, 'Saul Bellow: Politics and the Sense of Reality', in *The Traditional and the Anti-Traditional: Studies in Contemporary American Literature*, edited by Ohashi Kenzaburo (Tokyo: n.d.), pp. 43–56.

CRITICAL STUDIES OF SAUL BELLOW (2)

Essays in Periodicals

Allen, Michael, 'Idiomatic Language in Two Novels by Saul Bellow', *Journal of American Studies*, 1 (1967), pp. 275–80.

Bailey, Jennifer, 'A Qualified Affirmation of Saul Bellow's Recent Work', *Journal of American Studies*, 7 (1973), pp. 67–76.

Baker, Carlos, 'Bellow's Gift', *Theology Today*, 32 (1976), pp. 411–13.

Baker, Sheridan, 'Saul Bellow's Bout with Chivalry', *Criticism*, 9 (1967), pp. 109–22.

Baruch, Franklin R., 'Bellow and Milton: Professor Herzog in his Garden', *Critique*, 9 (1967), pp. 74–83.

Bayley, John, 'By Way of Mr. Sammler', *Salmagundi*, 30 (Summer 1975), pp. 24–33.

Belitt, Ben, 'Saul Bellow: The Depth Factor', *Salmagundi*, 30 (Summer 1975), pp. 57–65.

Berets, Ralph, 'Repudiation and Reality Instruction in Saul Bellow's Fiction', *Centennial Review*, 20 (1976), pp. 75–101.

Bezanker, Abraham, 'The Odyssey of Saul Bellow', *Yale Review*, 58 (1969), pp. 359–71.

Bigsby, C. W., 'Saul Bellow and the Liberal Tradition in American Literature', *Forum* (Houston), 14 (Spring 1976), pp. 56–62.

Borrus Bruce, J., 'Bellow's Critique of the Intellect', *Modern Fiction Studies*, 25 (1979), pp. 29–45.

Boyers, Robert, 'Nature and Social Reality in Saul Bellow's *Mr. Sammler's Planet*', *Critical Quarterly*, 15 (1973), pp. 34–56.

Bradbury, Malcolm, 'Saul Bellow's *The Victim*', *Critical Quarterly*, 5 (1963), pp. 119–28.

Bradbury, Malcolm, 'Saul Bellow's *Henderson the Rain King*', *Listener*, 30 January 1964, pp. 187–8.

Bradbury, Malcolm, 'Saul Bellow's *Herzog*', *Critical Quarterly*, 7 (1965), pp. 269–78.

Bradbury, Malcolm, 'The It and the We: Saul Bellow's New Novel', *Encounter*, 45 (November 1975), pp. 61–7.

Bromwich, David, 'Some American Masks', *Dissent*, 20 (Winter 1973), pp. 35–45.

Burns, Robert, 'The Urban Experience: The Novels of Saul Bellow', *Dissent*, 24 (Winter 1969), pp. 18–24.

Campbell, Jeff, 'Bellow's Intimations of Immortality: *Henderson the Rain King*', *Studies in the Novel*, 1 (1969), pp. 323–33.

Casey, J. B., 'Bellow's Gift', *Virginia Quarterly Review*, 5 (1976), pp. 150–4.

Cecil, L. Moffitt, 'Bellow's Henderson as American Imago of the 1950s', *Research Studies*, 40 (1972), pp. 297–300.

Chapman, Sara S., 'Melville and Bellow in the Real World: *Pierre* and *Augie March*', *West Virginia Philological Papers*, 18 (1970), pp. 51–7.

Chase, Richard, 'The Adventures of Saul Bellow', *Commentary*, 27 (1959), pp. 323–30.

Christhilf, Mark M., 'Death and Deliverance in Saul Bellow's Symbolic City', *Ball State University Forum*, 18, No. 2 (1979), pp. 9–23.

Cohen, Sarah Blacher, 'Comedy and Guilt in *Humboldt's Gift*', *Modern Fiction Studies*, 25 (1979), pp. 47–57.

Cronin, Gloria L., 'Faith and Futurity: The Case for Survival in *Mr. Sammler's Planet*', *Literature and Belief*, 3 (1983), pp. 97–108.

Crozier, Robert D., 'Theme in *Augie March*', *Critique*, 7 (Spring-Summer 1965), pp. 18–32.

Detweiler, Robert, 'Patterns of Rebirth in *Henderson*', *Modern Fiction Studies*, 12 (1967–68), pp. 405–14.

Dougherty, David C., 'Finding Before Seeking: Theme in *Henderson the Rain King* and *Humboldt's Gift*', *Modern Fiction Studies*, 25 (1979), pp. 93–101.

Edwards, Duane, 'The Quest for Reality in *Henderson the Rain King*', *Dalhousie Review*, 53 (1965), pp. 246–55.

Eiland, Howard, 'Bellow's Crankiness', *Chicago Review*, 32, No. 4 (Spring 1981), pp. 92–107.

Eisinger, Chester E., 'Saul Bellow: Love and Identity', *Accent*, 18 (1958), pp. 179–203.

Fisch, Harold, 'The Hero as Jew: Reflections on *Herzog*', *Judaism*, 17 (Winter 1968), pp. 42–54.

Freedman, Ralph, 'Saul Bellow: The Illusion of Environment', *Wisconsin Studies in Contemporary Literature*, 1 (Winter 1965), pp. 50–65.

Friedman, Melvin J., 'Dislocations of Setting and Word: Notes on American Fiction Since 1950', *Studies in American Fiction*, 5 (Spring 1977), pp. 79–98.

Fuchs, Daniel, 'Saul Bellow and the Modern Tradition', *Wisconsin Studies in Contemporary Literature*, 15 (Winter 1974), pp. 67–89.

Galloway, David D., '*Mr. Sammler's Planet*: Bellow's Failure of Nerve', *Modern Fiction Studies*, 19 (1973), pp. 17–28.

Gerson, Steven M., 'The New American Adam in *The Adventures of Augie March*', *Modern Fiction Studies*, 25 (1979), pp. 117–27.

Gindin, James, 'The Fable Begins to Break Down', *Wisconsin Studies in Contemporary Literature*, 8 (Winter 1967), pp. 1–18.

Glenday, Michael K., '"The Consummating Glimpse": *Dangling Man*'s Treacherous Reality', *Modern Fiction Studies*, 25 (1979), pp. 139–48.

Glickman, Susan, 'The World as Will and Idea: A Comparative Study of *An American Dream* and *Mr. Sammler's Planet*', *Modern Fiction Studies*, 28 (1982–83), pp. 569–82.

Goldberg, Gerald J., 'Life's Customer, Augie March', *Critique*, 3 (Summer 1960), pp. 15–27.

Gordon, Andrew, '"Pushy Jew": Leventhal in *The Victim*', *Modern Fiction Studies*, 25 (1979), pp. 129–38.

Guerard, Albert J., 'Saul Bellow and the Activists: On *The Adventures of Augie March*', *The Southern Review*, 3 (1967), pp. 582–96.

Guttman, Allen, 'Bellow's *Henderson*', *Critique*, 7, No. 3 (Spring-Summer 1965), pp. 33–42.

Guttman, Allen, 'Saul Bellow's Mr. Sammler', *Wisconsin Studies in Contemporary Literature*, 14 (1972), pp. 157–68.

Handy, William J., 'Saul Bellow and the Naturalistic Hero', *Texas Studies in Literature and Language*, 5 (1964), pp. 538–45.

Harris, James Neil, 'One Critical Approach to *Mr. Sammler's Planet*', *Twentieth Century Literature*, 18 (1972), pp. 235–70.

Hollahan, Eugene, 'Editor's Comment', *Studies in the Literary Imagination*, 17, No. 2 (Fall 1984), pp. 1–6. This is a special issue of this periodical, with the general title 'Philosophical Dimensions of Saul Bellow's Fiction'.

Hux, Samuel, 'Character and Form in Bellow', *Forum*, (Houston), 12 (1974), pp.34–8.

Jefchak, Andrew, 'Family Struggles in *Seize the Day*', *Studies in Short Fiction*, 11 (1974), pp.297–302.

Kazin, Alfred, 'My Friend, Saul Bellow', *Atlantic*, 225 (January 1965), pp. 51–4.

Klug, M. A., 'Saul Bellow: The Hero in the Middle', *Dalhousie Review*, 56 (1975), pp. 262–78.

Kulshrestha, Chirantan, 'Affirmation in Saul Bellow's *Dangling Man*', *Indian Journal of American Studies*, 5 (1975), pp. 21–36.

Leach, E., 'From Ritual to Romance Again: *Henderson the Rain King*', *Western Humanities Review*, 14 (1960), pp. 223–4.

Malin, Irving, 'Saul Bellow', *London Magazine* (January 1965), pp. 43–54.

Markos, Donald, 'Life Against Death in *Henderson the Rain King*', *Modern Fiction Studies*, 17 (1974), pp. 193–205.

Mathis, James C., 'The Theme of *Seize the Day*', *Critique*, 7, No. 3 (Spring-Summer 1965), pp. 43–5.

Mellard, James M., 'Consciousness Fills the Void: *Herzog*, History, and the Hero in the Modern World', *Modern Fiction Studies*, 25 (1979), pp. 75–91.

Meyers, Jeffrey, 'Breughel and *Augie March*', *American Literature*, 49 (1977), pp. 113–19.

Michelson, Bruce, 'The Idea of Henderson', *Twentieth Century Literature*, 27 (1981), pp. 309–24.

Morahg, Gilead, 'The Art of Dr. Tamkin: Matter and Manner in *Seize the Day*', *Modern Fiction Studies*, 25 (1979), pp. 103–16.

Morrow, Patrick, 'Threat and Accommodation: The Novels of Saul Bellow', *Midwest Quarterly*, 8 (1967), pp. 389–411.

Mudrick, Marvin, 'Who Killed Herzog? Or, Three American Novelists', *University of Denver Quarterly*, 1 (1966), pp. 61–97.

McSweeney, Kerry, 'Saul Bellow and the Life to Come', *Critical Quarterly*, 18 (1976), pp. 67–72.

Nault, Marianne, 'Humboldt the First', *American Notes and Queries*, 15 (February 1977), pp. 88–9.

Newman, Judie, 'Saul Bellow: *Humboldt's Gift* – The Comedy of History', *Durham University Journal*, 72, No. 1 (December 1979), pp. 79–87.

Newman, Judie, 'Bellow and Nihilism: *The Dean's December*', *Studies in the Literary Imagination*, 17 No. 2 (Fall 1984), pp. 111–30.

Opdahl, Keith, '"Stillness in the Midst of Chaos": Plot in the Novels of Saul Bellow', *Modern Fiction Studies*, 25 (1979), pp. 15–28.

Opdahl, Keith, '"Strange Things, Savage Things": Saul Bellow's Hidden Theme', *Iowa Review*, 10 (1979), pp. 1–15.

Overbeck, P. T., 'The Women in *Augie March*', *Texas Studies in Literature and Language*, 10 (1968), pp. 471–84.

Podhoretz, Norman, 'The New Nihilism and the Novel', *Partisan Review*, 25 (1958), pp. 576–90.

Porter, M. Gilbert, 'Is the Going Up Worth the Coming Down? Transcendental Dualism in Bellow's Fiction', *Studies in the Literary Imagination*, 17, No. 2 (Fall 1984), pp. 19–38.

Rans, Geoffrey, 'The Novels of Saul Bellow', *Review of English Literature*, 4 (October 1963), pp. 18–30.

Raper, J. R., 'Running Contrary Ways: Saul Bellow's *Seize the Day*', *Southern Humanities Review*, 10 (1976), pp. 157–68.

Richmond, Lee J., 'The Maladroit, the Medico, and the Magician: Saul Bellow's *Seize the Day*', *Twentieth Century Literature*, 19 (1961), pp. 15–26.

Rodrigues, Eusebio L., 'Bellow's Africa', *American Literature*, 43 (1971), pp. 242–56.

Rodrigues, Eusebio L., 'Saul Bellow's Henderson as America', *Centennial Review*, 20 (1976), pp. 189–95.

Rodrigues, Eusebio L., 'Beyond All Philosophies: The Dynamic Vision of Saul Bellow', *Studies in the Literary Imagination*, 17, No. 2 (Fall 1984), pp. 97–110.

Roudané, Matthew C., 'A Cri de Coeur: The Inner Reality of Saul Bellow's *The Dean's December*', *Studies in the Humanities*, 1 (1984), pp. 1–17.

Rovit, Earl, 'Bellow in Occupancy', *American Scholar*, 34 (1965), pp. 292–8.

Salter, D. P. M., 'Optimism and Reaction in Saul Bellow's Recent Work', *Critical Quarterly*, 14 (1972), pp. 57–66.

Shulman, Robert, 'The Style of Bellow's Comedy', *Publications of the Modern Language Association of America*, 83 (March 1968), pp. 109–17.

Siegel, Ben, 'Artists and Opportunists in Saul Bellow's *Humboldt's Gift*', *Contemporary Literature*, 19 (1978), pp. 143–64.

Smith, Herbert J., '*Humboldt's Gift* and Rudolf Steiner', *Centennial Review*, 22 (1978), pp. 478–89.

Stock, Irwin, 'The Novels of Saul Bellow', *Southern Review*, 3 (January 1967), pp. 13–42.

Tanner, Tony, 'Saul Bellow: An Introductory Note', *Salmagundi*, 30 (Summer 1975), pp. 3–5.

Trachtenberg, Stanley, 'Saul Bellow's *Luftmenschen*: The Compromise with Reality', *Critique*, 9 (Summer 1967), pp. 37–61.

Trachtenberg, Stanley, 'Saul Bellow and the Veil of Maya', *Studies in the Literary Imagination*, 17 No. 2 (Autumn 1984), pp. 39–58.

Tripathy, Biyot K., 'End-Game: Terminal Configurations in Bellow's Novels', *Modern Fiction Studies*, 33 (1987), pp. 215–31.

Trowbridge, Clinton W., 'Water Imagery in *Seize the Day*', *Critique*, 9 (Summer 1967), pp. 62–73.

Uphaus, Suzanne Henning, 'From Innocence to Experience: A Study of *Herzog*', *Dalhousie Review*, 46 (1966), pp. 67–78.

West, Ray B., 'Six Authors in Search of a Hero', *Sewanee Review*, 65 (1957), pp. 498–508.

Wirth-Nesher, H. and Andrea Cohen Malamut, 'Jewish and Human Survival on Bellow's Planet', *Modern Fiction Studies*, 25 (1979), pp. 59–74.

Yetman, Michael, 'Who Would Not Sing for Humboldt?', *English Literary History*, 48 (1981), pp. 935–51.

Young, James Dean, 'Bellow's View of the Heart', *Critique*, 7 (Spring 1965), pp. 5–17.

Zeitlow, E. R. 'Saul Bellow: The Theater of the Soul', *Ariel*, 4 (1973), pp. 44–59.

REVIEWS OF BELLOW'S FICTION

Aldridge, John, 'Saul Bellow at 60: A Turn to the Mystical', *Saturday Review*, 6 September 1975, p. 25.

Bell, Pearl, 'Bellow's Best and Worst', *New Leader*, 1 September 1975, p. 20.

Boyers, Robert, 'Losing Grip on Specifics', *Times Literary Supplement*, 24–30 March 1989, p. 299.

Gaddis, William, 'An Instinct for the Dangerous Wife', *New York Times Book Review*, 24 May 1987, pp. 1 and 16.

Gilman, Richard, 'Saul Bellow's New Open, Spacious Novel About Art, Society and a Bizarre Poet', *New York Times Book Review*, 17 August 1975, pp. 2–3.

Gross, Beverley, 'Dark Side of the Moon', *The Nation*, 8 February 1970, p. 154.

Harwell, Meade, 'Picaro from Chicago', *Southwest Review*, 39 (1953), pp. 273–6.

Holloway, David, 'It's a Sad, Sad World', *Daily Telegraph*, 24 October 1987, p. 11.

Josipovici, Gabriel, 'A Foot on the Stockyard and an Eye on the Stars', *Times Literary Supplement*, 2 April 1982, p. 371.

Kemp, Peter, 'America's Carnival of Excess', *The Sunday Times*, 25 October 1987, p. 32.

Kermode, Frank, 'The American Thinker Prince', *Guardian*, 28 June 1984, p. 10.

Lodge, David, 'Dead Reckoning', *Times Literary Supplement*, 10 October 1975, p. 1173.

Mount, Ferdinand, 'Bellow's American Follies', *Sunday Telegraph*, 25 October, 1987, p. 16.

Newman, Charles, 'Lives of the Artists', *Harper's Magazine*, 251 (October 1975), pp. 82–5.

Perrick, Perry, 'The Days of Naked Lunches', *Sunday Times*, 2 April 1989.

Podhoretz, Norman, 'The Language of Life', *Commentary*, 16 (1953), pp. 378–82.

Popkin, Henry, 'American Comedy', *Kenyon Review*, 16 (1954), pp. 329–34.

Raider, Ruth, 'Saul Bellow', *Cambridge Quarterly*, 2 (1966–67), pp. 172–83.

Read, Forrest, '*Herzog*: A Review' *Epoch*, 14 (winter 1964), pp. 81–96.

Rushdie, Salman, 'The Big Match', *New Statesman*, 2 April 1982, p. 22.

Schorer, Mark, 'A Book of Yes and No', *Hudson Review*, 7 (1954), pp. 136–41.

Schwartz, Delmore, 'Adventure in America', *Partisan Review*, 21 (1954), pp. 112–15.

Stern, Richard G., 'Henderson's Bellow', *Kenyon Review*, 21 (1959), pp. 655–61.

Strawson, Galen, 'Professor Crader's Satellite', *Times Literary Supplement*, 23–29 October 1987, pp. 1157–58.

Sullivan, Walter, 'Terrors Old and New: Bellow's Romania and Three Views of the Holocaust', *Sewanee Review*, 90 (1982), pp. 490–2.

Taylor, Paul, 'Pontificating Away in the Spiritual Ice Age', *Literary Review*, October 1987, pp. 21–2.

Taylor, Paul, 'Is He Trying to be Satirical or What?', *Literary Review*, April 1989, pp. 20–1.
Towers, Robert, 'A Novel of Politics, Wit and Sorrow', *New York Times Book Review*, 10 January 1982, p. 22.
Towers, Robert, 'Mystery Women', *New York Times Book Review*, 27 April 1989, pp. 51–2.
Tuohy, Frank, 'An Irish Intelligence', *Guardian* 1 April 1982, p. 10.
Updike John, 'Toppling Towers Seen by a Whirling Soul', collected in his *Hugging the Shore: Essays and Criticism* (New York: 1984), pp. 255–63.
Warren, Robert Penn, 'Man with no Commitments', *New Republic*, 129, 2 November 1953, pp. 22–3.
Webster, Harvey Curtis, 'Quest Through the Modern World', *Saturday Review of Literature*, 19 September 1953, pp. 13–14.

BIBLIOGRAPHIES

Cronin, Gloria L. and Blaise H. Hall, *Saul Bellow: An Annotated Bibliography*, 2nd edn (New York and London: 1987).
Field, Leslie, and John Z. Guzlowski, 'Criticism of Saul Bellow: A Selected Checklist', *Modern Fiction Studies*, 25 (1979), pp. 149–71.
Lercangée, Francine, *Saul Bellow: A Bibliography of Secondary Sources* (Brussels: Centre for American Studies, 1977).
Nault, Marianne, *Saul Bellow: His Works and his Critics: An Annotated International Bibliography* (New York: 1977).
Noreen, Robert G., *Saul Bellow: A Reference Guide* (Boston: 1977–78).
Schneider, Harold W., 'Two Bibliographies: Saul Bellow, William Styron', *Critique*, 3 (Summer 1960), pp. 71–91.
Sokoloff, B. A. and Mark E. Posner, *Saul Bellow: A Comprehensive Bibliography* (Folcroft, Pennsylvania: 1971). Edition limited to 150 copies.

OTHER WORKS CITED

Adams, Henry, *The Education of Henry Adams: An Autobiography* (London: 1919).
Allen, Donald (ed.), *The Human Universe and Other Essays* (New York: 1967).
Ayer, A. J. (ed.), *The Humanist Outlook* (London: 1968).
Blackmur, R. P., *Henry Adams*, edited by Veronica A. Makowsky (New York: 1980).
Clayton, John, 'Alain Robbe-Crillet: The Aesthetics of Sado-Masochism', *Massachusetts Review*, 18 (1977), pp. 106–19.
Conrad Joseph, *The Collected Letters of Joseph Conrad, Volume 1, 1861–1897*, edited by Frederick R. Karl and Laurence Davies (Cambridge: 1983).
Dostoyevsky, Fyodor, *The Brothers Karamazov* (Harmondsworth, Middlesex: 1958).
Faulkner, Peter, *Humanism and the English Novel* (London: 1976).
Fiedler, Leslie, *Waiting for the End* (New York: 1964).
Forster, E. M., *A Passage to India* (Harmondsworth, Middlesex: 1961).

Fossom, Robert H. and John K. Roth, *The American Dream*, British Association for American Studies Pamphlets in American Studies, No. 6 (South Shields: 1981).

Fromm, Erich (ed.), *Socialist Humanism: An International Symposium* (London: 1967).

Hemingway, Ernest, *A Farewell to Arms* (New York: 1929).

Krupnick, Mark, *Lionel Trilling and the Fate of Cultural Criticism* (Evanston, Illinois: 1976).

Kurtz, Paul (ed.), *The Humanist Alternative: Some Definitions of Humanism* (London and Buffalo, New York: 1973).

Lewis, R. W. B., *The American Adam: Innocence, Tragedy and Tradition in the Nineteenth Century* (Chicago: 1975).

Lodge, David, *The Modes of Modern Writing: Metaphor, Metonymy, and the Typology of Modern Literature* (London: 1977).

Lowell, Robert, *Selected Poems* (London: 1965).

Mailer, Norman, *Advertisements for Myself* (London: 1965).

Maritain, Jacques, *True Humanism*, translated by M. R. Adamson (London: 1938).

Olderman, Raymond, 'American Fiction 1974–76: The People Who Fell to Earth', *Contemporary Literature*, 19 (1978), pp. 497–527.

Podhoretz, Norman, *Making It* (New York: 1967).

Rahv, Philip, 'Trials of the Mind', *Partisan Review*, 4 (April 1938).

Reichley, A. James, *Religion in American Public Life* (Washington DC: 1985).

Williams, William Carlos, *The Collected Earlier Poems of William Carlos Williams* (New York: 1951).

Williams, William Carlos, *In the American Grain* (London: 1966).

Index